Politics and Beef in Argentina
Patterns of Conflict and Change

Institute of Latin American Studies
Columbia University

Politics and Beef
in Argentina

Patterns of
Conflict and Change

Peter H. Smith

Columbia University Press
New York and London   1969

Peter H. Smith is
Assistant Professor of History
at the University of Wisconsin

10331

The Institute of Latin American Studies of Columbia University was established in 1961 in response to a national, public, and educational need for a better understanding of the contemporary problems of the Latin American nations and a more knowledgeable basis for inter-American relations. The major objectives of the Institute are to prepare a limited number of North Americans for scholarly and professional careers in the field of Latin American studies and to advance our knowledge of Latin America and its problems through an active program of research by faculty, by graduate students, and by visiting scholars.

Some of the results of this research program are published from time to time by the Institute of Latin American Studies. This book, *Politics and Beef in Argentina: Patterns of Conflict and Change* by Peter H. Smith, is another volume in the series. The author was associated with the Institute of Latin American Studies as a graduate student and as a research scholar. The faculty of the Institute believes that his book on Argentina contributes to one of our major objectives, namely to improve public and scholarly knowledge of Latin America and to contribute to the advancement of inter-American relations. We are grateful to the Ford Foundation for financial assistance which has made this publication program possible.

To My Parents

Acknowledgments

THIS book could never have been written without other people's help. It would be impossible to name all the Argentines who have aided my efforts, but special thanks are due to Dr. Julio Olivera, then Director of the Instituto de Investigaciones Sociales y Económicas of the University of Buenos Aires, where I was given office space and help from the staff and other researchers; to the members of the Centro de Sociología Comparada of the Instituto Torcuato di Tella; to the Instituto de Desarrollo Económico y Social; and to the Instituto de Investigaciones Históricas of the Facultad de Filosofía y Letras at the University of the Littoral, Rosario. During the course of my research in 1965, all of these organizations arranged seminars for the scrutiny of my methods and analysis.

In England, Professor R. A. Humphreys was kind enough to lend me office space in the Institute of Latin American Studies at the University of London. Dr. D. C. M. Platt furnished expert guidance to the British sources. A seminar at the Latin American Centre, St. Antony's College, Oxford, provided a further test for some of my conclusions and contentions.

Courteous and invaluable assistance has come from many librarians, especially the staffs at the Banco Tornquist, the Biblioteca del Congreso Nacional, the Biblioteca Nacional, the Confederación de Asociaciones Rurales de Buenos Aires y La Pampa, the Confederación General de Trabajo, the Junta Nacional de Carnes, the Ministerio de Agricultura y Ganadería, the Sociedad Rural Argentina, and various faculties of the

University of Buenos Aires, all in Buenos Aires; the Federación Agraria Argentina in Rosario; the British Museum, the Public Record Office, and Canning House in London; the Library of Congress and the National Archives in Washington; the New York Public Library; and the University of California, Berkeley.

Generous financial support has come from the Foreign Area Fellowship Program, the Joint Committee on Latin American Studies of the Social Science Research Council and the American Council of Learned Societies, and the Center for Comparative Studies at Dartmouth College.

Earlier versions of the study have been read by Ezequiel Gallo (h.), Professor David Felix, Professor Tulio Halperín Donghi, Professor Joseph Love, Ing. José Minola, Professor K. H. Silvert, Professor Arnold Strickon, Dr. Richard Weinert, and a board of dissertation examiners at Columbia University. Cristina Cacopardo and Ruth Sumners lent able assistance to the research. Shirley Martin and Lucille Flanders typed successive drafts of the manuscript with efficiency and cheer. Professor Lewis Hanke, my adviser at Columbia, has provided thoughtful guidance and criticism from the moment that this project was conceived. Comments and help from all these people have been extremely beneficial; the mistakes that remain are naturally mine alone.

Finally, I thank my wife, Mary Grant Smith, for her encouragement, for her suggestions, and for having understood.

Madison, Wisconsin
October 1968

Contents

Abbreviations

Anales	*Anales de la Sociedad Rural Argentina*
Boletín	*Boletín de la Unión Industrial Argentina* (Title varies.)
Concejo Deliberante	Concejo Deliberante de la Municipalidad de Buenos Aires, *Diario de Sesiones*
Diputados	Cámara de Diputados de la Nación, *Diario de Sesiones*
Senadores	Cámara de Senadores de la Nación, *Diario de Sesiones*
P.R.O.	Public Record Office, London
F.O.	British Foreign Office
N.A.	National Archives, Washington
D.S.	Department of State, Decimal File
D.A.	Department of Agriculture
Corr. Am. Leg./Emb.	Correspondence of the American Legation/ Embassy, Buenos Aires

Introduction

THE first half of the twentieth century formed a critical stage in the political development of Argentina. At the beginning of the period, power was concentrated in the hands of an aristocratic, landowning elite; by the middle 1940s, power had passed to Juan Domingo Perón, leader of a surging urban lower class. The intervening years were marked by intensive modernization, at least insofar as expanding parts of the country's population came to take part in the political process. In an effort to explore some of the pressures, alignments, and modes of behavior which characterized politics during those years, this book studies the patterns of conflict and consensus relating to the Argentine beef industry between about 1900 and 1946.

The struggles over the production of cattle and beef probably provide as accurate a barometer to Argentina's over-all political climate as any other single issue of the time. Other problems—such as the wheat industry or organized labor—are clearly deserving of study, but livestock raising ranks high on the list of importance and priority. Cattle production has been a mainstay of the national economy ever since the Wars of Independence, and the Anglo-Argentine beef trade gained about half of the country's foreign exchange between 1900 and 1942.[1] Stockraising formed the economic base for the enrichment of Argentine *estancieros,* the backbone of the landed

[1] [Sociedad Rural Argentina], *Anuario de la Sociedad Rural Argentina* (Buenos Aires, 1928), p. 72, and Junta Nacional de Carnes, *Estadísticas básicas* (Buenos Aires, 1964), p. 20.

aristocracy. The predominance of British and United States capital in the meat packing business involved the interests of foreign investors, whose role in politics has long been a source of concern. But beef has also affected Argentine citizens of all social strata, for whom it has been a source of national pride as well as physical nourishment. As the beef industry goes, some have even said, so goes the Argentine nation.

Almost inevitably, the size and diversity of economic interests led to political conflict. When Americans threatened to take over the overseas trade early in the century, British and local investors turned to the Argentine government for help. During World War I some pro-consumer congressmen complained about inflation, and strikes in the packinghouses prompted decisive political measures. A post-war collapse in the cattle market angered many stockmen, who demanded legislative protection against the alleged malpractice of foreign-owned packinghouses. Late in the twenties, the British and Americans fought once again. When the Depression brought another drop in cattle prices, ranchers supported the controversial Roca-Runciman Pact with Britain and lobbied for a special law in Congress. In 1935, as the Argentine Senate undertook a full-scale investigation of the industry, the public assassination of a Senator stirred political passions which have persisted to the present. After a subsequent struggle between rival groups of ranchers, urban consumers and packinghouse workers started to assert their interests; and the workers, especially, played a vital role in lifting Juan Perón to power.

Aside from its intrinsic value, concentration on the meat industry provides an opportunity to examine the types and significance of political conflict concerning rural sectors of production. This theme has been overlooked in much of the literature on developing societies, which seems to assume that industrialization is a basic and necessary feature of social modernization.[2] Yet as we shall see in Chapter I, Argentina's eco-

2 For example see James S. Coleman, "The Political Systems of the Developing Areas," in Gabriel A. Almond and James S. Coleman, eds., *The Politics of the Developing Areas* (Princeton, N. J., 1960), p. 532; and Gino Germani, *Política y sociedad en una época de transición: de la sociedad tradicional a la sociedad*

nomic development was built mainly on raw-material exports and the importation of manufactured goods. An exploration of the pressures and tensions that emerged in connection with the meat industry, which neatly exemplified this process of growth, should yield considerable insight into the character of political conflict in a country whose economic modernization was based on commercial agriculture instead of industrialization.

Within this framework, specific attention will be devoted to the behavior of the "middle sectors"—urban groups whose economic strength is presumably derived from industrial activity. It has been frequently argued that these classes challenged the rural aristocracy and sought to reorganize the social and economic structure in agreement with their "modern" values; eventually, they tried to mobilize support among the lower classes and thus take charge of a general assault upon the Establishment. According to one analysis, this process began in Argentina as early as 1892, with the formation of the Radical Party—"from the start the party of the middle sectors, particularly those in Buenos Aires." [3] From that date forward, the argument goes, these ambitious reformers sought to take over power from the historic ruling groups. They won control of the State through free elections in 1916, held on until a military coup d'etat in 1930, then struggled against a conservative coalition until the advent of Perón. For a full half-century the dominant political theme was urban-rural class conflict: the challenge of the rising middle sectors against the landed aristocracy.

Though this interpretation has become a source of mounting

de masas (Buenos Aires, 1968), esp pp. 69–126. More flexible analyses have recently been contributed by S. N. Eisenstadt, *Modernization: Protest and Change* (Englewood Cliffs, N. J., 1966); Barrington Moore, Jr., *Social Origins of Dictatorship and Democracy: Lord and Peasant in the Making of the Modern World* (Boston, 1966); and C. E. Black, *The Dynamics of Modernization: A Study in Comparative History* (New York, Evanston, London, 1966). Also see Alfred Stepan, "Political Development Theory: The Latin American Experience," *Journal of International Affairs*, XX, no. 2 (1966), 223–34.

[3] John J. Johnson, *Political Change in Latin America: The Emergence of the Middle Sectors* (Stanford, Calif., 1958), p. 98.

controversy, it has been applied frequently to the case of Argentina [4] and will be taken as a reference point throughout this book. Nevertheless, the notion that political modernization is typified by class-oriented urban-rural conflict needs to be tested against the possibility that the process might be characterized, instead, by the development of intra-class conflict within the rural sector.

DEFINITIONS, ASSUMPTIONS, AND PROCEDURE

The following analysis views politics as the resolution of conflicting claims of interest groups. An "interest group" is taken to be "any group that, on the basis of one or more shared attitudes, makes certain claims upon other groups in the society for the establishment, maintenance, or enhancement of forms of behavior that are implied by the shared attitudes." [5] In particular, this study will deal with groups whose basic interests were economic, and the initial conflicts between them were consequently related to economic issues.

Though it is assumed that such economic interests can determine political behavior, I shall be giving systematic consideration to the possibility that political conflicts in Argentina might be influenced by other significant factors: ideological commitment, regional identification, class allegiance, party loyalty, or personal charisma. Indeed, a basic purpose of the analysis is to look for changes in the patterns of alliance, allegiance, and over-all comportment.

It is taken for granted that groups, in the pursuit of their

[4] Either explicitly or implicitly, the middle-class thesis has been promoted by such standard works as Ysabel F. Rennie, *The Argentine Republic* (New York, 1945); George Pendle, *Argentina*, 3rd edition (New York, London, Toronto, 1963); James R. Scobie, *Argentina: A City and a Nation* (New York, 1964); and Arthur P. Whitaker, *Argentina* (Englewood Cliffs, N. J., 1964). Also see Peter G. Snow, *Argentine Radicalism: The History and Doctrine of the Radical Civic Union* (Iowa City, 1965).

[5] David E. Truman, *The Governmental Process: Political Interests and Public Opinion* (New York, 1953), p. 33.

interests, seek power: that is, effective influence in making decisions that involve sanctions or deprivations. Power should not be confused with participation in the struggle for it. Although the two frequently go together, it is conceivable that those in power might regard competition as an unnecessary waste of resources, either when their control of the situation is assured or when their own interests are not affected. Participation in debates or other political contests can reveal a group's desire for power, but does not mean that it exercises influence.

The relative nature of power makes it necessary to distinguish between its various types, which differ according to the kind of sanctions or weapons employed. *Political* power refers to influence on the policies of the government and its component institutions, such as the Executive branch or the Congress; ideally, political strength is obtained and applied with the knowledge of the public. *Economic* power is derived from the control of money, goods, services, or labor. Under the so-called free enterprise system, the accumulation and exertion of economic strength is a generally private matter. *Social* power, which is both public and private, concerns influence on the criteria and allocation of "status" or prestige.

These distinctions provide the basis for my operational definition of "class," which depends upon the combined distribution of social and economic power. As explained in Chapter I, those who possess a great deal of socio-economic strength are said to belong to the upper class; those who lack strength are in the lower class; those in between fall somewhere in the "middle sectors." Hopefully, socio-economic position affords a valid indication of the "life chances" and cultural attributes which pertain to the concept of class. Yet these objective criteria must be matched by subjective factors, such as "class consciousness," before class conflicts can emerge in the political arena.

In an effort to locate the origins of conflicts, the participant groups will also be identified as either "rural" or "urban" in nature. The distinction is not easy to define. As recent studies indicate, mere residence in the city or country does not provide a conclusive index to attitudes and interests.[6] For groups directly connected with the beef industry, whose character and composition can be analyzed with care, I shall employ economic criteria to supplement the purely social ones. Despite some metropolitan habits, for instance, wealthy stockmen residing in the city of Buenos Aires will be regarded as an essentially "rural" interest group because of their pastoral holdings and commitment; packinghouse workers, employed in large-scale industry, will be considered truly "urban." For groups outside the beef industry, I shall simply suggest a concurrent hypothesis: that the interests of the city and its residents are not necessarily opposed to those of the country. In testing this proposition, it should become possible to examine the quality— as well as the fact—of urban life in Argentina.

Using the differentiation between various types of power, I shall try to examine the extent to which the distribution of political power corresponds to the distribution of social or economic power. One characteristic aspect of the politics of Argentine beef, as we shall discover, was the persistent attempt by aggrieved groups to transfer their economic complaints to the political system, thereby transforming private grievances into public issues. Whether or not such groups were able to rectify imbalances in one system through recourse to another will be a central concern of this analysis, as the question helps throw some general light upon the sources, types, allocation, and usage of power in Argentina prior to Perón.[7]

Another important aspect of intergroup conflict is the degree to which outside sectors are drawn into the struggles between the original competing groups. Whether or not outside sectors decide to take part in the fight provides some indication of how they perceive their own interests and go about pursuing them; and if it occurs, the spreading of a conflict can eventually determine its outcome, as the rival groups seek allies of varying

[6] Stepan, "Political Development Theory," esp. 226–31.
[7] See Robert A. Dahl, *Who Governs? Democracy and Power in an American City* (New Haven and London, 1961), for his usage of the concepts of "cumulative inequalities" and "dispersed inequalities."

strength in other areas.[8] In consideration of this problem, I shall take pains to explore the evolving responses of selected peripheral groups to the battles starting within the Argentine beef industry.

Furthermore, this analysis will give special attention to the meaning and role of ideology under conditions of political conflict. It is my hypothesis that ideological rhetoric not only expresses basic values and articulates group interests, but can also define and possibly transform the character and significance of a struggle. As E. E. Schattsneider has put it, perhaps a bit too strongly: "the definition of the alternatives is the supreme instrument of power. . . . He who determines what politics is about runs the country, because the definition of alternatives is the choice of conflicts, and the choice of conflicts allocates power." [9]

One form of issue redefinition that recurs in developing societies takes the shape of anti-imperialism, usually declaring that foreign interests pose a threat to the economic independence of the nation. Protagonists seek to make group interests synonymous with national interests; what is good for the group is good for the country, and support for the group becomes a patriotic duty. Though the tactic now seems commonplace, its function should not be overlooked. While the manifest purpose of anti-imperialist ideology is to attack foreign interests, its latent (and more important) function might be to advance the interests of one local group against another local group, usually by identifying the opponent with hated "alien" interests. This is not to say that nationalists do not bear a genuine resentment against what they see as foreign domination. But there can also be an internal dimension to anti-imperialism, and a meaningful understanding of its usage and significance should take this possibility into account.

In sum, this book raises a series of related questions about conflicts, power, and political behavior in early twentieth-cen-

[8] This idea of the "socialization" of conflict is developed in E. E. Schattsneider, *The Semisovereign People: A Realist's View of Democracy in America* (New York, 1960).

[9] *Ibid.*, p. 68. The quote is italicized in the original.

tury Argentina. (1) Where did the struggles break out? Were the conflicts drawn along urban-rural lines, or initiated within the rural sector? Did the fights take place within or between classes? (2) Who fought whom? How were the issues defined, and what were the goals of the participant groups? (3) Who won? How was power distributed? Did the political system reflect the allocation of economic strength, or did it provide an effective instrument for the correction of economic imbalances? (4) How were the victories achieved? What governmental institutions were used? Was ideology invested with a political function? Was the support of outside sectors sought or obtained by the competing groups?

These questions will be approached through a careful analysis of the reaction of selected interest groups to major developments and crises within the Argentine beef industry. As background, Chapter I will attempt to outline some major trends in the country's development during the early twentieth century. Chapter II will deal with the economic functions, composition, and leadership of the interest groups concerned. Chapters III through IX will trace the responses of the groups to successive changes in economic circumstances from the start of the century to the middle 1940s, with particular emphasis upon the emergence and resolution of conflicts and the behavior of the participants. Conclusions will come after that.

Admittedly, this conceptual framework does not cover the subject completely. While stress is placed on the competition between interest groups, relatively little attention is paid to competition within each group. Largely for lack of data and space, the analysis deals mainly with the composition, aims, and actions of the leadership, not the rank and file, of the various groups. Nor does it deal at much length with some of the intangible factors, such as family ties, that can help account for patterns of alignment and cohesion. In addition, the selection of only one concrete issue—control of the meat industry—yields no indication as to whether or not these same leaders exercised influence in other areas. On the basis of this analysis, therefore, it would be hazardous to draw sweeping conclusions about the allocation of power in Argentina up to 1946.[10] Even so, it is hoped that this study will not only offer some generalizations about the politics of beef in the first half of this century, but also provide some suggestions and hypotheses for further research on this critical phase of political change in Argentina and for similar cases elsewhere.

[10] In *Who Governs?*, for instance, Dahl examines three such "issue-areas" in his effort to determine the distribution of power in New Haven, Connecticut.

I

Argentina: The Process
of Modernization

AROUND the middle of the nineteenth century, Argentina started making significant strides along her road to "modernization," a general concept which refers essentially to the rationalization of human behavior. According to C. E. Black's definition, the process involves the adaptation of "historically evolved institutions . . . to the rapidly changing functions that reflect the unprecedented increase in man's knowledge, permitting control over his environment, that accompanied the scientific revolution." [1] As they covered an infinite range, the forces of modernization were also unevenly felt; changes in one area were not always matched by parallel changes in other areas, and some groups were more deeply affected than others. Despite the dangers of generalization, it would be useful to outline some of the salient economic, social, political, and ideological developments that took place in Argentina mainly between the 1880s and the 1940s.

TRADITIONAL SOCIETY AND
LIBERAL DOCTRINE

A full half century after the declaration of political independence, Argentina was still a largely "traditional" society.[2] The

---

[1] *Dynamics of Modernization*, p. 7.

[2] For an archetypical picture of traditional society see Germani, *Política y sociedad*, pp. 116–26.

economy retained a primitive character. The census of 1869 showed that barely one and a half million inhabitants lived in the sprawling territory of more than a million square miles, and were engaged mostly in subsistence farming or small-scale rural enterprise.[3] A few trading centers dotted the interior, and some ranchers produced hides and salted meat for export in the province of Buenos Aires. But for the most part, the vast, rich *pampas* in the countryside were totally unused. Controlled generally by hostile Indians, the fertile lands to the west symbolized the country's underdevelopment—and also pointed the way to its future.

The social structure was as traditional as the economy. Largely because of Juan Manuel de Rosas' policy of giving public properties away, there had emerged a landholding elite, engaged principally in the raising of livestock. Since the possession of land conferred power, wealth, and prestige upon the owners, these estancieros formed a formidable aristocracy. Below them were the *gauchos,* the peons, and a few tenant farmers. Between the upper and lower classes was an extremely thin middle layer: industrialists were almost nonexistent; the professions were run by the landowners' sons; merchants were not numerous.

The political system reflected this state of stagnation. Long after the liberation from imperial Spain, violence remained the basic instrument of power. Despite legal provisions for elections, popular participation was negligible; in the well-known phrase, political decisions were made by bullets rather than ballots. It was the heyday of the local strongman. Even after Rosas' dictatorship and the fratricidal wars that followed, regional *caudillos* roamed the countryside in open defiance of the central government. Though the Constitution of 1853 announced the formal association of the "Argentine Confederation," changed in 1860 to the "Argentine Nation," primary loyalties were devoted to the provinces rather than to the republic.

Faced with this array of problems, the leaders who came into

[3] Gino Germani, *Estructura social de la Argentina: análisis estadístico* (Buenos Aires, 1955), p. [21].

power after Rosas' defeat—especially Bartolomé Mitre and Domingo F. Sarmiento—started programs that were derived essentially from the nineteenth-century liberal doctrine of individual freedom. Though they continued to employ some authoritarian methods of political control, they drew up plans for representative government. With some modifications, the Argentine constitutions of 1853 and 1860 bore strong resemblance to their model in the United States. Presidents would be named for six-year terms by an electoral college, whose members would be chosen by popular suffrage. A bicameral Congress was set up, the lower house elected by direct vote and the upper house elected by the provincial legislatures. Authority was also divided. The provinces were given the right to establish their own governments, and all powers not specifically accorded to the national State were conceded to the local administrations— though this rule was sharply qualified by a provision allowing the central government to "intervene" in the provinces whenever such action seemed necessary.[4]

In economics, liberal doctrine held that individuals should be free to pursue their personal gain with minimal interference by the State. What was good for the citizen was good for the community; under the unfailing control of the "invisible hand," each person's pursuit of prosperity would necessarily lead to the benefit of society at large. For international dealings, laissez-faire theory maintained that the maximum wealth of all nations could best be achieved by free trade.

Though leading Argentine thinkers adopted this framework, they made two significant modifications. First, unlike Adam Smith, whose vision in *The Wealth of Nations* was more or less static, they stressed the dynamic characteristics of economic growth and regarded reliance on exports and trade as a prelude to the ultimate and desirable goal of industrialization.[5] Second, they assigned a positive role to the State. In their view, the

[4] Texts of the Constitutions of 1853 and 1860 can be found in Faustino Legón and Samuel W. Medrano, *Las constituciones de la República Argentina* (Madrid, 1953), pp. [409]–64.

[5] See Ricardo M. Ortiz, *El pensamiento económico de Echeverría (trayectoria y actualidad)* (Buenos Aires, 1953), esp. pp. 32–33.

government's most pressing task was to increase manpower by encouraging European immigration: hence Juan B. Alberdi's aphorism, "to govern is to populate." Furthermore, the State should provide concessions for the foreign capital that was badly needed for transportation networks, the improvement of ports, and some local industries.[6] Along with liberal injunctions about the rights of economic freedom and the inviolability of private property, these prescriptions for State action were written into the country's Constitution.

By the 1870s national leadership had passed from the post-Rosas intellectual reformers to the landed aristocracy, long an influential group in politics. Through the stabilizing policies of Mitre and Sarmiento, government by chaos had turned into government by an upper-class elite. This was the era of the well-bred and vastly talented "Generation of 1880," a small group of men who held the keys to social, political, and economic power. Led by Julio A. Roca, hero of the Conquest of the Desert from the Indians, they and their followers governed the country during the essentially formative years of its development.

These aristocrats employed a stark brand of nineteenth-century liberalism in order to justify their policies and power. Their outlook was based on the pseudo-science of Herbert Spencer as well as the theories of Adam Smith, stoutly maintaining that competition was the guiding principle of life: if an aristocracy governed Argentina, that was due to natural law. Along with laissez-faire, the survival of the fittest was the watchword of the day. Partly conditioned by the widespread vogue of positivism, Argentina's leaders ardently pursued the materialistic goal of economic growth.[7]

[6] Juan Bautista Alberdi, *Obras escogidas,* ed. Hilmar D. Di Giorgio, I (*Bases y puntos de partida para la organización política de la República Argentina*) (Buenos Aires, 1952), esp. 175, 71.

[7] See Thomas F. McGann, *Argentina, the United States, and the Inter-American System, 1880–1914* (Cambridge, Mass., 1957); and Oscar E. Cornblit, Ezequiel Gallo (h.), and Arturo A. O'Connell, "La generación del 80 y su proyecto: antecedentes y consecuencias," in Torcuato S. di Tella, Gino Germani, and Jorge Graciarena, eds., *Argentina, sociedad de masas* (Buenos Aires, 1965), pp. 18–58.

THE ECONOMIC SYSTEM: EXPORTS
AND IMPORTS

The steady growth and increasing accessibility of consumer markets in Europe during the late nineteenth century created strong international demands for goods that could be easily produced in Argentina, chiefly meat and cereals. The Generation of 1880 was anxious to exploit this opportunity, and took a series of steps to develop the country's rural sectors. Such a policy would strengthen the landowners' economic and political position, and offered a promising avenue for growth. As a result of these efforts, an economic system that prevailed through the 1930s was set up: Argentina exported raw materials to Europe, mainly Great Britain, and imported manufactured goods from abroad.

As Alberdi had recommended, immigration was actively encouraged. Colonization started in the 1850s, a law of 1876 provided for land ownership on easy terms, and by 1880 Roca's campaign against the Indians opened up vast territories for cultivation. Attracted by these conditions, immigrants flocked to Argentina in great numbers. Some were discouraged by the practical difficulties of acquiring land, or by economic crises as in 1890, and made their way back to Europe; others came merely as migrant workers, like the Italian *golondrinas* (or "swallows") who would harvest one crop in Argentina and another one at home. But net immigration was immense. Coming to a country with only 1.7 million residents in 1869, foreigners added more than 2.6 million residents in the following 40 years!

Another major plank in the liberal platform was the attraction of foreign capital, particularly for the construction of railroads. The interior could not be opened up without communications, and cattlemen and wheat farmers needed transportation for their goods and access to the ports. A series of extravagant concessions by Argentine governments eventually bore fruit. In 1880 there were only 2,300 kilometers of track in the coun-

Figure 1.1. *Net Immigration to Argentina, 1870–1910*

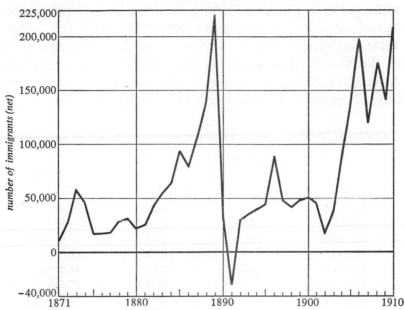

Source: Data in James R. Scobie, *Revolution on the Pampas: A Social History of Argentine Wheat, 1860–1910* (Austin, Texas, 1964), p. 169.

try; by 1910 there were nearly 25,000.[8] Significantly enough, the lines all radiated from the city of Buenos Aires—the country's leading port—and most of them ran through agricultural and pastoral production zones in the provinces of Buenos Aires, Santa Fe, Entre Ríos, and Córdoba.[9]

With rising demand abroad, increasing manpower at home, and facilities for transportation, Argentine exports became the most dynamic element in a rapidly growing gross national product.[10] According to the best available statistics, total output

[8] Juan A. Alsina, *La inmigración en el primer siglo de la independencia* (Buenos Aires, 1910), p. 59.

[9] See the map in Scobie, *Revolution on the Pampas,* p. 41; or, for the position of the provinces, map on p. 37.

[10] The value of Argentine exports increased at the average annual rate of approximately 7 per cent between 1880 and 1920, according to data in Dirección General de Estadística, *Anuario de la Dirección General de Estadística correspondiente al año 1912* (Buenos Aires, 1914), 11, 44; and the *Anuario de la Sociedad Rural Argentina,* p. 72.

increased by roughly 4.5 per cent a year from 1900 to 1930, while per capita income (despite the immigration) grew at an annual average rate of 1.2 per cent.[11] Up until the middle 1940s, agriculture and livestock accounted for a larger share of the G.N.P. than manufacturing. During this whole era, Argentina's economic modernization was based upon commercial agriculture, rather than upon industrialization.

Table 1.1. *Size and Distribution of G.N.P., 1900–1904 to 1945–1949*

	Average G.N.P. (Billions of Pesos, 1950 Prices)	Agriculture, Livestock %	Manufacturing %
1900–04	10.8	33.0	13.8
1905–09	15.9	27.8	14.4
1910–14	19.9	25.2	15.6
1915–19	19.1	31.0	15.3
1920–24	25.5	28.3	16.4
1925–29	33.2	25.7	17.7
1930–34	33.9	25.1	18.4
1935–39	39.8	24.3	20.4
1940–44	45.9	24.7	21.0
1945–49	57.0	18.5	23.5

Sources: Economic Commission for Latin America (United Nations), *El desarrollo económico de la Argentina* (Mexico, 1959), I, 15. And the mimeographed version of this same ECLA publication, "El desarrollo económico de la Argentina" (Santiago de Chile, 1958), E/CN.12/429/Add. 4, Pág. 4.

Undeniably, the steadily increasing importance of manufacturing posed a potential threat to this economic structure and its accent on international trade, as industrialists consistently clamored for tariff protection. Yet this challenge was somewhat modified by the relationship between the rural and industrial sectors. During this period, most manufacturers in Argentina processed products from the countryside (such as wool and beef) and therefore shared some common interests with the landowners. As late as 1935, foodstuffs accounted for 47 per cent of all industrial production, while textiles con-

[11] Economic Commission for Latin America (United Nations), *El desarrollo económico de la Argentina* (Mexico, 1959), I, 15.

tributed another 20 per cent.[12] Deep conflicts between the two sectors were delayed until the 1940s.

Despite successful growth, the reliance on exports, imports, and foreign capital involved one basic weakness: Argentina was extremely vulnerable to economic influence from abroad. First, the encouragement of capital from overseas placed a high proportion of the country's fixed investments—from 1900 to 1929, between 30 and 40 per cent—under the control of foreign citizens.[13] Second, and more important, the extraordinary dependence on exports and imports left Argentina at the mercy of the world market. Up to the 1930s exports amounted to about one-quarter of the country's G.N.P.; imports were equally large. As revealed in the figures below, reductions in overseas trade could have catastrophic effects on the country's economy.

Table 1.2. *Exports and Imports in the Argentine Economy, 1900–1904 to 1945–1949*

	Exports as % of G.N.P.	Imports Compared to G.N.P. (as %)
1900–04	27.1	26.1
1905–09	25.4	28.6
1910–14	22.5	28.7
1915–19	24.0	17.5
1920–24	25.1	21.2
1925–29	23.8	24.8
1930–34	21.9	14.7
1935–39	19.1	14.8
1940–44	13.0	6.4

Source: ECLA, *El desarrollo económico,* I, 18, 26.

Generally speaking, the export-import pattern of economic growth established by the Generation of 1880 prevailed throughout the 1930s. Rural production and international

[12] Computed from data in Adolfo Dorfman, *Evolución industrial argentina* (Buenos Aires, 1942), p. 67.

[13] ECLA, *El desarrollo económico,* I, 28. Most of these investments were British, as shown in Dorfman, *Evolución Industrial,* p. 289.

trade were the dominant features of the Argentine economy. How this fact affected the country's politics will be one concern of this book.

THE SOCIAL STRUCTURE:
EMERGING GROUPS AND CLASSES

Argentina's economic development was accompanied by far-reaching changes in the country's social structure. Stimulated by the immigration from abroad as well as by natural growth, the national population swelled from 1.7 million people in 1869 to 7.9 million in 1914 and then to 15.9 million by 1947.[14] Almost inevitably, this increase in size helped bring an end to the traditional class system which had so long prevailed, basically consisting of a landed elite on the top and a rural peonage on the bottom.

This expanding population provided the skill, expertise, and manpower that were essential to economic growth. Many immigrants moved into the interior regions of Entre Ríos, Santa Fe, and Córdoba as "colonists," tenant farmers, and foremen, where they assisted the breeding of cattle and sowing of grain. As the rural sectors stepped up production for export, other groups appeared in the cities to serve them; export houses, transportation companies, processing industries, and the professions acquired increasing importance. Thus the country's development created an intricate network of economic interests and also gave rise to primarily urban middle-class groups, many of whose members had come from abroad.[15]

The attractions of urban life, combined with an eventual shortage of available land and rural occupations, led to the growth of Argentina's cities. As shown in the following table, much of the urban expansion took place in Greater Buenos Aires, which contained 28 per cent of the national population

[14] Germani, *Estructura social*, p. [21].
[15] Scobie, *Revolution on the Pampas, passim;* and Germani, *Política y sociedad*, esp. p. 195.

by 1947. In all, nearly half the people of Argentina lived in urban areas by the middle 1940s.[16]

Table 1.3. *Urban Growth in Argentina, 1895–1947*

	% of National Population	% in Buenos Aires	Number of Urban Centers
1895	24	17	8
1914	36	24	18
1947	47	28	46

Source: Germani, *Estructura social,* p. 69.

One result of this trend was the appearance of an urban lower class, composed essentially of manual laborers. According to one estimate, this group may have nearly 60 per cent of the population in the city of Buenos Aires by the early twentieth century. But its character was more important than its size. By the 1940s, the lower-class "masses" in Buenos Aires were approximately 90 per cent literate. They were mobile, as nearly one-third of the city's residents had migrated from the interior. As a byproduct of this process, they were composed increasingly of native Argentines rather than European immigrants.[17] While they found it more and more difficult to find employment, especially during the Depression,[18] their economic interests called for industrialization. Combined with their mounting political resources, their implicit opposition to the export-import economic structure eventually posed a serious challenge to Argentine leadership.

On the basis of census materials, it seems fair to use the socio-economic attributes of differing occupations in order to gain some idea of Argentina's class structure (though I shall also stress family background and social prominence in dealing with

[16] In this context I have considered population centers of 20,000 or more inhabitants as "urban," while the official records (and Gino Germani) put the minimum at 2,000.

[17] Germani, *Estructura social,* pp. 210, 219, 232; Germani, *Política y sociedad,* p. 230.

[18] Between 1910–14 and 1940–44 the economically active population dropped from 42.2 per cent to 37.7 per cent: ECLA, *El desarrollo económico,* I, 37.

specific historical actors). Four crude categories emerge from the analysis. (1) The upper class or "aristocracy," which enjoyed great social prestige and economic strength, typically based on land ownership. (2) The upper middle class, usually prosperous but not prestigious. (3) The lower middle class, which had little economic strength and virtually no social power, but could at least entertain opportunities for upward ascent. (4) The lower class, standing at the bottom of the socio-economic ladder and confronted by major obstacles to upward mobility. Large segments of the middle and lower classes lived in urban areas, and many members of these strata were immigrants from Europe. Though precise computation is impossible, the relative size of the different classes is roughly estimated in the following table.

Table 1.4.   *Class Structure in Argentina, 1914–1947*

	1914 (%)	1947 (%)
Upper Class	1	1
Middle Classes	32	39
(Upper)	(8)	(7)
(Lower)	(24)	(32)
Lower Class	67	60
Total	100	100

Source: Adapted from Germani, *Estructura social*, pp. 198, 220–22, with methodological problems and techniques discussed on pp. 139–51.

The possibility that these developments would give rise to class conflict, involving either the middle classes or the lower class, would depend largely upon the interests, aspirations, and self-identification of the people involved. But whether or not class struggles occurred, Argentina's social modernization was eventually bound to exert pressures on the political system, as expanding parts of the population sought to take part in politics.[19]

[19] See Karl W. Deutsch, "Social Mobilization and Political Development," *American Political Science Review*, LV, no. 3 (September, 1961), 493–514. My treatment of political modernization implicitly follows the proposal, made by Samuel P. Huntington, that emphasis be devoted to four problems: mass

THE POLITICAL SYSTEM:
CENTRALIZATION AND EXPANSION

Under the Generation of 1880, Argentina was run by upper-class aristocrats whose political strength came from several sources. They gained control of the army; they openly rigged elections; they made the only major political party (*Partido Autonomista Nacional*, or P.A.N.) a tool of the administration; and they restricted the decision-making process to their own circles. Congress was not widely used as a forum for the expression of interests, and most significant decisions were made by "*acuerdo*"—literally by informal "agreement" with members of the Executive branch, not by presenting the issues and alternatives to the public.

Apparently seeking to consolidate their rule, leaders of this Generation made a deliberate effort to centralize power. In 1880 they strengthened national unity by turning the city of Buenos Aires into the country's capital. They set up a central bank in 1891, giving the State exclusive control over the issuance of currency. In 1893, as H. S. Ferns has written, consolidation of the national debt struck "the last blow at the federal structure of Argentine politics: more deadly than the interventions and military thrusts of the past." [20] Government budgets sharply increased, as shown in Figure 1.2 on the following page, while the national State consistently accounted for over 70 per cent of total public expenditures.

The consolidation of power took many forms. An expanding work load made it necessary to augment the number of ministries from five to eight. In 1901, a military conscription law bluntly reminded all Argentine males of their duty to the nation, whose international role was steadily gaining importance.

mobilization, interest articulation, elite broadening, and institutional development. See Merle Kling's essay "The State of Research on Latin America: Political Science" in Charles Wagley, ed., *Social Science Research on Latin America: Report and Papers of a Seminar on Latin American Studies in the United States Held at Stanford, California, July 8–August 23, 1963* (New York and London, 1964), pp. 195–96.

[20] *Britain and Argentina in the Nineteenth Century* (London, 1960), p. 477.

The central government also asserted its authority with increasing frequency. The number of national laws, for instance, climbed from barely over 1,000 in 1880 to more than 11,000 in 1920; that same year, the most powerful province of all—Buenos Aires—had only 4,000 laws of its own. (See Figure 1.3.) Though they were not always strictly enforced, major political decisions came to be made by the State.

centralization

While this centralization of authority tended to tighten the aristocrats' grip on the reins of power, other pressures forced them to broaden the base of the political system and relinquish some of their control. As noted above, Argentina's economic modernization spread rapidly into the interior and engaged important new groups, from landowners to merchants, in the production and export of raw material goods. Yet this redistribution of economic power, without corresponding changes in the social and political arenas, provoked discontent among three major factions: (1) the *nouveaux riches* landowners of the upper Littoral; (2) descendants of old aristocratic families who were somehow unable to cash in on the economic growth; (3)

Figure 1.2. *National and Provincial Budgets, 1895–1914*

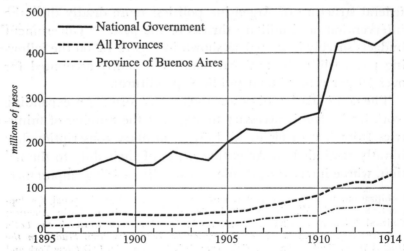

Source: *Tercer censo nacional, levantado el 1º de junio de 1914*, X (Buenos Aires, 1917), 351–55.

Figure 1.3.   *Total Number of National Laws, 1875–1940*

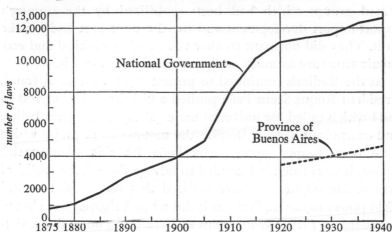

Sources: Jerónimo Remorino et al., ed., *Anales de la legislación argentina, 1852–1940,* 4 vols. (Buenos Aires, 1953–1955), and Cámara de Diputados de la Provincia de Buenos Aires, *Diario de Sesiones,* 1915–1940.

middle-class members who took part in the process of expansion, often as merchants, but who were excluded from strongholds of power.

As Ezequiel Gallo (h.) and Silvia Sigal have carefully argued, these three social elements combined to form the Radical Party.[21] In 1890, as the country plunged into a short but sharp depression, a group called the Civic Union rose up against the ruling aristocracy. The revolt was ended by "acuerdo," when Bartolomé Mitre struck a compromise with the government, but two years later the movement's dissenting faction established the "Radical" Civic Union. Led first by Leandro Alem and then by Hipólito Yrigoyen, the Radicals boycotted all elections and made two more attempts at revolution. They failed each time, but the significance was clear: these groups wanted political power.

Thus the Radical Party was born. Though the notion still needs testing, this does not appear to have been an exclusively urban middle-class movement, intent upon industrialization

21 "La formación de los partidos políticos contemporáneos: la U.C.R. (1890–1916)," in Di Tella et al., eds., *Argentina, sociedad de masas,* pp. 124–76.

and the overthrow of the aristocracy. Rather, the Party represented groups which had been mobilized by the country's export-import development and for the most part had a stake in it. They did not want to alter the existing political and economic structure so much as they wanted to control it.

As the Radicals continued to protest against electoral fraud, President Roque Saenz Peña pushed a bill through Congress in 1911 which called for universal male suffrage, the secret ballot, and compulsory voting. Despite the mountains of praise which have been heaped upon Saenz Peña for this "democratic" action, it was evidently intended to salvage the existing political system. He might well have realized that the decision would yield power to the Radicals, as it did when Yrigoyen was elected President in 1916, but he seems to have understood the underlying commitment of middle-class leaders to the existing political and economic structure and did not regard them as a threat to it.[22] In a way, the Saenz Peña law was a tacit "acuerdo"; as such, it was one of the last major political decisions of its kind.

With the application of the voting law in 1912, the Argentine political system retained its constitutional form but underwent three important modifications. First and foremost, the popular base was widened. All Argentine males over 18 years old were now registered to vote; about 70 per cent usually went to the polls.[23] Such high voter participation sharply contrasts with the apathy that greeted elections before, and clearly suggests that Argentine politics entered a truly competitive stage. As Saenz Peña had apparently foreseen, these changes strengthened the legitimacy of the existing governmental structure—but they also meant that an active and participant "public," or "audience," would play a significant role in politics.

Second, the national Congress gained importance both as a forum for the expression of interests and as a decision-making center. Under the previous "acuerdo" system, Congress had

22 See his comment in Ministerio del Interior, *Las fuerzas armadas restituyen el imperio de la soberania popular* (Buenos Aires, 1946), I, 9.

23 *Ibid.*, I, 402–603; and Germani, *Política y sociedad*, p. 225n. As these figures imply, the legal provision for compulsory voting was not universally followed.

Figure 1.4. *Total Congressional Activity, 1900–1942*
(Trend Line Based on Three-Year Running Averages)

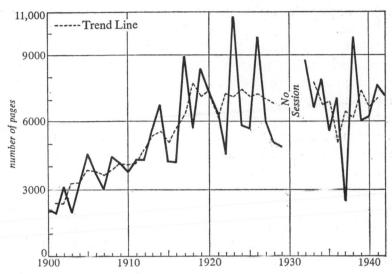

been nothing but a puppet of the ruling machine. Now, as Radicals, Socialists, and other parties won seats in the parliament, it won recognition as a legitimate and relatively open arena for conflicts and their resolution. As shown in Figure 1.4, the annual activities of the national legislature (measured by the total number of pages in the *Diario de Sesiones* of both houses) greatly increased in the 1910s and 1920s, as opposition groups and their spokesmen took part in the political process.[24] Despite its continuing superiority, the Executive no longer enjoyed near-absolute authority. For this reason, many of the conflicts over the beef industry took place principally within the halls of Congress.

Third, and in view of these developments, the political parties were strengthened. Before, the pro-government P.A.N. had exercised a virtual monopoly, which it occasionally shared with the conservative Mitre wing of the Civic Union. Opposition parties were relegated either to conspiracy, like the

[24] The break in 1930–31 is due to the suspension of the Congress after the revolution of 1930.

Radicals, or to obscurity, like the Socialists. Now these and other parties had definite and positive functions to perform, and they provided articulate vehicles for the expression of many opinions.

Thus the Argentine political system survived the transition from decision by "acuerdo" to decision by parliamentary procedure, though the President continued to exercise predominant influence. While power was reapportioned between the Executive and Congress and elections became more hotly contested, the authority of the central government not only increased; it also became the ultimate prize of politics.

IDEOLOGIES OF ANTI-IMPERIALISM

This over-all phase of economic, social, and political modernization was also characterized by the expression of economic nationalism or "anti-imperialism." As an ideology, nationalism is taken to be the assertion of superiority, strength, or independence of a nation—which may in turn be defined as a community of people with sovereign political authority. Despite its association with commonly recognized symbols, nationalism is subject to varying interpretations and does not necessarily acknowledge a consensus about civic responsibilities or the nation's destiny. As it developed in Argentina, this ideology came to stress the defense of national economic independence from the more powerful countries in Europe or the United States and their alleged "imperialist" designs.

One of the Argentine quests for economic independence took the shape of what I shall call "traditional" anti-imperialism, which rejected the basic validity of modernization on the ground that it required the adoption of alien and materialistic values. Near the turn of the century a whole spate of novels attacked the Generation of 1880 and its accent on development, while Juan Agustín García took a despondent look at the country's economic progress. If Argentina would never be anything more than a colossal *estancia*, crisscrossed by railroads and bursting with wealth, he said, "I would rather live in the most miserable corner of the earth where there still lives a feeling for beauty, goodness, and truth." [25] As José Enrique Rodó's *Ariel* became popular reading, Manuel Gálvez argued that Caliban had captured Argentina as well as the United States:

The present times demand that all of us Argentines gather what strength we have in order to revive the spiritual life of the country. This spiritual life, so intense in the past, ended with the coming of the materialistic and transitory age that we are now going through. We have abandoned those nationalist ideals which were once the noblest feature of the Argentine people, in order to concern ourselves merely with increasing our wealth and accelerating the progress of the country.[26]

It was time to forsake the shimmering falsehoods of progress, money, and modernity. Argentina needed to recover the spiritual purity of its rural past, symbolized by such romantic figures as the gaucho of the pampas.[27]

Despite its cultural emphasis, this ideology can be regarded as a form of anti-imperialism. It consistently maintained that the major corrupting agent in Argentine society was foreign economic penetration. The identification of materialism with foreign domination led to a double conclusion: if avaricious values were to be conquered, the foreigners would have to be driven out, and vice versa. Though the doctrine's content was anti-economic as well as anti-imperialistic, it could be employed for economic purposes.

This equation between the alien and the unspiritual led to frequent claims of cultural superiority over the more economically advanced nations, especially the United States. Manuel Ugarte neatly captured this feeling of defensive pride. As he wandered through the streets of New York City, he recalled, memories of the remote and backward Argentine interior gave him a sense of satisfaction. "That world might be

25 Quoted in Alejandro Korn, *Obras completas*, ed. Francisco Romero (Buenos Aires, 1949), p. 200. The tone of this remark runs throughout the whole of García's *Sobre nuestra incultura* (Buenos Aires, n.d.).

26 *El diario de Gabriel Quiroga* (Buenos Aires, 1910), pp. 51–52; explicit references to Caliban appear on pp. 185, 214.

27 See Madaline Wallis Nichols, *The Gaucho: Cattle Hunter, Cavalryman, Ideal of Romance* (Durham, N. C., 1942), esp. pp. [58]–63.

absurd, it might be uncomfortable, it might be barbarous: but it was mine." [28] Inherent in this outlook was the notion that Argentina was basically better than the more developed countries, and the pursuit of their example would only carry her downhill.

This kind of anti-imperialism frequently assailed the egalitarian values of modern society. Adolfo Saldías, among others, found patriotic inspiration in the tyrannical Rosas regime,[29] and Juan Agustín García maintained that an authoritarian State "has constituted the Argentine ideal ever since 1810. Like modern-day Germany and Italy, our country aspired to unity, and this unity can only be achieved under a strong and omnipotent State which overcomes all individual resistance in its irresistible march. This State contains its own ideal of progress and growth, regardless of the more or less capricious will of the people." [30] Rather than nineteenth-century liberalism and its emphasis on laissez-faire, García demanded order: morality and the collective good, not fraudulent notions of liberty, were the fundamental issues. Not surprisingly, several of these traditionalists became exponents of Argentine fascism in the 1930s.

The appearance of this creed revealed an important ideological rift in Argentina, particularly within the ranks of the aristocracy. Some members of the upper class adopted a liberal belief in progress and change. Others maintained firm faith in traditional values, glorifying sanctity and order. In pure form, the creeds were diametrically opposed: materialism vs. spiritualism, liberty vs. hierarchy, internationalism vs. isolationism, democracy vs. authoritarianism. The result of this difference was sometimes conflict but more often confusion, as many aristocrats settled for vague, eclectic, and inconsistent combinations of the two beliefs.

[28] *The Destiny of a Continent,* ed. J. Fred Rippy, trans. Catherine A. Phillips (New York, 1925), pp. 10–11.
[29] *La evolución republicana durante la revolución argentina* (Buenos Aires, 1906).
[30] *Sobre nuestra incultura,* p. 69.

Yet it should be recognized that, as general prescriptions for economic policy, these doctrines were in harmony. The traditional emphasis on rural values could easily be translated into a justification of agricultural activity and the importation (rather than the money-grubbing production) of manufactured goods. Thus traditional anti-imperialism could rationalize the export-import economy that was originally inspired by liberal doctrine. As the expansion of the political system required the landed elite to find a means of identifying its interests with those of the nation at large, traditional nationalism neatly suited such a need. In fact, one typical feature of political debate came to be the aristocracy's assiduous cultivation of a patriotic "agrarian myth" that emphasized the rural features of the Argentine heritage.

A second form of nationalism, which I shall call "modern," regarded foreign imperialism as an obstacle to, and not an agent of, economic development. Instead of rejecting the notion of material progress, this ideology sought to regain and assert national sovereignty through the attainment of economic self-sufficiency. This could only be reached, according to the argument, by relaxing commercial links with the outer world and embarking upon an intensive program of industrialization. This would free Argentina from the unpredictable whimsies of the world market, lead to heightened prosperity, and increase the country's prestige. The entire logical structure was based upon a fundamental premise: that national greatness is derived from economic strength.[31]

The stress on economic self-sufficiency led to persistent and mounting demands for the protection of native industries, particularly through import quotas and elevated tariffs. Starting as early as the 1870s, pleas for tariff protection reached a peak of intensity during and just after World War I, which spawned a great number of local industries. Sparks of resentment smoldered through the 1920s, as Argentina's economy recovered from the wartime shock, then flared up again in the 1930s. The

[31] *Boletín*, XXXII, no. 591 (March, 1918), 1, and no. 598 (October, 1918), 244.

Depression, it was claimed, pointed up the risks and folly of reliance on foreign markets. For many Argentines, *"Bastarse a sí mismo"* became the slogan of the day.[32]

Modern anti-imperialism also emphasized the need to protect indigenous resources, especially mineral and petroleum deposits, from foreign exploitation. Such resources were essential requisites for progress, according to this view, and should be kept intact for use by Argentines alone. It was primarily in this context that modern nationalists conceived their ardent resentment of foreign capital, especially the "trusts" from the United States. Regarded with hatred, fear, and a hint of grudging admiration, large-scale foreign firms were held as symbols of rapacity and greed.

The two major planks in the pro-industrial platform, tariff protection and resource preservation, both called for active economic intervention by the State. In recognition of this demand, for instance, the Argentine government set up its own agency to exploit petroleum deposits in the 1920s. Though proponents of industrialization sometimes vacillated on this point, they generally supported State action.

Modern nationalism had far-reaching implications. Challenging the liberal doctrines of free trade and laissez-faire, it called for a total revision of economic priorities. Industrialization, not agriculture and stockraising, should become the primary source of national wealth. This argument could be readily turned against the landed aristocracy, whose hegemony had presumably kept the country in its "backward" and "dependent" economic state. On an ideological plane, there were considerable grounds for conflict between the proponents of traditional and modern anti-imperialism.[33]

There were, in sum, three separate economic ideologies cur-

[32] *Ibid.*, XVII, no. 417 (September, 1903), 1; XXVIII, no. 550 (October, 1914), 1–4; XLIV, no. 746 (February, 1931), 23–25.

[33] This ambiguity is typical of rapidly developing societies. See Mary Matossian, "Ideologies of Delayed Industrialization: Some Tensions and Ambiguities," in John H. Kautsky, ed., *Political Change in Underdeveloped Countries: Nationalism and Communism* (New York and London, 1962), pp. 252–64.

rent in early twentieth-century Argentina: liberal laissez-faire, traditional anti-imperialism, and modern anti-imperialism. They all carried different messages and could be applied to different purposes. How they were used, by which groups, with what intentions and with what results, will be one constant concern of the following analysis.

II

Overview: The Industry and Interest Groups

ARGENTINE beef bore profound political importance for two main reasons. Tied to foreign markets and financed largely from abroad, the meat industry epitomized the country's export-import pattern of economic growth.[1] Furthermore, the production and consumption of meat involved the interests of several significant groups. Almost immediately, conflicts between the groups became major national issues. To understand how these struggles shaped up, it is necessary to begin by examining the background and the structure of the industry.

EARLY DEVELOPMENT

The first factor in the eventual rise of Argentine beef was the appearance of foreign demand, especially in Britain. There, as population increased and the Industrial Revolution moved thousands of people from the country to the cities, demographic changes and improved purchasing power of the wage-earning masses altered dietary habits and taste: British consumers wanted meat, rather than bread and potatoes. Demand steadily outstripped supply, and when natural disasters (wet-

---

[1] Unless otherwise specified, "meat" will be used to mean "beef" throughout this book. Lamb and mutton were important export products, of course, but they are excluded from this analysis because (1) their relative economic significance dropped off after 1900, and (2) they do not seem to have generated much political debate.

ness, droughts, and plague) cut down the number of cattle it became abundantly clear that Victorian England would have to rely on meat importation.[2]

One of the most promising places for large-scale beef production anywhere in the world was Argentina. The flat, fertile pampas offered unrivaled pasturing grounds. Though most of the country's cattle was of a low-grade *criollo* type, used primarily for hides and jerked meat, some European bulls were imported as early as the 1840s; in 1866, a group of farsighted cattlemen founded the Argentine Rural Society for the purpose of improving the quality of stock. Roca's Conquest of the Desert opened up additional grazing areas, and the phenomenal growth of the railroads provided a means of getting livestock to the port of Buenos Aires.

The problem was getting it from there to Europe. Shipments on the hoof were clumsy and costly, and raw meat spoiled during oceanic voyages. It was not until the 1860s that Charles Tellier invented an ammonia-compression refrigerating plant. In 1876, a cargo of beef, mutton, and small game was dispatched from Rouen, bound for Buenos Aires in a ship which Tellier fittingly named *Le Frigorifique;* the meat arrived in an edible (if not delectable) state. The next year, with improved refrigeration, Argentine beef on board the *Paraguay* reached France in first-rate condition.[3]

After this technical problem was solved, pioneer efforts in Argentina's refrigerated meatpacking industry were made by the British. In 1882 George W. Drabble founded the country's first *frigorífico*, the River Plate Fresh Meat Company, and began exporting mutton and lamb the next year. The Las Palmas Produce Company was started with English capital in 1886. In 1902 some British investors combined with other for-

[2] T. W. Fletcher, "The Great Depression of English Agriculture 1873–1896," *The Economic History Review*, 2nd ser., XIII, no. 3 (1961), 417–32; Viscount Astor and B. Seebohm Rowntree, *British Agriculture: The Principles of Future Policy* (London, New York, Toronto, 1938), Chapter III, pp. 28–54; William Ashworth, *An Economic History of England 1870–1939* (New York and London, 1960), pp. [3]–26 and esp. pp. [46]–70.

[3] Simon G. Hanson, *Argentine Meat and the British Market: Chapters in the History of the Argentine Meat Industry* (Stanford, Calif., 1938), pp. 18–47.

eign groups to finance construction of the massive La Plata Cold Storage Company. Another English firm, the Smithfield & Argentine Meat Company, was established in 1903. Major Argentine investments were limited to the Sansinena Company (1884), the Frigorífico La Blanca (1902), and the Frigorífico Argentino (1905). Britain dominated the business in these years.[4]

Argentine beef exports started spectacular growth at the turn of the century, when a coincidental series of events wrought long-lasting changes in the world market. A crisis in the French wool industry discouraged Argentine ranchers from breeding sheep, and many turned to the raising of cattle. As beef supplies increased, competition fell off in the international market. The Boer War drastically reduced the herds in South Africa, creating demand for the armies as well; drought took a heavy toll on Australian stock; increasing domestic consumption and labor strikes in Chicago cut down United States shipments abroad. Most important of all, the Anglo-Argentine trade in cattle on the hoof was brought to a sudden halt with the closing of British ports to steers from areas with hoof-and-mouth disease; if meat were to enter London from the Plate, it would have to be in canned or frozen form. As a result of these factors, Argentina soon became the United Kingdom's leading source of frozen beef.[5]

United States capital moved into the Argentine beef industry with Swift & Company's purchase of the giant La Plata Cold Storage plant in 1907, and immediately stepped up growing demands on the stockmen. The Americans wanted to ship meat in soft condition, as some other packers had started to do, rather than frozen solid. Refrigerated at 28°–30° Fahrenheit, chilled beef was more perishable than frozen—it lasted only about 40 days—but was also better tasting. In order to make the process

---

[4] *Ibid.*, esp. pp. 51–70, 131–35. British investors and their partners controlled nearly two-thirds of the country's meat-freezing capacity by 1905; but since Argentine firms tended to concentrate on the domestic market, the foreign companies held an even higher proportion of the export trade. See the data in Juan E. Richelet, *The Argentine Meat Trade: Meat Inspection Regulations in the Argentine Republic* (London, 1929), p. 19.

[5] Hanson, *Argentine Meat,* p. 129.

worthwhile, the Americans wanted top-quality beef and promptly encouraged Argentine ranchers to produce it.

This development added another major category to the kinds of cattle bred for slaughter in Argentina. (1) Now there were "chillers," the top-grade calves which had usually been fattened on special alfalfa pastures. (2) Next came the "freezers," sometimes fattened and sometimes not, still an important item in the export trade. (3) Beef for domestic consumption was usually of fair-to-middling quality, frequently from cows instead of calves. The best Argentine beef was sent abroad: an English rib roast came from substantially better stock than the local *bife de chorizo*. (4) Of distinctly lower quality was the cattle used for conserved and canned beef, thin, scrawny animals that found their way into anything from Liebig's Extract to corned beef hash.

Overseas demand for chilled beef grew sharply after World War I, and by the mid-1920s chilled was by far the leading item in Argentine meat exports. Approximately 90 per cent of these shipments were sent to Great Britain. Much of the frozen and canned meat, on the other hand, was sold in continental Europe.[6] (See Figure 2.1 on the following page.)

The major socio-political significance of the chilled beef trade lay in the division of Argentine ranchers into two groups: *criadores,* who bred the high-grade cattle and nurtured them through the age of weaning at eight to ten months; and *invernadores,* who fattened the animals until they were ready for slaughter at two or possibly three years of age, then sold them to the packers. This separation of labor rested primarily on geographical bases, since only the land in the western part of the province of Buenos Aires and similar areas—flat, dry ground in which alfalfa flourished—could be used for the feeding of chillers. (The principal zones for breeding and fattening are outlined in the map on the page after next.) [7] Before going to

6 Junta Nacional de Carnes, *Estadísticas básicas,* p. 15. Freezer cattle for the European trade were sometimes placed in a separate category, known as "Continental," but this classification will be employed rarely in this study.

7 The fattening zone, in the map and throughout this study, is taken to have included the following counties or *partidos.* In the province of Buenos

Figure 2.1. *Exports of Frozen and Chilled Meat, 1880–1930*
(Thousands of Tons)

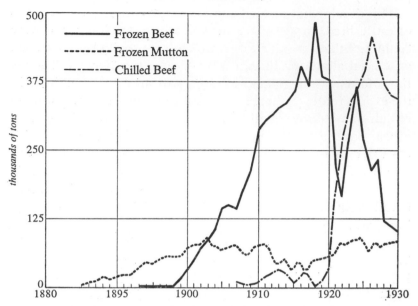

Source: Ricardo M. Ortiz, *Historia económica de la Argentina,* II (Buenos Aires, 1964), 11.

slaughter, virtually all chiller cattle produced in the southeast of Buenos Aires, Córdoba, Corrientes, Entre Ríos, La Pampa, San Luis, and Santa Fe were sent to the special grounds for grazing.

The separation between breeders and fatteners [8] was contingent entirely upon the trade in chilled beef and, as such, was a product of the industry's development. It started around

Aires: Adolfo Alsina, Bolívar, Carlos Casares, Carlos Tejedor, Caseros, General Pinto, General Villegas, Guaminí, Lincoln, Nueve de Julio, Pehuajó, Pellegrini, Rivadavia, Trenque Leuquén. Córdoba: General Roca, Juárez Celman, Marcos Juárez, Unión. Entre Ríos: Diamante, Gualeguay, Gualeguaychú, Victoria. Santa Fe: Caseros, Constitución, General López, Rosario, San Lorenzo. La Pampa: Atreucó, Capital, Catriló, Chapaleufú, Maracó, Quemú Quemú, Rancul, Realicó, Toay. This list differs slightly from the one in Carl C. Taylor, *Rural Life in Argentina* (Baton Rouge, La., 1948), p. 254.

[8] At the expense of literary gracefulness, cattlemen—as a general group—will be referred to as stockmen, ranchers, and livestock producers; invernadores will be called fatteners; criadores will be called breeders. Packinghouse managers are also called packers.

Major Cattle Production Zones in Argentina

▨ Breeding Grounds
⣿ Fattening Grounds

City of Buenos Aires

FALKLAND ISLANDS
(MALVINAS)

JUJUY
LOS ANDES
SALTA
FORMOSA
CATAMARCA
TUCUMAN
SANTIAGO DEL ESTERO
CHACO
CORRIENTES
MISIONES
LA RIOJA
SAN JUAN
CÓRDOBA
SANTA FE
ENTRE RÍOS
SAN LUIS
MENDOZA
LA PAMPA
BUENOS AIRES
NEUQUÉN
RÍO NEGRO
CHUBUT
SANTA CRUZ
TIERRA DEL FUEGO

1912,[9] blurred during World War I, then crystallized during the decade of the 'twenties. It was much less apparent in the preparation of freezers and not at all evident in the growing of cattle whose meat would be conserved or consumed in Argentina.

If the chilled beef trade was the most profitable part of the industry, the domestic market was by far the most voluminous. Much if not most of this local trade took place in Greater Buenos Aires, which offered a ready and large-scale market. Urban demand was an important consideration for the country's cattle producers, especially for the raisers of lower-grade stock who were automatically excluded from the profits to be made in the exportation of chilled meat.

Table 2.1. *Consumption and Exportation of Argentine Beef, 1915–1935*

	Slaughtered for Export		Slaughtered for Home Consumption	
	Number (Million Head)	% Total	Number (Million Head)	% Total
1915	1.4	38.7	2.2	61.3
1920	1.4	41.7	2.0	58.3
1925	3.1	38.7	5.0	61.3
1930	2.1	32.8	4.4	67.2
1935	1.9	27.6	5.1	72.4

Source: Junta Nacional de Carnes, *Estadísticas básicas*, p. 8.

In these various ways, the structure and development of the Argentine beef industry led to the formation of five major interest groups: (1) the packinghouse managers; the cattlemen, eventually divided into (2) breeders and (3) fatteners; (4) the consumers in Greater Buenos Aires; and (5) the packinghouse workers. The list is by no means definitive—butchers, railroad owners, and shipping agents might also be included—but it identifies the groups of greatest importance. Their economic interests were defined by their positions in the beef industry, which have been schematized (and vastly simplified) in Figure

[9] Horacio V. Pereda, *La ganadería argentina es una sola* (Buenos Aires, 1939), p. 26.

Figure 2.2. *General Structure of the Argentine Beef Industry*

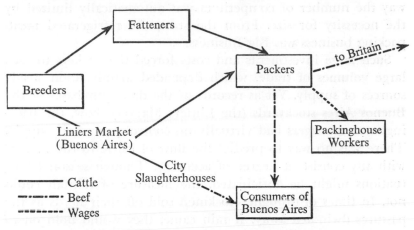

2.2. Before dealing with the interaction of these groups, it is necessary to consider their character, composition, and leadership.

THE PACKERS

The packers performed an intermediary function. They bought cattle ready for the kill and sold meat to be consumed. The absolute prices of cattle and meat did not much matter in themselves; what was important was the margin between these prices, for that was where the packinghouse made or lost its profit. The preservation and expansion of this margin was the paramount interest of the packers. Their purpose was to buy as low as possible and to sell as high as possible.

Meatpacking was and still is a complicated business, marked by dozens of pitfalls and risks. Large amounts of capital were needed to construct a plant, which required at least £200,000 by the end of the nineteenth century. The costs of maintenance and labor were also considerable. Losses were therefore expensive. At the same time, this situation meant that small- and middle-sized entrepreneurs were excluded from the industry (except, of course, as stockholders). It was impossible for someone to start out with a little packinghouse and, through alertness and clean living, turn it into a large packinghouse. In this way the number of competitors was automatically limited by the necessity for size. From the start, the refrigerated meat-packing business was Big Business.

Such large investments and costs forced the packers to seek large volumes of trade, which depended mainly upon steady sources of supply. Yet as records of the daily purchases at the Buenos Aires stockyards (the Liniers Market) show, the pack-inghouse managers had virtually no control over their supply. There was no way to predict the flow of cattle to the market with any consistent degree of accuracy. Though seasonal fluc-tuations might be anticipated, the measure of rainfall could not. In times of drought, stockmen sold off their herds as the pastures dwindled away; if rain came, they would hold on to their calves a little longer, waiting for the animals to reach top weight. In the meantime, the packers faced the prospect of scarcity and gluts. Oversupply meant lower purchase costs, of course, but it could also mean a lower price for meat as well. Scarcity was disastrous, no matter how low the costs and how high the price of meat: if there was no volume, there was no profit.

Under these conditions the packers took whatever steps they could to assure fairly predictable supplies, especially of the much-demanded chillers. They bought large quantities of cattle on the ranches, rather than at Liniers, because that gave them (and not the cattlemen) control over the timing of the pur-chase. Frequently, they made advance agreements with some of the fatteners, often at predetermined prices that would turn out to be higher than the going Liniers rates at the actual mo-ment of purchase. Any losses incurred this way were willingly absorbed by the packers.[10]

Their next major hazard was transportation. Speed in transit to Europe was particularly important for chilled beef, whose perishability made time a precious matter. If the meat was not

[10] Perhaps as a measure of their confidence in such agreements, most major packers refrained from vertical integration before the 1940s. During the Perón era they started buying cattle lands; Swift & Company, a partner in the Inter-national Packing Company, is now one of the largest landowners in the country.

retailed within 40 days after slaughter, it had to be "frozen down" and sold at a loss. As it was, most boats took about a month to reach Britain because of stops in Brazil, leaving only a week or ten days for distribution and sale of the beef. This situation, trying in itself, was aggravated by the limited availability of refrigerated hulls for shipment to Britain, which usually had to be reserved for months ahead. Competition for cargo space was naturally brutal; ultimately, it was a question of survival.[11]

The strain of this competition eventually induced the packers to come to a series of agreements for the partition of transportation facilities. (Their specific conditions will be discussed in the chapters that follow.) As explained by the managers, the point of these "pools" was to enable their members to share available shipping tonnage and to regulate supplies for the British market so that, particularly in view of the perishable nature of chilled beef, the timing and quantity of shipments could be adjusted to the market's power of absorption.

Despite their avowed or intended purposes, the pools amounted to an apportionment of the British market for Argentine (and Uruguayan) beef. Though they consequently had some impact on the retail price of meat at London's Smithfield Market, their influence in Britain was limited by strong competition from Canada, Australia, New Zealand, South Africa, Brazil, Scotland, and the rest of the United Kingdom. The real power of the pools was exercised in the Argentine cattle market, where the packers enjoyed a virtual monopsony (buyer's monopoly). A partition of shipping space naturally implied a partition of the cattle to be purchased for export. If a rancher was not satisfied by the price offered by one packinghouse, he could not just go to another—not if the quotas had already been filled. The frequent buyers' markets were particularly onerous for those who sent their cattle to Liniers; those who sold from the ranches had at least a little bargaining room. While the

11 The shipping problem was not an artificial bottleneck, since the limitations in cargo space reflected limitations in the capacity of the British market to absorb Argentine beef at prevailing prices. When demand increased, additional transportation facilities were usually available.

transportation agreements made no direct reference to cattle prices, whatever pressure they exerted on prices was in a downward direction.

Though British and American packers sometimes fought for control of the market, these pools were in effect about 80 per cent of the time under study. As a result, the half-dozen major packinghouses possessed an awesome amount of economic power. Yet it is important to remember that these concerns were private and nearly all foreign-owned, so they had little direct representation in Argentine politics.[12] They could lobby for their interests in various ways. They could recruit Argentine lawyers as company spokesmen. It was possible for the British and United States embassies to exert diplomatic pressure on the packers' behalf—which is not to say that they necessarily did. But if the packers had a weakness, it was in the political sphere.

As a group, the men who managed the packinghouses generally lived in Buenos Aires or its suburbs. At the same time, their economic function was to "service" the pastoral sector, rather than foster domestic industrialization; because of their consequent interests, they can be identified as "rural" or at least "rurally oriented." Their extensive social contacts with the landed aristocracy, in addition to their economic power, would also put the leading packinghouse managers (even foreign citizens) in the general category of the upper class.

CATTLEMEN: BREEDERS AND FATTENERS

By force of tradition and circumstance, Argentine ranchers never tended toward cohesiveness or cooperation. The strain and solitude of life on the pampa had bred fierce pride in their social and economic independence. Though communications had greatly improved by the early twentieth century, the heritage of individualism was reinforced by an era of unusual pros-

---

[12] Some of the companies were legally registered in Argentina, but their ownership and management still made them decidedly foreign.

perity. As large landowners acquired fantastic fortunes, they built baronial mansions on their ranches, constructed palaces in Buenos Aires ("townhouses" was the euphemism), spent half their time in England or France. They dined and lounged in the Círculo de Armas, the Club del Progreso, and the Jockey Club. Their tours through the Continent created the image of the Argentine Playboy, and a new saying cropped up in Europe's capitals: "as rich as an Argentine." To say the least, this kind of prosperity made collective action look unnecessary.

As the export trade progressed, the division of labor between breeders and fatteners formed two separate groups with often divergent economic interests. The fatteners dealt almost exclusively in chiller steers, which the packers normally preferred. If markets were limited abroad, they therefore tended to compete against those who bred freezers and canners. And within the chiller trade, the fatteners bought calves from the breeders and sold cattle to the packers; they were concerned not so much with the absolute price of their goods as with their cost-price margin. This point is central to an understanding of their political behavior, for their desire to buy cattle cheaply frequently put them at odds with the breeders and on the side of the packers.

The fatteners stood in a flexible position. Their land happened to be excellent for agriculture as well as for grazing. So if wheat looked like a better short-run investment than cattle, they could rent out portions of their land to tenant farmers. Or they could continue buying cattle with an exact knowledge of their inventory, anticipating sales within a year or possibly two. Only a sudden, steep drop in cattle prices—after buying from the breeders and before selling to the packers—could bring them any harm.

Socially, the fatteners usually departed from the hidebound ways of their ancestors. There was little to do on the ranches, since the cattle required abundant pastures and minimal care, so they did not always reside in the country. On the contrary, their need for contact with the packers and the attractions of urban leisure normally brought them to the city. Although their interests and background were decidedly rural, they lived and worked in Buenos Aires as much as on the pampa.

The breeders generally followed a more traditional way of life. Their occupation demanded steady attention to the breeding, birth, and upbringing of cattle. As a result, they spent less time in Buenos Aires or in Europe than the fatteners. They had two major outlets for their stock: (1) sale to the fatteners, and (2) sale of cattle at the Liniers Market, usually cows for domestic consumption.[13] Thus they sent their herds to the fattening zone, auctioned them off at rural fairs, or packed them on trains for Liniers. By necessity if not by choice, the breeders were men of the country.

They did not form an entirely cohesive unit. When foreign demand was limited or controlled, competition between different kinds of export beef could lead to internal rivalry. Those who bred high-quality steers naturally preferred to sell them for chilled beef, in which the fatteners and packers also had an interest; sometimes, this alignment placed them in opposition to breeders of lesser-grade stock. But the political consequences of this division were not especially significant. Breeders of chiller steers usually grew freezers and even some canners as well; and within the chiller trade, of course, they still opposed the fatteners and packers. For the most part, Argentine cattlemen pursued their economic interests as either breeders or fatteners.

It is impossible to measure the size of these two groups with any definite precision, mainly because of their tendency to overlap. Some important fatteners owned ranches in the breeding grounds, and wealthy breeders occasionally rented land for feeding. Particularly in the central portions of the province of Buenos Aires, cattle were often grown and grazed on the same ranch. Yet some general indication of their size can be taken from the Livestock Census of 1937, which listed 300,000 cattle owners of one kind or another. Subtracting those with less than

---

[13] Though the packers were active at Liniers, a relatively small proportion (perhaps as little as 10 per cent) of the cattle bought on this market were used for the export trade. Agustín Ruano Fournier, *Estudio económico de la producción de las carnes del Río de la Plata* (Montevideo, 1936), p. 242.

200 head, the approximate minimum then needed for significant participation in the foreign or municipal meat trade, we find that there were about 25,000 "cattlemen" in the major production areas, and that the fattening zone accounted for about one quarter of that total.[14] Broken down by province, the results shape up as follows:

Table 2.2.   Cattlemen in Breeding and Fattening Zones, 1937

		Breeders		Fatteners	
Province	Total	Number	%	Number	%
Buenos Aires	13,039	10,043	77.1	2,986	22.9
Córdoba	2,841	1,468	51.7	1,373	48.3
Corrientes	1,870	1,870	100.0	—	—
Entre Ríos	1,869	1,176	62.9	693	37.1
La Pampa	1,363	477	35.0	886	65.0
San Luis	512	512	100.0	—	—
Santa Fe	3,174	2,675	84.3	499	15.7
Totals	24,668	18,231	73.9	6,433	26.1

Source: Argentine Republic, *Censo nacional agropecuario, año 1937,* vol. entitled *Ganadería* (Buenos Aires, 1939), 723–92.

As a group, the fatteners tended to be relatively large-scale stockmen. With 1937 data for the province of Buenos Aires, a rough index of their "bigness" can be calculated by dividing the percentage of fatteners in the provincial total of large-scale cattlemen (those with more than 3,000 head) by the percentage

---

[14] The procedure for calculating the number of cattlemen, as a single group and as divided into breeders and fatteners, was worked out in a series of discussions with Ing. José Minola, a professor at the Facultad de Agronomía y Veterinaria of the University of Buenos Aires. To some degree these figures tend to be inflated because they were compiled by partido, and quite a few cattlemen either owned or rented land in more than one partido. Some owners of dairy cows are also doubtless included. On the other hand, these calculations are lower than some estimates because they omit ranchers with less than 200 head and all those in marginal production zones (Chaco, Formosa, Misiones) on the grounds that they had no meaningful participation in the beef industry, since most of their cattle was used for local consumption, hides, or dried beef. In any case, my aim has been to estimate the number of cattlemen with a direct interest in the politics of the beef industry, and this seems like a reasonable attempt. The cattlemen from the major production zones with more than 200 head owned approximately 63 per cent of all the stock in the entire nation.

of fatteners in the provincial total of all stockmen: the result is 1.65. Similar indices also show that the fattening areas contained less than their share of middle-sized stockmen (0.64) and small commercial ranchers (0.94).[15]

Table 2.3.   *Relative Size of Fatteners in the Province of Buenos Aires, 1937*

Number of Cattle Owned	A. % of Fatteners in Each Size Group	B. % of Fatteners in Entire Province	Index (A ÷ B)
200–1,000	21.6	22.9	0.94
1,000–3,000	14.7	22.9	0.64
Over 3,000	37.9	22.9	1.65

These statistics provide partial confirmation for the notion, widely held in Argentina, that breeders belonged to the middle class and fatteners belonged to the upper class. Due to their flexible market position and their larger landownings, the fatteners undoubtedly had more economic strength than the breeders; for some ranchers, this imbalance might well have carried some social overtones. Yet it would be both dangerous and misleading to attribute class characteristics to these groups in simplistic fashion. At least for the leadership, with which this study mainly deals, there is no evidence that differences in economic power were matched by corresponding differences in social power. Many prominent breeders possessed the wealth to import English stud bulls, and came from aristocratic families; for every Anchorena among the fatteners, there was a Martínez de Hoz or a Pereda among the breeders. Generally speaking, the socio-economic disparities among the rank and file do not appear to have been supported by feelings of class consciousness; both groups drew most of their leaders from the upper class.[16]

15 The computation for this index is limited to the province of Buenos Aires partly because of its importance, but especially because the over-all excellence of the land and livestock within provides a legitimate basis for comparison. The quantitative criteria for distinguishing between "small," "middle-sized," and "large" ranching operations are frankly arbitrary.

16 During one polemic, a pro-breeder newspaper, *Edición Rural*, asserted

As shown in the map and Table 2.2, there were some regional differences between the breeders and the fatteners. Though both groups were mainly concentrated in the powerful province of Buenos Aires, many breeders were scattered throughout the less-favored areas of Córdoba, Corrientes, Entre Ríos, La Pampa, San Luis, and Santa Fe. With Argentina's long history of inter-provincial strife, it was likely that conflicts between these two groups would be occasionally colored by regional considerations.

Nevertheless, the basic difference between them derived from their economic functions and interests. When cattle prices declined, the packers and the fatteners could both conceivably protect their cost-price margins at the expense of the breeders. Whatever social and regional overtones crept into such conflicts were secondary to the dominant economic issue. One group raised cattle, the other group fattened it: this was the major distinction.

THE ARGENTINE RURAL SOCIETY

Until the 1930s, the only major institution that represented the ranchers' interests was the Argentine Rural Society. The extent of this organization's political influence has long been a source of speculation and debate: some present-day pundits claim that it virtually governed pre-Peronist Argentina, while its defenders maintain that its purposes were purely apolitical.[17] As a means of exploring this issue, it would be useful to analyze the Society's representation in the presidential Cabinets. Despite the increasing activity of Congress, the Executive branch

that 750 fatteners controlled 92 per cent of the chiller calves sold for meat to be exported: February 6, 1939. This would definitely suggest that the bulk of the fattening business was dominated by the upper class. Yet the passion of argument throws some doubt upon the reliability of the source; and besides, this datum does nothing to indicate that some breeders were not aristocratic as well.

[17] There is an incredible dearth of analytical material on the Rural Society, the most serious effort to date being in José Luis de Imaz, *Los que mandan* (Buenos Aires, 1964), pp. 85–105. Also see Taylor, *Rural Life*, pp. 396–400; and, for general background, Jorge Newton, *Historia de la Sociedad Rural Argentina* (Buenos Aires, 1966).

was still the most powerful part of the government. In addition, the ministries provide some meaningful clues about the distribution and types of political influence. Cabinet members wielded influence in eight different areas—such as Finance, Foreign Affairs, or Agriculture—and there was relatively little encroachment between the varying spheres. Thus we can discern not only whether the Society had access to power; within limits, we can also discover where its influence was strongest.

The Rural Society enjoyed remarkable representation in government. Between 1910 and 1943, five out of the nine different presidential administrations were led by men who belonged to the Society; that is, *over half* the Chief Executives were prominent ranchers. Out of some 93 appointments to the Cabinets during the same period, no less than 39—more than 40 per cent—were given to members of the Society.[18] Furthermore, as shown in the table below, the Society tended to control ministries of major importance, notably Foreign Relations, Finance, and the military posts. The institution's influence was particularly apparent with regard to livestock and farming. Of the 14 appointees to the Ministry of Agriculture, 12 belonged to the Society, controlling that ministry well over 90 per cent of the time. It was also the governmental custom to consult the Society on all major pastoral problems.

Perhaps the most provocative finding is that the Rural Society generally survived the vicissitudes of party politics. Table 2.4 indicates that the Society was strongly represented in the Cabinet before, during, and after the Radical administrations of 1916–1930. (The political implications of this fact will be discussed in subsequent chapters.) And in each of these different periods, roughly 15 per cent of all the seats in the

18 Key government officials—including the President, the Minister of Agriculture, and some other Cabinet members—were given honorary membership in the Rural Society during their tenure of office. Such an ingratiating process of "cooptation" was naturally intended to assure the Society of adequate representation and sympathetic hearings within the upper circles of power. All my references to Society membership here and elsewhere refer only to full-time, not honorary, association with the Society. Here and throughout the remainder of this study, the ministers considered in analyses of various Cabinets will not include interim or short-term appointees.

Table 2.4. *Rural Society Representation in Inaugural Cabinets, 1910–1943* [a]

(X = Member of Rural Society)

	Term	President	Vice-Pres.	Interior	Foreign Affairs	Finance	Army	Navy	Agriculture	Public Works	Justice and Publ. Instr.
Saenz Peña	1910–14	X	X	X	X	X		X	X	X	
De la Plaza	1914–16	X	None					X	X		X
Yrigoyen	1916–22				X	X		X	X	X	
Alvear	1922–28	X				X	X		X		X
Yrigoyen	1928–30		X						X		
Uriburu	1930–32		X		X	X			X	X	
Justo	1932–38	X	X		X		X				X
Ortiz	1938–41	X			X						
Castillo	1941–43		None						X		

[a] For the sake of simplicity, this table does not account for the replacement of ministers during the course of each administration.

Congress were held by members of the Society.[19] This institution had great political power; the question is how it was used.

Notwithstanding its official claim to stand for all the nation's ranchers, the Society represented limited interests. Controlled by a secret admissions procedure, membership fluctuated between 2,000 and 5,000 from 1900 to 1946, usually hovering around the 2,500 mark. So if the estimates taken from the 1937 census are correct, the Society included only about *10 per cent* of the ranchers engaged in the livestock trade.[20] The other 90 per cent, despite their direct and permanent interest in decisions affecting the beef industry, had no organized means of expressing its interests in the years before the Depression. Local livestock organizations had negligible power and prestige. And most of them were linked to the Society itself; around 1918, a Confederation of Rural Societies was founded to unite the local associations—under the parental leadership of the Argentine Rural Society.

Given the exclusiveness of membership, it seems fair to identify members of the Rural Society as upper-class aristocrats. They were men of wealth and good family. Approximately 75 per cent of the Society's members listed residences in the city of Buenos Aires, where the institution's headquarters were located.[21] This means that they were prosperous enough to own townhouses as well as cattle ranches; it also suggests that they took part in the social life of the traditional elite. As much as any other single institution, the Rural Society stood for the landowning aristocracy.

Yet there could still be divisions within the Society, as the membership included both breeders and fatteners. Internal struggles usually focused on the biennial elections for the institution's President and 18-man Board of Directors, which

19 Based on my biographical analyses of both houses of Congress for 1913, 1923, and 1933. Another 15 per cent of the legislators had surnames which appeared on the Society's lists; in all likelihood, these men were related to members of the institution.

20 If all livestock owners in the country are counted, the percentage plummets to roughly 1 per cent!

21 Taylor, *Rural Life*, p. 399.

made all policy decisions and faced a General Assembly of members only once a year.[22] The fatteners possessed a slight advantage over the breeders in competing for membership on the Board, since they more often lived in the city of Buenos Aires—where the ballots were cast and the decisions were taken. But this was not always the case. Throughout this study, it will therefore be necessary to take the composition of the Board of Directors into constant consideration.

THE URBAN CONSUMERS

The largest, least coherent group of all was the consumers of Greater Buenos Aires. They numbered almost two million people in 1914, fully 24 per cent of the national population; by 1947 the count climbed to 4,600,000, about 28 per cent of all Argentines.[23] They were essentially "urban," of course, and as diverse and disparate as the city was itself: immigrants, stevedores, clerks, industrialists, bankers, and small businessmen. They came from all walks of life: some were rich, some were poor, some were in between. What they had in common was their life in Buenos Aires. Given the long history of conflict between this city and the countryside, this fact alone was enough to distinguish them from the residents of the interior.

Despite their heterogeneous characteristics, most urban consumers belonged to the lower-middle and especially the lower classes. About 65 per cent of the population in Buenos Aires around 1914 fell within the lower class.[24] Since many of the city's middle-class residents identified their interests with those of the upper-class producers of meat, as I shall try to show in some detail, those who regarded themselves as consumers generally belonged to the urban working class.

Their function in this context was consuming meat. They ate incredible amounts of it: *bife de lomo, bife de chorizo, bife a caballo, asado de tira, puchero*—as much as 250 pounds a year

[22] See *Estatutos de la Sociedad Rural Argentina* (Buenos Aires, 1927).
[23] Germani, *Estructura social*, p. 69.
[24] *Ibid.*, pp. 219–20.

for every person.[25] Their interest was to acquire a steady supply
of beef as cheaply as possible. They wanted more meat for less
money. The price of cattle at Liniers and the price of meat in
London were not immediately relevant to them. Most of the
beef they bought was prepared in local or municipal slaughterhouses, though a significant portion—between 20 and 30 per
cent [26]—came from the export-oriented packinghouses. The consumers therefore had a limited, but vital, stake in the politics
of beef.

As the consumers had little direct representation in the industry itself, their interests were articulated mainly in the
political sphere, usually through two major institutions. On the
local level there was the Municipal Council (*Concejo Deliberante de la Municipalidad de Buenos Aires*), a city assembly
whose members were elected by popular vote. On the national
level there was the Congress. On both these planes, the most
consistent spokesmen for the consumers belonged to the Socialist Party, founded by Juan B. Justo, which drew most of its
support from the lower and lower-middle classes.[27] When someone spoke up for the consumers, it was almost always a Socialist.

THE PACKINGHOUSE WORKERS

The final group with direct interests in the beef industry to
be considered in this study consisted of laborers in the packinghouses. Recruited mainly from the lower-class masses in the
city and suburbs of Buenos Aires and employed in large-scale
industry, they were plainly "urban" in nature and outlook.
Their number was significant, if not overwhelmingly large: as

[25] N.A., D.A., Foreign Agricultural Relations: Reports, Argentina, Meat
(1918–34), file "Argentina, 1924–1932." In the United States, the per capita consumption of all meats (including pork) has amounted to a comparatively paltry
150 pounds a year: U.S.D.A. Agricultural Marketing Service, *Meat Consumption
Trends and Patterns* [by Gertrude Gronbech], Agriculture Handbook No. 187
(Washington, 1960), p. 4.

[26] Junta Nacional de Carnes, *Informe de la labor realizada desde el 1o de
octubre de 1935 hasta el 30 de septiembre de 1937* (Buenos Aires, 1937), p. 109.

[27] Though some Socialists were middle-class in origin and outlook, the party
was recognized as a significant vehicle for the promotion of lower-class political
interests before the 1940s—if just because it was the only one.

early as 1914 there were more than 15,000 such workers, and by 1946 the total had risen to nearly 46,000.[28]

To say the least, their working conditions were difficult. Men and women got up around four in the morning to slaughter and dress beef for daily distribution in the local market. Hours and wages depended on the size of the kill, which varied according to demand and was restricted by the packinghouse pools. Labor that was performed on blood-soaked floors, in dank freezing-rooms, or next to whirring knives posed countless hazards to health. The workers' interest was not only the classic demand for more money and less toil; the improvement of conditions was for them a central issue.

Despite their numbers and their grievances, the workers did not have much economic strength. Until the early 1930s, as we shall see below, the laborers were organized by company rather than for the industry as a whole. This naturally meant that the closely knit managers had an immense advantage in bargaining, negotiations, and other forms of conflict, partly because they kept an industry-wide black list on all intractable employees. The packers could offer jobs on a take-it-or-leave-it basis. More often than not, the workers felt compelled to take it. Frustrated by their lack of economic power, they eventually took to pursuing their goals through political action.

OUTSIDE ECONOMIC SECTORS

When struggles concerning the Argentine beef industry became public issues, their outcome could naturally depend upon the opinions and actions of other groups. To some extent the mere articulation of interests in a national forum, like the Congress, tended to widen the conflicts. If present, spokesmen for un-involved constituencies would have to listen to the debates and vote on bills or resolutions; the literate public at large, through coverage in the daily press and other news media, would also

[28] These figures, which include workers in the freezing establishments in the sheep-raising Patagonia, are taken from the *Tercer censo nacional*, VII (Buenos Aires, 1919), 535, and the *IVᵒ censo general de la Nación, 1947*, III (Buenos Aires, 1949), 106.

become alert to the matter at hand. In this way outside opinion and influence might conceivably be brought to bear. Yet such expansion of struggle was largely institutional and, for the original nonparticipant, involuntary. Meaningful inquiry into the attitudes and behavior of outside groups would have to go beyond the halls of Congress.

For this reason, I have included three other sectors in this study: (1) industrialists, (2) farmers, and (3) labor. In one way or another, they all had tangential relationships to the beef industry that would, hypothetically at least, have engaged them in the conflicts before still other sectors had been mobilized.

The importance of the industrialists' response is derived in part from their increasing weight in the national economy, but more specifically from the potential rivalry between this mainly middle-class group and the traditional landowners. Did the manufacturers of this period, many of whom processed products of the countryside, take sides in rural conflicts? Did they support the stockmen in struggles with the packers, or were they consistently opposed to the aristocracy? In more general terms, did they seem to want to build a whole new social and economic system, or gain upper status within the old order?

Wheat farmers had an ambiguous perspective on the beef industry. Though they were rural people, they had reasons to resent the stockmen. The zones that were used for fattening livestock were also excellent areas for the cultivation of wheat. Further, many farmers were tenants of the cattle fatteners, planting grain for two or three years and then sowing the land with alfalfa. To what extent did the farmers participate in the politics of beef? Did they complain about the usage of prime agricultural land for grazing? Did their grievances and complaints as tenant farmers ever put them on the side of the breeders against the property-owning fatteners?

Labor's demands were articulated in uneven and largely ineffective fashion until 1932, when the General Confederation of Labor—or C.G.T.—was founded. Worker activity then greatly intensified. With regard to the beef industry, labor leaders had a direct interest in the improvement of wages and working conditions for those who toiled in the meat-freezing plants. But this sector's attitude is significant for deeper reasons, since it eventually formed the political base for the rise of Perón. Did the C.G.T. openly support the packinghouse workers? Did it also use beef industry politics as a means of attacking the traditional aristocracy? Did it support one rural group in its struggles against another, or attack the nonindustrial economic structure as a whole?

THE CONTESTANTS AND THEIR POWER

In summary, the rapid development of the Argentine beef industry in the twentieth century led to the emergence of five distinct interest groups. According to my (partly economic) criteria, three were essentially rural or rurally oriented: the breeders, the fatteners, and the packers. To one degree or another, their leaders could also be identified with the upper class. The other two groups, consumers and laborers, were decidedly urban and predominantly lower class. Presumably, this competitive line-up provides a meaningful and concrete opportunity to examine the original locus (rural or urban) of intergroup struggles, the possibility of their transition from one area to another, the political response of Argentina's "middle sectors" and the question of class conflict.

Because of their mutual relationships to the beef industry, fights between these groups were bound to break out over economic issues: cattle prices, meat prices, wages and working conditions. Though generalization is necessarily imprecise, the economic power of the competing groups can be fairly reliably ranked. First would come the packinghouse managers, who exercised predominant control over the whole industry. Second, after their appearance as a separate unit, would be the fatteners, who handled the bulk of the profitable chiller trade and could pass along price reductions with relative ease. Third, in a rurally oriented society, were the cattle breeders. Fourth and fifth, in uncertain order, were the urban consumers and the packing-house workers.

In times of conflict, it would only be logical for economically vulnerable groups to try offsetting their weakness by asserting political strength. Resort to the political arena could make public issues out of private grievances, redefine the conflicts, engage some measure of popular interest, perhaps mobilize active support among outside groups—and, above all, bring the power of the State to bear on the question at hand. Which groups resorted to this mechanism, how, when, and with how much success will be the basic subject of what follows.

III

Yankees, War, and Trusts

THE first major group conflict in the modern Argentine beef industry came after the start of the twentieth century. In its early stages of development, the preparation and export of frozen meat had not established many solid interests. The British had secured a near-monopoly over the meat-freezing business, it is true, but without stirring much of a fuss: there was little to monopolize. Then the great stimulus to the international trade after 1900 ushered in a period of prosperity and contentment.[1] The British-owned packing companies rang up some remarkable profits, and Argentine stockmen reaped the benefits of rising cattle prices.[2] Both the packers and the producers worked in a kind of economic euphoria. It would not last for long.

ENTER THE IMPERIALISTS

In 1907 Swift & Company, the largest meatpacking firm in the United States, bought out the largest plant in Argentina, the freezing-works at La Plata. Almost immediately, Swift started to promote the breeding of top-quality calves for use in the preparation of chilled beef. Two years later a mighty Chicago combine known as the National Packing Company (Swift, Armour, Morris) purchased an Argentine-owned plant at La

[1] Some ranchers complained about the British prohibition against Argentine cattle on the hoof and about the prices offered by the packers. P.R.O., F.O. 6/473, 482, 495; Diputados, 1902, I (July 23), 502–7 and 1906, I (May 28), 154–73; Horacio C. E. Giberti, *Historia económica de la ganadería argentina* (Buenos Aires, 1961), pp. 177–79. But they did not mount any major political action.
[2] See price statistics in the *Anuario de la Sociedad Rural Argentina*, p. 261.

Blanca. It was simultaneously heard that Sulzberger & Sons, another American firm, was negotiating with the Frigorífico Argentino. British interests were seriously challenged; by 1910, in fact, Chicago-based packinghouses were shipping over half the chilled beef that was exported from the Plate.[3]

The British turned to both their government and the cattlemen for help. In London, company representatives proposed (unsuccessfully) that the Board of Trade support an amalgamation that would assure Britain of its meat supply and yield an annual interest to the Crown. In Argentina, pro-British propagandists denounced the perils of American penetration. The prestigious *Review of the River Plate* gravely warned its readers that the American firms would join forces to suppress competition in the cattle market, so Argentine producers would eventually suffer as much as British consumers.[4] Without much courtesy to local legislators, the *Buenos Aires Herald* advised the country's ranchers to "Trust no trust; tolerate no 'control' of any source of national industry because control in one quarter means an encroachment on all quarters and finally control of everything from a box of matches to a vote in the Senate." [5]

This anti-American campaign was transferred to the Chamber of Deputies in June 1909, when Carlos and Manuel Carlés introduced a bill to prohibit any "trusts or joint action" in the meatpacking business. Though representing the city of Buenos Aires, the Carlés brothers came from a prominent cattle-owning family and spoke in behalf of ranching interests.[6] They were

[3] Hanson, *Argentine Meat*, p. 159. For British awareness of the problem see the Legation's annual reports for 1908–11 in P.R.O., F.O. 371/598, 824, 1045, 1295.

[4] Hanson, *Argentine Meat*, pp. 147–48.

[5] June 16, 1909.

[6] Throughout this book, biographical data on participants in conflicts over the meat industry are taken from sources in the section of the Bibliography entitled "Biographical Data on Political Participants." All the operative variables should be self-explanatory except my working concept of "class," which I have based mainly upon (1) occupation, (2) membership in social clubs—the Argentine Rural Society, the Jockey Club, and the Círculo de Armas, (3) self-description, (4) contemporary comments, and (5) family status or reputation as reported by informants. The data are imperfect but seem to provide a fair index to socio-economic power; they are particularly good for telling whether or not individuals belonged to the aristocracy.

specifically concerned with price-fixing agreements on animals destined for slaughter, and asserted that fear of the Chicago "Beef Trust" was amply justified by experience: "the day which that powerful syndicate succeeds in gaining irresponsible control of our incipient meat trade, it will treat the docile, defenseless, and individualistic Argentine ranchers with the same or even greater ruthlessness that the 'Beef Trust' has treated its English clients, other packinghouses, and stockmen from its own country, all in behalf of the 'trustsmen.' " [7]

At first glance, this looks like a standard example of antiimperialism. The introductory speech explicitly complained about foreign attempts to "found an empire within our republic." But it was not so simple as that. The Carlés brothers went out of their way to welcome most foreign investments, especially praising the British. The whole inspiration for their bill, in fact, had come from the United Kingdom: "Our friends the English," they acknowledged, "have for some time been putting us on the alert about the danger of the Yankee 'Beef Trust.' " [8] The brothers were speaking for British investors as well as for Argentine ranchers. What looked like anti-imperialism, therefore, was actually a kind of inter-imperialism.

The basic point of the Carlés proposal was to gain the support of cattlemen and transfer the Anglo-American conflict from the economic system to the political system. But most ranchers, who profited greatly from the packers' competition, were reluctant to act. As illustrated in Figure 3.1, cattle prices (with allowances for seasonal fluctuations) were steadily rising. Understandably, if complacently, cattlemen denied that there was anything to fear: as Abel Bengolea, president of the Argentine Rural Society, stated, "The North American trust can never dictate prices or conditions to the ranchers . . . for the

---

[7] Diputados, 1909, I (June 21), 155–59.

[8] *Ibid.* A British report on the meat market, supervised by Winston Churchill, had been released two months before: Committee on Combinations in the Meat Trade, "Report of the Departmental Committee Appointed to Inquire into Combinations in the Meat Trade," *Parliamentary Papers*, 1909 (Cd. 4643), XV, 1–31, and "Minutes of Evidence Taken before the Departmental Committee on Combinations in the Meat Trade," *Ibid.*, 1909 (Cd. 4661), XV, 33–383.

Figure 3.1.   *Liniers Prices for Cross-Bred Steers, 1908–1911*

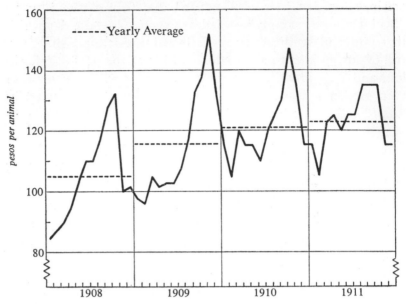

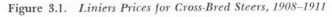

Source: *Anuario de la Sociedad Rural Argentina,* p. 261.

meat trade of today is subject to the law of supply and demand." [9] The Carlés bill was ignored.

Despite the Anglo-American rivalry, market conditions remained tolerable for the packers until late in 1910, when the
continually heavy shipments of chilled beef by American firms
finally glutted the British market. While prices sagged at London's Smithfield Market, the competition forced the packers to
keep up the prices for Argentine cattle. The companies began
to take some losses; by the end of 1911, the situation was un-
bearable. So the packers joined together in a "pool," distributing total shipments among the different groups as follows:
Americans, 41.35 per cent; British, 40.15 per cent; Argentine,
18.5 per cent.[10] For better or for worse, United States capital
took over the leadership of the Argentine meatpacking industry.

The pool arrangement worked to the satisfaction of all major

[9] *La Prensa,* June 14, 1911.
[10] Hanson, *Argentine Meat,* pp. 162–63.

interests for as long as it lasted. There were no abrupt oscillations in the prices for cattle or meat, and the packers made
some handsome profits.[11] Then in February 1913, Armour completed the expansion of its La Blanca plant and—possibly anticipating the growth of a United States market for Argentine beef
—threatened to pull out of the pool unless it received a 50 per
cent increase in its share of the market.[12] British packers viewed
the prospects with alarm, and persuaded an Argentine representative in London to wire home in hopes of preserving the
pool. Saenz Peña's Minister of Agriculture, himself a cattleman,
replied that his department would take no action against the
Americans "unless the purpose of a trust were discovered." [13]
After that, Armour management refused to accept a 10 per cent
raise in its quota. On April 5, 1913, the first packinghouse pool
came to an end.

Bitter competition ensued. The British market was swamped
with chilled beef, and prices broke badly at Smithfield. As conditions deteriorated, the British again tried to stimulate political action. On May 27, packinghouse spokesmen asked the
British Minister in Buenos Aires to advise the Foreign Office
of the "expediency of supporting and encouraging the Argentine Government to resist [the] growing power of the American
meat trust." [14] Though not eager to act, perhaps because the
meatpacking rivalry provided beef cheaply for British consumers,[15] the Foreign Office consulted the Board of Agriculture
before dispatching instructions. Defending the interests of home
cattle farmers, the Board suggested that Argentine authorities
might be encouraged to limit the exports of each packinghouse

[11] *Ibid.,* pp. 169–70.

[12] The National Packing Company had been broken up by anti-trust action
in the United States, and the La Blanca plant taken over by Armour alone. At
this time the United States was revising tariff schedules; Congress abolished
import duties on fresh meat later in the year, thus opening a new market for
Argentine products.

[13] Hanson, *Argentine Meat,* pp. 173–74.

[14] P.R.O., F.O. 368/785, Gaisford to F.O., May 27, 1913; and Tower to Grey,
May 28, 1913. Also see the mounting concern in such pro-British press organs
as the *Buenos Aires Herald,* May 14–June 24, 1913, and the *Review of the
River Plate,* May 16, 1913, 1229–31.

[15] P.R.O., F.O. 368/785, marginal note on Gaisford to F.O., May 27, 1913.

(thus reducing competition from abroad). As a result, the British Minister conveyed assurances that His Majesty's Government "will watch with sympathetic concern any action taken to prevent the establishment by foreign firms of a monopoly in the meat export trade." [16] But the primary purpose of the note was not to help the packers; it was to protect British stockmen from foreign competition.[17]

Argentina's leadership was hesitant. Adolfo Mugica, the Minister of Agriculture, drafted a bill to tax excessive exports and thus limit the output of each packinghouse. Spokesmen for the Rural Society opposed the plan, though its members were almost evenly divided. After weeks of speculation, an informal meeting was held in Mugica's office with General Julio Roca, the eminent ex-President, and other leading cattlemen. The group concluded that no action should be taken against the Americans unless they threatened the interests of Argentine ranchers.[18] It was a classic instance of decision by "acuerdo."

In response to a petition from British and Argentine companies [19] Mugica then agreed to "investigate" the problem, and sent a questionnaire to Swift and Armour representatives. The Americans asserted that heavy shipments of meat were made only in fulfillment of long-standing contracts, that the drop in London prices was entirely "due to the natural play of supply and demand," and that they could still "do business" at going rates. There were no illegitimate imbalances in economic power that would justify governmental intervention; to prove the point, they opened their books to the government. Strongly impressed by this testimony, Argentine authorities turned away from the Americans and buttonholed the British. For both con-

16 P.R.O., F.O. 368/785, Board of Agriculture to F.O., May 30, 1913; F.O. to Gaisford, June 2, 1913; Tower to Grey, June 11, 1913.

17 A secondary purpose might have been to prevent a monopoly whose operation could have been detrimental to the long-run interests of British consumers. Concern for consumers played a major part in British thinking, as shown by the Committee on Combinations in the Meat Trade, "Report," 1909, cited above; and a marginal note in P.R.O., F.O. 368/379, Townley to Grey, December 9, 1909.

18 P.R.O., F.O. 368/785, Gaisford to Grey, May 15, 1913; Tower to Grey, May 19, 1913; Tower to Grey, May 28, 1913; Tower to Grey, June 11, 1913.

19 La Nación, June 15, 1913; Review of the River Plate, June 13, 1913, 1487.

sumers and producers, Mugica now argued, the best way to combat any meat trust would be to reopen British ports to cattle on the hoof from Argentina.[20]

THE CATTLEMEN DIVIDED

The intrusion of United States capital into the beef industry separated Argentine ranchers into two main groups: those who sold to the Americans, and those who still sold to the British. It is unlikely that this division had fattener-vs.-breeder overtones, for the chilled beef trade in which the Americans specialized accounted for only a small portion of the trade at this time (see Figure 2.1). The distinction was probably more one of habit than function. But in this way, Argentine stockmen acquired a stake in the welfare of the various packinghouses. Thus the struggle between investment interests from Great Britain and the United States opened a rift in the ranks of the cattlemen.

The anxious allies of the British sought to bring the issue into the political arena soon after the pool had been broken. It should be remembered that power had not yet passed to the Radicals. Roque Saenz Peña was still President, and his Cabinet was recruited from the aristocracy: virtually all the ministers came from the upper class, and more than half belonged to the Rural Society. Conservative or pro-administration delegates also controlled the Congress, even after the electoral reforms of 1911–12, holding over 80 per cent of the seats in the Chamber of Deputies. The Radicals had only 12 per cent, the Socialists much less than that.[21] In 1913 the aristocracy maintained the upper hand.

As an indication of Congress' increasing importance, por-

20 P.R.O., F.O. 368/375, Tower to Grey, June 13 and June 18, 1913. Also see Mugica's comments in Diputados, 1913, II (June 25), 316–317; and Ministerio de Agricultura, *Comercio de carnes*, I (Libro rojo) (Buenos Aires, 1922), 26–27.

21 These figures differ widely from the data in Eduardo Zalduendo, *Geografía electoral de la Argentina* (Buenos Aires, 1958), pp. 226–27. Zalduendo lists only 60 Deputies for the year 1913, apparently because his information is taken from the 1912 election tally only. My base total of 120 Deputies is taken directly from the *Diario de Sesiones*.

trayed in Figure 1.4, action took place in the national Chamber
of Deputies. On May 13 Carlos Carlés reintroduced the bill that
he and his brother presented in 1909.[22] A month later Juan J.
Atencio requested permission to interpellate Mugica about the
possible existence of a meat trust in Argentina.[23] Though he
claimed to represent consumers as well as producers, it is clear
that Atencio and his supporters spoke out mainly in behalf of
British packers and their cattle-raising clients.[24]

Addressing the Chamber on June 25, Mugica related how he
had drafted a bill to tax excess exports, abandoned the plan,
and finally concluded that there was no trust. He praised the
Americans for their cooperation, failed to see any aggressive
intentions in their expanding shipments, and argued that "the
alarm caused by the attitude of the Anglo-Argentine packinghouses is largely unjustified." Since the boost in cattle prices
was good for cattlemen and the whole country, the government
had decided to take no action on "a simple commercial matter."
If a trust were ever discovered, however, Mugica pledged his
support for general anti-trust legislation.[25]

Atencio retaliated with a strong rhetorical plea in behalf of
Argentine consumers. As he explained it, the sharp rise in livestock prices and excessive meat exportation had driven local
retail prices of beef to intolerable heights. In the meantime,
consequent profits had blinded ranchers to the American tactic
of breaking the pool in order to monopolize the market and
then exploit producers as well as consumers. The current bonanza also threatened to deplete Argentine herds and thus rob
the country of one of its leading resources. In behalf of both

22 Diputados, 1913, I (May 13), 57–62.

23 Ibid., I (June 13), 1087–90.

24 Atencio himself came from a wealthy family in the cattle-raising province
of Buenos Aires. As for the British connection, His Majesty's Minister noted
that one manager of a London-based firm was working hard to arouse sentiment against the Americans: "For this purpose, I understand that Argentine
Deputies are being sedulously provided with material for future speeches, as
soon as the meat question may be brought up in Congress." P.R.O., F.O.
368/785, Tower to Grey, June 25, 1913. And see N.A., D.S., 835.6582/2, Garrett
to Secretary of State, July 9, 1913 (also in Corr. Am. Leg., 1913, V, 865.82); and
the retrospective comment by Juan B. Justo in Diputados, 1922, VII (April 16,
1923), 419.

25 Diputados, 1913, II (June 25), 312–19.

consumers and cattle production, Atencio proposed two major measures: a livestock census, and a general anti-trust law like the Sherman Act in the United States. Later on he further suggested the establishment of a mixed-enterprise packinghouse supported by the State and private Argentine capital.[26]

Atencio's argument was reinforced by Estanislao Zeballos, ex-president of the Rural Society,[27] and sharply attacked by pro-Americans. Abel Bengolea, still president of the Society and now a Conservative Deputy, claimed that the activity of the Chicago-based packinghouses posed no threat of any kind to Argentine interests. In theory, he said, it was impossible to set up a "trust" without controlling the bases of production; since the Americans could never hope to own all the ranches, they would not be able to establish a genuine trust. In practice, there was no conflict of interests anyway. Concentration of the market in American hands would actually favor the stockmen, since the expanded volume in trade would assure the packers of their profits and allow them to pay more for cattle. And there was no reason for the packers to drive the ranchers bankrupt; in view of growing demand in Europe and maybe in the United States, killing the Argentine cattle industry would be as senseless as "killing the goose that laid the golden egg." [28]

With regard to the consumers, Bengolea pointed out that the domestic and foreign markets dealt with different kinds of meat. The expansion in volume and value of exports was therefore not related to the rising cost of local beef. Drought (which had prevented cows from calving), taxes, and an excessive number of butcher shops—not the foreign packinghouses—were responsible for the inflation. In conclusion, Bengolea wholeheartedly supported the government's inaction.[29]

This logic was also pursued by Emilio Frers, another ex-president of the Rural Society, whose discourse took on a sharp ideological note. Limitations on packinghouse exports, he warned, would be "an enormity and a fallacy":

26 *Ibid.* (June 25), 320–28; and (July 2), 413.
27 *Ibid.* (July 2), 417–30.
28 *Ibid.* (June 27), 342–45.
29 *Ibid.*, 346–50.

It would be a singular . . . and I think unprecedented fact, that in want-
ing to intervene in the commercial struggle between various companies,
we should once more back away from the policy of industrial and commercial liberty which has brought so much glory and so much wealth to
the republic, and which we have with just pride considered as one of our
first conquests over the colonial regime. Monopoly by private enterprise
is a thousand times more preferable than an industrial monopoly under
the State, because it is possible, at least possible, to defend oneself from
the first, while the second can turn into a truly invincible economic tyr-
anny, and economic tyrannies are generally the instrument of political
tyrannies.[30]

To hear Frers tell it, the country's democratic heritage was
hanging in the balance.

Despite its evident sincerity, this homage to laissez-faire had
an immediate and definite political function. These speeches
were made before a dual audience: the Congress, with representatives from nonpastoral areas, and the political public at
large. The proponents of laissez-faire were anxious to stave
off interference in the economic sphere, by the government (at
any level) or by outside groups, and to let the packers continue
their competition. Nineteenth-century liberalism was aptly
suited to their purposes. Emphasis on the sanctity of free trade
and its consecration in the Argentine Constitution would
denigate ideas of State action and also discourage the public
from taking interest in the issue; if unfailing forces of the
market would eventually restore the situation to optimal
equilibrium, there was no need for popular concern. For the
moment, liberal economic theory helped to envelop the interests of the Chicago-based packers and their cattle-raising
clients in an aura of inviolable doctrine.[31]

As it had developed so far, the debate revealed some significant features. On both sides, the major spokesmen for
pastoral interests were cattlemen themselves; all the participant
Deputies, except Atencio, had at one time or another presided
over the Rural Society. This not only illustrates the power of
the institution but also indicates that there was little or no

30 *Ibid.*, 363–64.
31 Atencio was acutely aware of this procedure: Diputados, 1913, II (July 2),
412–13.

separation between political and economic leadership. Politics was not "professionalized," insofar as there was no discernible difference between the leaders and the led. Second, group participation in the dispute helped reveal the nature of the conflict. All the speakers came from the province of Buenos Aires; all belonged to the aristocracy; supporters of both sides represented either the Conservative Party or the conservative Civic Union.[32] The split was not regional, social, or political. It was economic. Some ranchers dealt with the British, others with the Americans: here was the heart of the issue.

The only interruption to this cattlemen's conclave came when Juan B. Justo, Socialist from the city of Buenos Aires, spoke out for the consumers. Dismissing Atencio's statement as "an alarm bell of the landowning class," he said that the true interests of consumers concerned products other than meat and also the reduction of some tariffs. There was nothing inherently wrong with a trust, he declared; it cut down on waste and duplication, reduced the costs of production, and heralded the advent of socialism. But the primitive structure of the Argentine economy made some kind of anti-trust scheme necessary. Instead of action by the State, however, Justo recommended the construction of public packinghouses under the administration of municipalities, provincial governments, or large cooperative associations.[33]

The debate yielded few concrete results. A parliamentary committee was set up to consider the feasibility of anti-trust legislation. All the spokesmen for the stockmen were appointed to it—while Justo, the one consumer representative, was not. A few weeks later the Saenz Peña administration submitted a Sherman-type act to Congress,[34] and then the committee on trusts came out with a series of bills: (1) an anti-trust measure which specifically prohibited price manipulation on articles "of prime necessity, to the detriment of the consumer"; (2) a

[32] The Civic Union was the conservative wing of the group that led the *Noventa* in 1890. For all practical purposes, cooperation with the ruling aristocracy made this party just about as conservative as the P.A.N.

[33] Diputados, 1913, II (July 2), 433–36.

[34] *Ibid.*, II (July 30), 606.

livestock census; (3) a proposal for a study on the compatibility of producer and consumer interests.[35]

Nothing happened after that. All the bills were shelved and forgotten. This inaction represented a victory for the pro-American stockmen and the Chicago-based companies over the other cattlemen and the Anglo-Argentine packers, who were unable to offset economic weakness by resorting to the State. Thus the faction with greater economic power displayed greater political power as well. This outcome was also a triumph for the current leaders of the Argentine Rural Society. The opposition had not been able to gather its forces. Atencio's attack on rising meat prices had not won support from the Socialists—if that was what he wanted—and Justo's exclusion from the anti-trust committee demonstrated the weakness of the consumers. The cattlemen still reigned supreme. This was government of the elite, by the elite, and for the elite.

THE WARTIME BEEF TRADE

The packers could not continue their competitive orgy forever. In September 1913, the Frigorífico Argentino closed down and was leased by Sulzberger & Sons. The following January, the River Plate and Las Palmas firms merged into the British & Argentine Meat Company. A month or so later negotiations were finally begun for the establishment of another pool, and agreement was apparently reached in June. The new percentages reflected the gains made by the Americans: Chicago-based plants controlled 58.5 per cent of the market, compared to 29.64 for the British and 11.86 per cent for the Argentines.[36]

Though the outbreak of World War I temporarily interrupted beef shipments to Europe, trade picked up after the British government announced in August 1914 that it would make all of the island's meat purchases; in January 1915,

[35] *Ibid.*, 614–17.
[36] Ortiz, *Historia económica*, II, 27–29; and David J. R. Watson, *Los criollos y los gringos: escombros acumulados al levantar la estructura ganadera-frigorífica, 1882–1940* (Buenos Aires, 1941), p. 47.

Figure 3.2.   *Argentine Beef Exports, 1912–1920*
(Thousands of Tons)

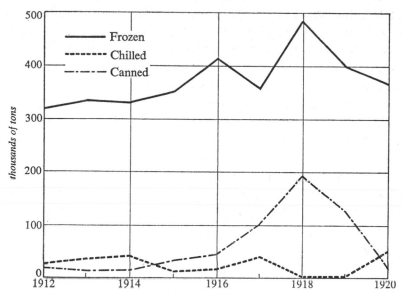

Source: Official document reprinted in Concejo Deliberante, 1934, II (July 31),
[1478].

Britain also started purchasing for France. Seeking to assure
supplies for Allied troops, the Board of Trade later leased
the Las Palmas plant for operation on the government's account.[37] Wartime demand was extraordinarily high, especially
for canned and frozen beef. Between 1914 and 1918, the total
slaughter for exports more than doubled.[38]

The commerce had varied effects. Speculation mounted
as many Argentines, aided by the government's liberal credit
policy, sought to cash in on the boom by investing in cattle.
The heavy strain on herds prompted numerous proposals to
prevent depletion of the livestock population.[39] The demand

[37] For information on the wartime policy of the British government see P.R.O.,
F.O. 368/926, 927, 1203; and Hanson, *Argentine Meat*, pp. 186–209.
[38] Junta Nacional de Carnes, *Estadísticas básicas*, p. 8.
[39] See the proposal by Gerónimo del Barco, Diputados, 1914, IV (September 19),
961–63. The next year the Executive introduced a bill for permission to limit
the exports of cows: *Ibid.*, 1915, I (July 12), 650. Then Del Barco reintroduced
his own bill: *Ibid.*, 1916, I (July 17), 911. But no such action was taken.

for canned and frozen beef temporarily suppressed the latent rivalry between breeders and fatteners, since canners and freezers did not have to go to special feeding grounds. The packers made staggering profits.[40] As long as volume continued to expand, however, there was little conflict between the producers and the packers; Atencio's attempt to revive the 1913 anti-trust bill was flatly voted down by the Congress of 1915.[41] For a while, intergroup conflicts were suppressed.

This state of contentment lasted until the middle of 1916. In that year, the breeders and particularly the fatteners of top-grade cattle began to suffer from the emphasis on conserved and frozen beef, as they were unable to sell their stock at customary chiller prices. As wheat prices also headed downhill, Pedro T. Pagés, one of the country's leading stockbreeders, proposed a "precautionary" bill for a national fund to buy out the foreign-owned packinghouses and thereby "counteract the frightful effects of the meat trust." [42] Conditions grew worse the next year, as shown in Figure 3.3. In June 1918, some cattlemen promoted expropriation of the packinghouses through a bond issue, which ranchers would gladly take up "to put an end to the exploitation of which cattle producers and the whole Argentine nation are at present the victims!" [43]

This change in economic circumstances, resulting from wartime conditions, realigned the interests of a significant group of stockmen and the packers. Whereas in 1913 most breeders and fatteners of top-quality stock had stoutly defended the packers, at least the Americans, they were opposed to them by 1917.

[40] Ministerio de Agricultura, *Comercio de carnes,* II (Libro verde) (Buenos Aires, 1923), 73.

[41] Diputados, 1915, III (September 17), 576–78.

[42] *Ibid.,* 1916, II (July 26), 1033–39.

[43] *Review of the River Plate,* July 26, 1918, 209; and Hanson, *Argentine Meat,* pp. 205–6. Also see Joaquín de Anchorena's comment in the *Informe de la Comisión Investigadora de los Trusts* (Buenos Aires, 1919), pp. 202–3. The packers' responses to these complaints are recounted in the *Review of the River Plate,* November 2, 1917, 1073–75; May 3, 1918, 1075–77; July 19, 1918, 143–45 and 149–51.

Figure 3.3. *Monthly Prices for Fat Stock at Liniers, 1916–1917*

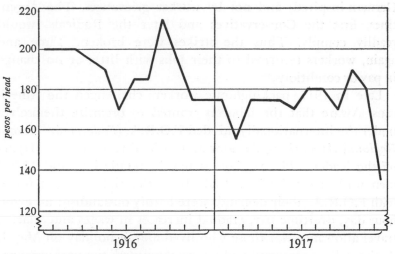

Source: *Anuario de la Sociedad Rural Argentina*, p. 261.

OPPOSITION TO THE WORKINGMEN

As this conflict was emerging between some cattle producers and the packinghouses, important developments were taking place on the national political scene. In 1916 the presidency was won by Hipólito Yrigoyen, head of the Radical Party and, according to historical myth, a partisan of labor. The government was now in the hands of those who drew support, in large part, from the country's middle sectors. With the Radicals in power, the action and attitudes of the State and the groups involved in the politics of beef take on special significance.

The new administration was soon tested by restive laborers, who were staging a series of strikes on railroads, in ports—and at the British-owned meatpacking plants. The responses were consistent. At the request of a packinghouse manager, His Majesty's Minister would ask the Argentine Ministry for Foreign Affairs to provide "adequate" police protection for the companies. Upholding the time-honored right of free men to work as they chose, he would deplore any violence and take care to point out that the strike was caused by "agitators" (sometimes German-inspired) and not by worker grievances. The Argentines, first the Conservatives and later the Radicals, would readily comply. Thus the strikes were broken. Time and again, workers returned to their jobs with little or no change in pay or conditions.[44]

Late in 1917, packinghouse workers challenged the Americans. Aware that the laborers wanted to organize themselves under the internationally minded F.O.R.A. (*Federación Obrera Regional Argentina*), Armour and Swift directors began laying off the leaders. The workers struck in retaliation, and 11,000 men walked off the job. Aside from the right to join forces with F.O.R.A., their demands were hardly outlandish: an eight-hour day, overtime pay, gradual increases in wages and salaries, travel allowances for those who lived afar, a holiday on May 1. As the strike progressed and violence erupted, the packinghouse workers received support from the powerful seamen's union, which boycotted all cargoes of Armour and Swift, and from the F.O.R.A. leadership.[45]

In this dispute the ranchers were quick to support the packers. Meeting under the auspices of the Rural Society, a group of prominent cattlemen exhorted Yrigoyen to take action against the strike, since shipments were stalled and producers had no market for their stock. Insisting that the movement was inspired by "elements outside the working personnel, known to the police as professional agitators," they demanded that the strike should be suppressed and workers sent back to the job.[46] Such a policy would be in their economic interest, of course, since low labor costs helped make it possible for the packers to pay high prices for cattle.

In view of their own impending conflict with the packers, the ranchers' response assumes added importance because it shows that a difference of opinion on one problem did not

[44] See P.R.O., F.O. 118/356, 394, 408, 423, 428, 430, 435, 471, 472.

[45] The description of the strike is taken mainly from Departamento Nacional de Trabajo, *Boletín del Departamento Nacional de Trabajo*, no. 40 (1919), 66–67 and no. 41 (1919), 56–65.

[46] *Anales*, LI, no. 10 (December, 1917), 771–72.

impede the perception of common interest on another. Though ranchers and packers engaged in intra-class battles on specific issues, without making any broad political or ideological commitments, they could still join hands in order to crush a challenge from the lower class.

Meanwhile, Yrigoyen held interviews with the British Minister and the American Ambassador, who each requested governmental intervention for the sake of Allied troops.[47] Then the President took his decision: he sent in the Navy to break up the strike! (Coincidentally, perhaps, both the Minister for Foreign Affairs and the Minister of the Navy belonged to the Rural Society.) He later pulled out the troops, but only after the F.O.R.A. threatened to call a general strike. In the end the strike was beaten—as F.O.R.A put it, "by the resistance of the capitalists and the support of the State." By February 1918, all the men were back at work again.[48]

The Radical administration's stand on these strikes is remarkable for two reasons. First, it throws some doubt upon the quality of Yrigoyen's oft-noted policy of neutrality in World War I. Second, it provides a meaningful precedent for the infamous "Tragic Week" of January 1919, when laborers and policemen waged bloody battles in the streets of Buenos Aires. It has sometimes been suggested that this ugly experience dampened Yrigoyen's pro-worker ardor and might explain his subsequently pallid position on labor issues. His action during the packinghouse revolt implies, on the contrary, that he had never really been a zealous advocate of labor reform. As spokesman for the middle classes, he had sided with the beef barons and the foreign capitalists instead of with the workers.[49]

[47] P.R.O., F.O. 368/1876, esp. Tower to Balfour, February 24 and March 2, 1918. N.A., D.S., 835.5045/31, 32, 34, 40, 41, Stimson to Secretary of State, November 30–December 11, 1917; and Corr. Am. Emb., 1917, II, 350 and VIII, 850.4.

[48] Departamento Nacional de Trabajo, *Boletín*, no. 41 (1919), 63. As a further illustration of labor's weakness, a strike against the municipal slaughterhouse of Buenos Aires also ended in ignominious defeat. See the *Review of the River Plate*, February 13, 1920, 423–25; February 20, 1920, 493; February 27, 1920, 567.

[49] Yrigoyen's over-all labor policy stands in need of intensive research. Samuel Baily says Yrigoyen was "sympathetic" to the worker cause, "but there was a

CONSUMER AGITATION

While wartime conditions annoyed some leading stockmen and drove the laborers to violence, they also imposed heavy sacrifices upon the consumers. In the midst of rising unemployment and general inflation, the price of meat soared from 50 centavos a kilo in 1914 to 71 centavos in 1919. One major reason for this price rise was a relative shortage of supply, since the increase in exports reduced the number of cattle available for domestic consumption. A decrease in tenant farming also created some rural unemployment, so many idle people sought jobs in the cities and added to urban demand.

Table 3.1. *Cost and Consumption of Beef in Argentina, 1914–1919*
(Index: 1936–1939 = 100)

	Cost-of-Living Index	Average Retail Beef Price (centavos/kilo)	Annual Kilos Per Person
1914	83.1	50	62.7
1915	89.0	67	60.3
1916	95.4	69	53.3
1917	112.3	62	55.8
1918	140.8	54	54.7
1919	132.7	71	49.7

Source: Junta Nacional de Carnes, *Estadísticas básicas,* pp. 13–14.

Several efforts were made to protect consumer interests, mainly by the Socialists. In August 1914, Perfecto Araya suggested that the municipality of Buenos Aires be granted the right to fix price ceilings for meat and bread, and the Socialist bloc in the Chamber of Deputies proposed a 15 per cent export tax on all cattle products.[50] Weeks later, the Socialists requested that tariffs be lifted on meat imported from Uruguay.[51]

limit to his understanding." Baily, *Labor, Nationalism, and Politics in Argentina* (New Brunswick, N. J., 1967), pp. 34–39. But the question remains: What was the limit, how was it defined, and how did it affect presidential policy?

[50] Diputados, 1914, III (August 17), 726–27; (August 19), 802–3.

[51] *Ibid.,* IV (September 4), 52–53; (September 21), 604. This bill was approved by the Deputies, 1917, VI (September 28), 404 mainly as a fiscal measure; and by the Senate in Senadores, 1917, II (September 30), 1176–77.

In February 1915, Enrique Dickmann—another Socialist—called
for export taxes on the grounds that meat and bread had become "inaccessible to the lower class." [52] Later that month,
some 70,000 people expressed their support for the measure
at a Buenos Aires demonstration.[53]

Toward the end of the war, both producers and consumers
were dissatisfied. The producers of top-grade stock felt they
were not being paid enough for their cattle; the consumers objected to the rising price and scarcity of meat. Under these
conditions it became possible for the leaders of these two groups
to forge an alliance against their mutual enemy, the packers.
Though ranchers and consumers were customarily opposed, a
rational perception of their economic interests provided the
chance to become political bedfellows, and they promptly set
about to make the most of it.

CONSUMER-CATTLEMAN ALLIANCE

First hints of a tactical alliance between representatives of the
two groups came in July 1917, when the Conservative Deputies
from the province of Buenos Aires reintroduced the general
anti-trust measure presented in 1913 by the committee on
trusts. These spokesmen undoubtedly stood for the cattlemen:
Buenos Aires was the country's leading pastoral province, the
Conservative Party was a traditional rancher stronghold, and
half the bill's proponents belonged to the Rural Society. In
his explanation of the plan, Adrian Escobar made it clear
that his group was ready to cooperate with consumers. Though
Argentina produced both meat and wheat in abundance, he
said, they were expensive at home "because their whole commercial and industrial procedure is manipulated by various
trusts which have taken complete possession of our market."
This situation was liable to get worse before it got better, and

[52] Diputados, 1914, VII (February 9, 1915), 522–24. Dickmann reintroduced
this bill two and a half years later, and with the help of the revenue-seeking
Radicals finally managed to have it passed into law as a temporary measure.
Ibid., 1917, II (June 20), 152–54.

[53] P.R.O., F.O. 368/1203, Tower to Grey, March 1, 1915. *Review of the
River Plate*, March 5, 1915, 501–3.

in preparation for the future "we must fight with energy against the trusts, those octopi which damage, detain, and destroy commercial independence and free production." [54] His appeal was eagerly followed, as Socialists lent their support; the bill was approved by unanimous vote.[55]

Since the slow-moving Senate failed to take immediate action, Horacio Oyhanarte and Juan B. Justo (one a Radical, the other a Socialist) recommended that the Deputies appoint a committee to investigate the trusts.[56] In apparent recognition of the producer-consumer alliance, the committee reflected a variety of interests: lawyers, doctors, sugar-cane growers, wheat farmers, and cattle ranchers all had their representatives. When Justo assumed the leadership of the committee, due to the first chairman's resignation, urban consumers finally gained a prominent forum in Congress.

The report, issued in September 1919, plainly reflected the pro-consumer bias of its authors.[57] The committee dealt with many more products than the Escobar group, which had confined its concern to meat and wheat. Furthermore, as shown in Figure 3.4, Justo and his colleagues by no means shared the anti-foreign or "anti-imperialist" emphasis expressed by the brothers Carlés. Who the producers were and where the trusts were centered bore little importance to consumer spokesmen, especially the internationally minded Socialists. What bothered them was the elevation of retail prices. So if they joined the cattle producers' attack upon the trusts, they did so for distinctly different reasons.[58]

Despite this divergence, the committee adopted an essentially pro-producer outlook in its section on the meat industry. The only difference lay in emphasis: instead of devising ways to reduce the profits of the companies and expand the profits of the

[54] Diputados, 1917, II (July 23), 668–76.

[55] According to Escobar's retrospective comment: Diputados, 1920, III (July 6), 134–40.

[56] Diputados, 1917, VII (January 10, 1918), 844.

[57] Octaviano S. Vera, Radical from Tucumán, issued a dissenting minority report in an apparent effort to exculpate the sugar trust.

[58] The graph is based on the number of pages devoted to each product and its "trust," and does not include the general introduction and conclusions.

Figure 3.4.   *Distribution of Emphasis in Anti-Trust Report*

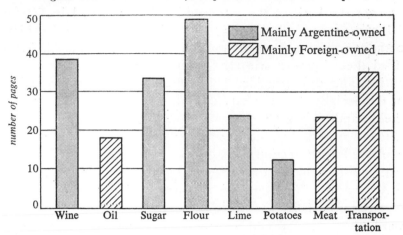

cattlemen, the report merely maintained that prices for Argentine stock should be on a par with analogous cattle prices in the other exporting countries of the world. Though evidence on the meatpacking "trust" was woefully imperfect, the committee asserted that it was necessary "to organize our own supplies [of meat], through municipal or regional packinghouses, and also to enter into direct contact with the great consuming markets abroad." Through devices of this kind, envisioned by Justo some years before, Argentina should enter the meatpacking business and take it away from the foreigners.[59]

This defense of the cattle producers deserves some special notice. It shows that the ranchers, by taking their complaints against the packers to Congress, had managed to gain support from Socialist spokesmen for the urban lower class. For both sides, such cooperation was undoubtedly a matter of political convenience. But whatever the motives, the result was plainly visible: the stockmen's struggle had moved from the countryside to the city.

Furthermore, the ranchers' frequent usage of nationalism

[59] *Informe de la Comisión Investigadora*, pp. [200]–1, 225. The committee seems to have been deeply influenced by the trust-baiting *Report of the Federal Trade Commission on the Meat-Packing Industry*, 6 vols. (Washington, 1919).

appears to have played a significant part in this process. It was not the basis of the partnership. As illustrated in Figure 3.4, the consumers' anti-trust campaign was not an anti-imperialist vendetta. But the ranchers' nationalistic rhetoric identified their interests with the economic independence of the nation, and thus provided a justification for the cooperation of the Socialists. If necessary, Socialist leaders could legitimize their stand to the Congress, the public, and their own constituents in terms of anti-imperialism; their behavior could be explained as protection of Argentine sovereignty. In this way, nationalism helped gain urban support for the stockmen.

At any rate, the committee's report concluded with the text of a comprehensive anti-trust bill. Any acts which tended toward "monopoly" would be prohibited by law. A "monopoly" could be created by those acts which, "without signifying technical or economic progress," arbitrarily and disproportionately increased the profits of the perpetrators and which obstructed—or were intended to obstruct—free competition. A host of sins was specified: price-fixing agreements, the hoarding of goods, the intentional destruction of products, "dumping" of goods or services at prices below cost, selling goods cheaper abroad than at home, price discrimination or favoritism, agreements to distribute production or markets or profits, agreements to impose fixed resale prices on buyers, differential transport fares, monopolistic holding companies, and interlocking directorates. Offending companies would be stripped of legal status and any State concessions, fined from 2,000 to 500,000 pesos, and directors and managers could be jailed for three months.[60]

PASSAGE OF THE BILL

The committee's bill was publicly endorsed by the Socialist Deputies in the next congressional session, when Escobar reintroduced his own project of 1917.[61] All the proposals dealing with trusts were submitted to a Committee on General Legis-

[60] *Informe de la Comisión Investigadora*, pp. 280–85.
[61] Diputados, 1920, III (July 6), 134–40.

lation, most of whose members were Radicals, which took nearly a year to make its recommendation. In June 1921, it finally presented a bill which resembled the Escobar plan much more than that of the Socialists. The measure was given speedy approval by the Chamber, and subsequent consideration of each article yielded significant changes. In the end, the bill that emerged from the Chamber looked like the anti-trust committee's proposal once again.[62] This debate was generally low-keyed; for the most part, Deputies seemed to regard the two plans as more or less interchangeable.

The most striking demonstration of the consumer-cattlemen alliance came when Justo, the country's leading Socialist, requested that a clause prohibiting agreements to limit production should not apply merely to basic consumer goods. His reason was that the clause in its original form *would protect only the consumers, and not the ranchers as well.* In his own words: "This law would not protect the livestock producers . . . against the downward maneuvers of the packers. If the companies stopped operations in order to make the price of steers go down, the consumer would suffer no harm. On the contrary, the price of [domestic] meat would go down. What would be damaged would be the country's cattle production. The packers could decide to stop slaughtering in order to buy cattle cheaper later on. . . ."[63] Justo's argument was widely supported by other sectors, especially the ranchers, and the alteration was made without delay.

The only point of serious contention concerned Justo's proposal (contained in the original Socialist bill) to prohibit selling goods abroad more cheaply than at home. Though Justo denied that this clause was intended for the packinghouses, rancher spokesmen seemed to think it might inhibit the exportation of beef. When the measure was brought to a vote, it was defeated by 35 to 28.[64] Support for Justo's idea came

[62] *Ibid.*, 1921, I (June 30), 691–705; (July 1), 730–47; (July 6), 759–93; (July 7), 808–45; II (July 8), 7.

[63] *Ibid.*, I (July 6), 772.

[64] *Ibid.*, 793. In spite of an apparent lack of a quorum, it was later ruled that this vote should stand. I (July 7), 806–8.

from the consumer constituencies—the city of Buenos Aires and regions outside the pastoral zone—and a handful of Radicals from livestock areas. Opposition came from the ranchers and their allies, from both the upper and the middle classes, including 23 members of the Radical Party. As shown by this dispute, the consumer-cattleman alliance was tenuously based on a single issue: opposition to the trusts. When their interests diverged on other problems, conflict immediately followed. And as in 1913, when consumers clashed with cattlemen, they lost.

Finally sanctioned by the Deputies, the bill went up to the Senate and languished for more than a year. This lackadaisical delay might well be attributed to the temporary improvement of the market for livestock, especially for chiller calves, so many stockmen felt less need for legislation. But in 1922—as will be fully discussed in the following chapter—prices for cattle began to decline. By the end of the year the crisis was acute. With an eye on these developments, President Marcelo T. de Alvear—Yrigoyen's handpicked successor, who took office in October 1922—urged the Senate to pass the anti-trust bill.[65]

The proposal was brought to the Senate floor on March 20, 1923 and promptly approved that same day. The only significant change came in response to a plea that a clause against the artificial raising of prices should also prohibit the artificial reduction of prices. As Juan Ramón Vidal, an outspoken defender of ranching interests, complained: "These laws on monopoly have undoubtedly been inspired to protect the consumers against the rise in prices, but this nation's problem is the defense of the producers. . . ."[66] The amendment passed without objection. On August 24, 1923, after ten full years of intermittent effort, the bill against the trusts became law.[67]

In retrospect, it is clear that the stockmen made up much the stronger half of the alliance with the consumers. Whenever their interests collided—in the debate of 1913, and in sub-

[65] Senadores, 1922 (February 1, 1923), 421.

[66] Ibid. (March 20, 1923), 586.

[67] After the Chamber of Deputies finally overrode one other change by the Senate and restored a clause prohibiting the sale of goods below cost ("dumping"). Diputados, 1923, V (August 24), 375.

sequent revisions of the anti-trust bill—the producers won decisive victories. The fluctuating intensity of the whole campaign against the trusts also tended to reflect the anxieties of the stockmen. In short, the ranchers had greater economic power and greater political power than did the consumers. The Socialists' role in this campaign should therefore not be regarded as any meaningful transition of power from rural to urban groups, or from the upper to the lower class. The ultimate success of the anti-trust efforts was largely, if not totally, dependent upon the cooperation, the tolerance, and the needs of the ranchers. Though consumers took part in the quest for political power, in actual fact they did not have it.

IV

⇝—⇝—⇝

Crisis!

THE wartime boom in the Argentine beef industry was promptly followed by collapse. Economic tensions of the crisis exerted great pressure on the nation's political system, which was completely controlled by the Radicals. In October 1922, Marcelo T. de Alvear took over the presidency with Yrigoyen's personal approval. The transition has generally been regarded as a milestone in the evolution of the Party: Yrigoyen came from the middle class, Alvear descended from the landed aristocracy, and the rank and file would soon be divided between the two men. The Congress was also in Radical hands; 103 out of 153 seats in the Chamber of Deputies were occupied by members of the Party. The Conservatives and Progressive Democrats held 14 seats each, while the Socialists had only 10.[1] Effective political action would require at least the tolerance, if not the active support, of the Radical Party.

THE COMING OF THE CRISIS

By the time hostilities ended in Europe, Argentine meat producers were riding for a fall. Tempted by the high and easy profits of the war and encouraged by liberal government lend-

[1] About 90 of the Deputies belonged to the Radical Civic Union, while 13 came from Radical splinter groups. The Progressive Democrats were moderate reformers who drew their basic support from wheat farmers and some ranchers in the province of Santa Fe. About a dozen seats in the Chamber were occupied by local politicians of a generally conservative character. Zalduendo, *Geografía electoral*, pp. 226–27.

ing, cattlemen expanded their herds; other groups, including businessmen, also put their money into livestock. As land values soared,[2] the supply of cattle increased: according to one official count, herds grew from less than 26 million head in 1914 to more than 37 million by 1922.[3] In the meantime, overseas demand was going down. As Great Britain and the Allies devoted their energies to the tasks of reconstruction, they were unable to maintain much purchasing power; they had also stockpiled large amounts of canned and frozen beef, and set about consuming that before importing more. Argentine exports were consequently reduced. About 2.9 million cattle were slaughtered for the international trade in 1918; only 1.2 million were used for that purpose in 1921.[4]

When the volume of trade then picked up, important changes took place in the composition of exports. The commerce in chilled beef, brought to a virtual halt by the war, at last got under way again. The shift was startling: as shown in Table 4.1, the proportion of chilled in total beef exports jumped from less than 12 per cent in 1920 to more than 60 per cent in 1922, later leveling off between 60 and 70 per cent. Almost all chilled beef was sent to Britain, as continental Europe consumed mostly lower-grade beef in canned or frozen form.

Partly because of the trade in chilled beef, the packers continued to make solid (if unspectacular) profits.[5] To protect their cost-price margins, they pushed down the prices for livestock. At the Liniers Market, the price for chiller steers plunged from 240 pesos in October 1920 to 113 pesos in May 1922. Despite a rapid recovery in the volume of slaughters and shipments after 1921, cattle values were cut by more than half.[6] Through the

[2] On the speculation see Raúl Prebisch, *Anotaciones sobre la crisis ganadera* (Buenos Aires, 1923), pp. 34–39.

[3] Junta Nacional de Carnes, *Estadísticas básicas,* p. 1; *Anales,* LVII, no. 18 (September 15, 1923), 11.

[4] Junta Nacional de Carnes, *Estadísticas básicas,* p. 8.

[5] Ministerio de Agricultura, *Los frigoríficos y el Ministerio de Agricultura: informes a la Comisión Investigadora del Honorable Senado de la Nación* (Buenos Aires, 1934), graph between pp. 18–19. And see Hanson, *Argentine Meat,* pp. 235–40.

[6] *Anuario de la Sociedad Rural Argentina,* p. 261. Although the decline in cattle prices was partly alleviated by a significant drop in the cost of living

Table 4.1.   *Chilled Beef Exports, 1920–1930*

	Chilled Tons Shipped	% of Total Beef Exports
1920	50,681	11.8
1921	148,386	36.6
1922	246,806	60.9
1923	326,888	52.5
1924	364,204	44.7
1925	372,473	50.6
1926	430,728	60.0
1927	466,689	61.0
1928	383,078	66.6
1929	357,959	65.2
1930	345,525	68.2

Source: Concejo Deliberante, 1934, II (July 31), [1478].

economic power of their pool, the packers managed to pass most of the postwar shock on to the ranchers.

Among the cattlemen, those who raised low-grade livestock on the upper Littoral, in and around Corrientes, probably felt the pinch more than anyone else. In the single year between 1919 and 1920, shipments of canned beef declined more than 90 per cent.[7] Prices doubtless descended as well. Though part of their herds might have been used for domestic consumption, the stockmen of the north were badly hurt.

The crisis took its toll in other cattle-raising regions. Though conclusive statistics are lacking, it does not appear that everyone suffered to the same extent. Large-scale and wealthy stockmen often managed to survive the shock: either they could afford to hold their cattle until prices improved; or they got good prices from the packers, who sometimes paid extra premiums for special breeding. Smaller ranchers, who sold freezer steers and did not get favors from the packers, felt the full impact of the crisis.[8] As shown in Figure 4.1, the price

between 1920 and 1923, the decrease in the real value of cattle was still sharp. Junta Nacional de Carnes, *Estadísticas básicas,* p. 14.

[7] Concejo Deliberante, 1934, II (July 31), [1478].

[8] Nemesio de Olariaga, *El ruralismo argentino: economía ganadera* (Buenos Aires, 1943), pp. 152–55; P.R.O., F.O. 371/5221, Macleay to Curzon, July 20, 1921; N.A., D.S., 835.6222/26, Spencer to Secretary of State, July 3, 1923.

Figure 4.1. *Index of Price Movements, 1919–1923*
(Index: 1915–1919 = 100; Based on Monthly Averages)

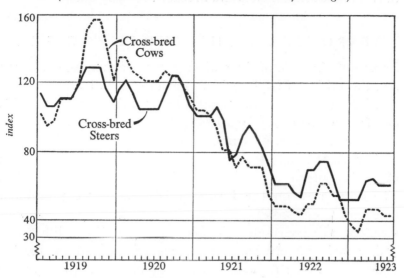

Source: *Anuario de la Sociedad Rural Argentina*, pp. 261–64.

index for cross-bred cows (which may be taken as a general indication of the smaller ranchers' plight, as cows were used for domestic consumption) started to fall in September 1919, while the index for chillers hung on a year longer; and when the cow price fell, it fell a good deal farther.

In a preliminary form, the difference between large and small ranchers foreshadowed the separation of fatteners from breeders. Still in its early development, the chilled beef trade had not yet completed the ranchers' division of labor. But many of the well-paid wealthy stockmen owned land in what would be the fattening zones, where they bred and fed their own steers. And many of the lesser-paid cattlemen would soon become breeders.[9] Insofar as the separation existed, it was apparent that the fatteners—after an initial cost-price squeeze—could respond to the crisis by lowering the prices they offered to breeders, who were left to fend for themselves.[10] Thus the different status of

[9] Olariaga, *El ruralismo argentino*, pp. 152–55.
[10] As one rancher observed at the middle of the crisis, "The fattener is the

larger and smaller ranchers was reinforced by a growing distinction between fatteners and breeders.

RESPONSE IN THE RURAL SOCIETY

Apparently because of these divergent consequences, cattlemen met the crisis with indecision. Generally, small ranchers and breeders advocated governmental intervention; large ranchers and fatteners counseled patience. This lack of consensus was clearly reflected in the changing policies of the Argentine Rural Society. At the end of the war the Society was led by Joaquín C. de Anchorena, a well-known aristocrat of fabulous wealth. The other men on the Board of Directors were prominent ranchers, many were or would become fatteners, and they managed to survive the market crash with little difficulty.[11] This was a group which had been treated well be foreign trade and foreign capital, and had every reason to leave the market undisturbed.

Their understandable conviction about the beneficial "laws" of supply and demand was repeatedly expressed throughout the years of crisis. In mid-1920, when prices for lower-grade stock were slipping down, the directors appointed some committees to investigate the drop—but shied away from any feeling of emergency.[12] In July 1921 the Society held an assembly to consider means of meeting the crisis. Although a wide range of solutions was propounded, from market investigations to cooperative packinghouses, Anchorena took a moderate

only dealer in livestock who . . . has been saved from the reputed cattle crisis. It is true that the first drop in prices brought him losses, but he could soon make up for them and today is in a better position because with a smaller capital [outlay] he obtains larger . . . profits than he got when the packers were paying high prices for steers." *La Prensa,* December 26, 1922. Also see N.A., Corr. Am. Emb., 1922, VIII, 861.3, report on "The Live Stock Crisis in Argentina" by D. S. Bullock, Agricultural Commissioner, Bureau of Markets and Crop Estimates, June 22, 1922, enclosed in Bullock to Riddle, July 24, 1922; (British) Department of Overseas Trade, *Report on the Financial and Economic Conditions of the Argentine Republic* [by H. O. Chalkley] (London, 1922), p. 22; and Hanson, *Argentine Meat,* pp. 217–18.

[11] Hanson, *Argentine Meat,* pp. 219–20.

[12] *Anales,* LIV, no. 14 (August 1, 1920), 883.

stand and proposed (later presiding over) an Organization for the Defense of Argentine Production in order to stimulate the foreign consumption of beef.[13] In the fulfillment of this task, the Organization freely consulted the packers.[14] Later that year, Anchorena specifically exonerated the packinghouse pool from any blame for the crisis. On repeated occasions, he and Ernesto Bosch flatly rejected the advisability of State intervention and confidently asserted that "natural" market forces would soon come back into balance.[15]

This do-nothing stance of the Rural Society underwent an abrupt change late in 1922, when the Anchorena-Bosch group was unexpectedly ousted from the Board of Directors in the institution's biennial elections. Led by Pedro Pagés, a prestigious breeder and part-time Conservative politician, the new Board quickly altered the Society's policy. Pagés laid the blame for the crisis squarely upon the packers, whose "monstrous" profits came at the expense of the stockmen. The only conceivable solution to the problem was economic intervention by the State. The Argentine government, Pagés declared, could not in good faith abandon the ranchers to the voracity of the foreign-owned packinghouse pool. Public action was needed, and this would have to include the establishment of an officially regulated minimum price for livestock.[16]

In support of this policy, Pagés set out to mobilize the ranchers. He formed a National Committee for the Defense of Production that was pointedly distinct from Anchorena's mild-mannered Organization. Rather than work with the packers, as in finding new markets, the Committee worked against them, and came out with a series of trust-baiting reports. In June 1923, the Society called a massive convention at Gualeguaychú

[13] *Ibid.,* LV, no. 15 (August 1, 1921), 587–88, 633–34.

[14] *Ibid.,* LV, no. 16 (August 15, 1921), 640.

[15] *Ibid.,* LV, no. 17 (September 1, 1921), 649–53; LVI, no. 19 (October 1, 1922), 574. Bosch assumed leadership of the Society when Anchorena resigned to take the less influential presidency of the Jockey Club, apparently because of criticism of his laissez-faire policy. See the *Review of the River Plate,* December 16, 1921, 1577–81.

[16] Pedro T. Pagés, *Crisis ganadera argentina* (Buenos Aires, 1922); and see *Anales,* LVII, no. 2 (January 15, 1923), 80.

in Entre Ríos. Cattlemen, particularly from the hard-hit breeding grounds up north, approved a sweeping program of national
legislation, pledged to meet again, and appointed a permanent
board of breeders alone to coordinate activities.[17]

POLITICAL PROPOSALS

Such demands for State action found promotion in the Congress,
where a large number of bills was introduced to protect Argentine ranchers from the packinghouse "trust." In mid-1921
Alberto Méndez Casariego, Progressive Democrat from Entre
Ríos, suggested an investigation of the market.[18] A subsequent
proposal called for the expropriation of any packinghouse
whose profits exceeded 20 per cent.[19] Another plan, introduced
by two Radicals in 1922, sought to prevent the purchase of
extremely heavy cattle by the packers, which forced breeders
to keep their stock longer than usual while the packers got
more meat from fewer animals and the fatteners prospered as
well.[20] Mario Guido, a Radical lawyer, then proposed that discrimination could be stopped if the packers had to buy stock
on the basis of live weight, rather than customarily offhand
estimates of beef yield.[21] Still later, a group of Radicals recommended the establishment of regional slaughterhouses and
freezing-rooms in order to protect the country's "true stock-
raisers ('verdaderos criadores')." [22]

Perhaps the most forthright call for governmental intervention was made by Manuel Mora y Araujo, a Radical who belonged to the Rural Society and raised cattle in Corrientes. On
June 24, 1921 he presented a bill to establish a minimum price
on the sale of cattle. The proposed price floors were notably
high, approaching the all-time peaks: 80 centavos per kilo of

[17] *Anales,* LVII, no. 12 (June 15, 1923), 455; LVII, no. 14 (July 15, 1923),
535–36.
[18] Diputados, 1921, II (July 15), 110–40.
[19] *Ibid.,* 1921, II (August 11), 475–79.
[20] *Ibid.,* 1921, V (February 8, 1922), 80–82.
[21] *Ibid.,* 1922, I (July 12), 625–29. Guido had introduced this bill on an earlier
occasion: *Ibid.,* 1920, IV (August 19), 281–85.
[22] *Ibid.,* 1922, I (July 13), 678–80.

meat for chillers, 50 centavos for canners. Such "regulatory" action would not obstruct the forces of the market, the Deputy contended, but release them for their natural interaction.[23] Support for the bill came mainly from small ranchers and breeders, who sought to uphold the absolute price of cattle (rather than a cost-price margin) and who had no special contacts with the packers.[24]

In December 1922 Matías G. Sánchez Sorondo—an aristocratic, conservative, brilliant, temperamental, and urbane urban lawyer—proposed a whole series of measures to deal with the crisis. One bill would require all buyers and sellers of cattle (the packers) to register with, and submit balance sheets to, the Argentine government. Another would set up a national meatpacking company, supported by public and private funds. A third called for the expansion of credit to stockmen. Still another measure provided for a sliding tax on cattle purchases, which would guarantee a minimum price of 73 centavos per meat kilo for chillers. Finally, Sánchez Sorondo won immediate approval for a Special Committee on Livestock Affairs which would investigate the crisis, consider alternative actions and recommend specific legislation to the Deputies.[25]

As this action took place in the Congress, the Yrigoyen government was slow to react to the crisis. Though Tomás A. Le Breton, as Ambassador to Washington, sent home a translation of the anti-trust findings of Woodrow Wilson's Federal Trade Commission—with its damning description of American meatpacking activities in the Plate region [26]—the report was not published at the time. The administration did propose a livestock

[23] *Ibid.*, 1921, I (June 24), 619–25.
[24] The minimum-price plan was supported, in principle, by the Pagés leadership of the Rural Society, the Liga Agraria, and the Rural Society of Curuzú Cuatiá, Corrientes. Diputados, 1921, II (July 29), 319; *Review of the River Plate*, July 29, 1921, 277. Theoretically, a bill of this kind could serve the interests of the fatteners. As one Deputy later remarked, minimum price plans often ignored "the damage which the breeders suffer at the hands of the fatteners." Diputados, 1923, VI (September 28), 831; and see José V. Liceaga, *Las carnes en la economía argentina* (Buenos Aires, 1952), p. 90. But the fatteners, who were able to protect their cost-price margin after the initial drop in 1921, had no real need for an official minimum price at this time.
[25] Diputados, 1922, V (December 14), 211–15, 230–31; (December 15), 259–60.
[26] *Report of the Federal Trade Commission*, I, esp. 160–80.

census, liberal lending to stockmen, and a drastic reduction in
rents for the sake of land tenants. Officials held frequent discussions with packers on ways to increase meat exports, and sent a
team to Europe to look for new markets.[27] By mid-1922 the
Yrigoyen government showed mounting concern, and drafted a
bill to challenge the meatpacking pool by purchase, expropriation, or construction of a State packinghouse.[28]

It was the Alvear administration, inaugurated in October
1922, which took decisive action. Le Breton stepped into the
Ministry of Agriculture and promptly started to tackle the problem. Main findings of the F.T.C. report were published in December as the *Libro rojo,* the first of a series of investigations
into the meat trade.[29] At the end of the year a livestock census
was taken. In January 1923, the President submitted two major
bills to Congress. One was a catch-all measure that called for
governmental inspection of company accounts, a requirement
that the packers register with the Ministry of Agriculture, and
the sale of all cattle on a live-weight basis; a key provision
would authorize the Minister of Agriculture to close down any
freezing-works on the grounds of suspicion alone. The other
proposed a national packinghouse in the city of Buenos Aires,
run directly by the State; according to Alvear's message, its purpose would be to reduce excess profits of intermediaries through
intensive competition and thus both raise the price of cattle
and lower the retail cost of meat.[30]

It might be tempting to relate this acceleration in governmental activity to the much-heralded contrast between Yrigo-

[27] Diputados, 1919, IV (September 16), 711; 1921, III (September 14), 566.
Review of the River Plate, July 15, 1921, 151; July 11, 1921, 215; March 31, 1922,
779–81; April 14, 1922, 901. (London) *Times Imperial and Foreign Trade Supplement,* July 22, 1922. And P.R.O., F.O. 371/5221, Macleay to Curzon, February 6, 1922.

[28] *Review of the River Plate,* July 18, 1922, 211; P.R.O., F.O. 371/5221, Hope
Vere to Balfour, August 3, 1922.

[29] Ministerio de Agricultura, *Comercio de carnes,* 3 vols. (Libro Rojo, Libro
Verde, Libro Azul) (Buenos Aires, 1922–1923).

[30] Diputados, 1922, VI (January 24, 1923), 3–9. Later in the year Le Breton
also made an unsuccessful effort to start a cattlemen's cooperative for control of Liniers: P.R.O., F.O. 371/8418, Alston to Curzon, July 10, September 7,
and October 23, 1923.

yen's middle-class orientation and Alvear's aristocratic heritage
or to their political animosity, but other explanations seem
more compelling. First, the Yrigoyen administration might
have realized the depth of the crisis only near the end of its
term, as prices continued to plunge. Second, and more important, the Argentine Rural Society shifted its stance. When Pagés
took over its leadership, late in 1922, the government's leading
source of advice and information on pastoral problems began
to advocate State action rather than laissez-faire; and it was then
that official policy changed. In testimony to the Society's extraordinary influence, the Alvear group was doubtless reacting,
at least in part, to the institution's new demands. Though it
remains a matter of speculation, it is more than conceivable
that the Yrigoyen administration would also have responded to
these pressures.[31]

THE POSITION OF THE PACKERS

As Argentine stockmen mounted their political attack, the packinghouse managers sprang to the defensive. They wanted to
stop or frustrate the campaign for special legislation in behalf
of the ranchers. That is, they wanted to keep the group conflict
within the economic system, where they could exercise their
power, and not let it escape into Argentina's political system.
In pursuit of this goal, packinghouse representatives marshaled
together a far-flung series of facts, figures, and doctrines.

The cornerstone of their argument was the contention that
the commerce in beef had always been, and should always be,
governed by the laws of supply and demand. The packers had
no "occult motive" behind their transactions, and did not strangle or restrain the trade.[32] Nor did they make exorbitant profits,

[31] As shown in Table 2.4, the Society had strong representation in both administrations and continued to control the Ministry of Agriculture. In fact
Yrigoyen gave five out of his eight ministerial appointments (63 per cent) to
members of the Society, while Alvear gave seven out of thirteen (54 per cent)
to Society members during his term.
[32] Compañía Swift de la Plata, *La industria frigorífica y el comercio de
carnes: información ilustrativa* (Buenos Aires, 1923), p. 5.

a claim which they supported with detailed calculations.[33] Whatever imbalances appeared within the market resulted from temporary over-supply and under-demand, while the unfailing invisible hand would restore the scales to equilibrium in due course. More often than not, the packers avoided all mention of the pool; but if they acknowledged it, they denied that such an agreement could "manipulate, restrain, or regulate prices for livestock." [34]

Opposing all legislative action on the crisis, they declared that any plan for live-weight cattle sales would be useless. There was no discrimination under the system of estimated yield. To be sure, the packers sometimes favored certain clients, but this was not connected with the sale procedure—it was simply sound commercial practice. The old system, they continued, was efficient and widely accepted. A live-weight system would either discourage transactions on the ranches, which provided stockmen with an opportunity to bargain, or the scales would cost too much to install all over the country. And even if cattle were sold by live weight, their commercial value would still depend upon the estimated beef yield. There was nothing to gain from the plan.[35]

Regarding the various bills for governmental inspection and control, particularly the Alvear-Le Breton proposal, the packers charged that all such measures would infringe upon the freedom of economic enterprise guaranteed in the Argentine Constitution. The key clause in the President's bill, permitting the Minister of Agriculture to shut down freezing plants at his own discretion, would hang over their heads like a Damocletian sword. It would subject them to political oppression, block their access to credit, incite a flight of foreign capital, force the sur-

---

[33] [Empresas Frigoríficas], *La verdad sobre la industria frigorífica: memorial presentado a la Comisión Especial de Asuntos Ganaderos de la Cámara de Diputados por las Compañías Frigoríficas, estudiando la faz económica del costo de producción y de la venta de la carne* (Buenos Aires, 1923), pp. 1–18. But David J. R. Watson, a manager of Sansinena, later declared that the packers overstated their costs and could have afforded to pay higher prices: *Los criollos y los gringos*, pp. [93]–96.

[34] Swift, *La industria frigorífica*, p. 19.

[35] *Ibid.*, pp. 37–39.

render of commercial secrets, and hold back economic progress: there would be no room for private initiative, "the source of the greatest advances in the industry." [36]

But of all the proffered schemes, the plan for the minimum price angered the packers the most. They condemned the bill as unconstitutional and unprogressive. On a more practical level, they contended that price-fixing would drive Argentine beef out of the international market, since Great Britain's lower- and middle-income groups would not be able to absorb the rise in prices. The consequent reduction in trade would either compel the packers to cut back on cattle purchases and buy only from special clients, or force them to suspend all operations.[37] The threat was hardly disguised: pass the minimum-price bill and cattle purchases will stop.

Instead of such self-defeating proposals, the packers suggested measures of a different kind—tax reductions, cutbacks in production costs, improvement of the herds. The only way the State should help, they maintained, was through diplomatic support in the conquest of new foreign markets.[38] All other plans should be abandoned. In clear reflection of their tacit alliance with large-scale producers and fatteners, the packers' position mirrored that of the Anchorena-Bosch group in the Argentine Rural Society.

However compelling these arguments might have seemed, their appeal was limited by the means available for propagation. First, the packers could count on the support of the English-language press. The *Buenos Aires Herald* and the *Review of the River Plate* carried long explanations of the packers' position and dared the ranchers to start their own packinghouse (if any group of cattlemen "found it was making too much money

[36] [Empresas Frigoríficas], *Memorial de las empresas frigoríficas presentado a la Cámara de Senadores, haciendo reparos al proyecto de ley de control del comercio de carnes* (Buenos Aires, 1923), pp. 7–15.

[37] [Empresas Frigoríficas], *Memorial de las empresas frigoríficas al Ministerio de Agricultura sobre la situación ganadera* (Buenos Aires, 1923), p. 18; and *La verdad*, pp. 21–24. For a detailed legal argument see the study by Mario A. Carranza, a manager of Swift: *La ley del precio mínimo: estudio jurídico* (Buenos Aires, 1923).

[38] *Memorial . . . a la Cámara de Senadores*, pp. 12–14; *Memorial . . . al Ministerio de Agricultura*, p. 18; Swift, *La industria frigorífica*, p. 24.

out of such a venture, we do not doubt that it could also find a remedy for such a tragic eventuality").[39] Second, the packers could make appeals to the Senate and Chamber of Deputies, but only as private petitioners. Third, they could try to enlist the aid of diplomats from Washington and London. But there is little evidence of concrete action in the diplomatic records.[40] On one occasion, His Majesty's Minister even seemed to criticize the packers' profits.[41] For the most part, the packers had to advance their interests in a private and foreign capacity. Despite their great economic power, they had no direct access to Argentina's political system.

THE PASSAGE OF LEGISLATION

As the competing groups defined their respective positions, the national Congress became the central arena for debate. Here the Deputies' Special Committee on Livestock Affairs, formed at Sánchez Sorondo's request, took up the task of defending the ranchers. Appointed in mid-December 1922, it represented a remarkably wide range of interests. Of its nine members, five were Radicals, two were Conservatives, one was a Socialist, and another a Progressive Democrat. Most of the major cattle-producing or beef-consuming regions were included: the city of Buenos Aires, the province of Buenos Aires, Santa Fe, Córdoba, Entre Ríos, and Corrientes. Only two members belonged to the

[39] *Review of the River Plate*, July 8, 1921, 85; and see the *Buenos Aires Herald*, esp. April 24, October 19, October 30, and November 8, 1923.

[40] At one point the United States State Department gave the Ambassador in Buenos Aires permission to "inform the Foreign Office that this government hopes there will be no action taken . . . which would tend seriously to affect invested American capital" in packinghouses. N.A., Corr. Am. Emb., 1923, VI, 850.3, Phillips to Embassy, September 1, 1923. Whether or not the Ambassador made such a statement, diplomatic activity does not appear to have played a significant role in this crisis. For other correspondence see N.A., D.A., Foreign Agricultural Relations: Reports, Argentina, Meat (1918–34), file "Argentina, 1918–1923."

[41] P.R.O., F.O. 371/5221, Macleay to F.O., July 14, 1921; *Review of the River Plate*, July 15, 1921, 151. The British kept out of the whole affair, and resisted Argentine pleas to take official action: P.R.O., F.O. 118/537, 538; F.O. 371/5521, 7173, 8418. Also see the comment by Stanley Baldwin, then president of the Board of Trade, in House of Commons, *Parliamentary Debates*, 5th ser., vol. 153 (April 10, 1922), 5–6.

Rural Society and are known to have been cattlemen; several others, including the committee chairman (Mario Guido), were professional lawyers.

Parenthetically, it is worth noting how the composition of this committee pointed up a trend toward "professionalization" in the politics of beef. Whereas livestock interests had been defended by ranchers in 1913, now they were promoted by lawyers—usually urban residents, though they might represent rural constituencies, and from either the upper class or the upper middle class. In view of their personal backgrounds, the members' energetic response to the cattle crisis also seems to suggest that those who were on their way up did not want to attack the rural aristocracy; they wanted to preserve it so they could join it.

At any rate, the Special Committee made its report to the Chamber of Deputies in April 1923, proposing a number of bills: (1) compulsory registration with the State for permission to slaughter cattle; (2) the creation of a commission to advise the President on pastoral matters, to oversee the application of all relevant laws, and to publish pertinent statistics; (3) the sale of cattle by live weight; (4) a sliding tax on cattle purchases to insure the payment of 36 centavos per live-weight kilo for chiller steers, 32 centavos for freezers, and 24 centavos for canners; (5) a National Packinghouse Company with a starting capital of 50 million pesos; (6) liberal loans to stockmen; (7) a public packinghouse in the city of Buenos Aires to cater to the domestic market; (8) a congressional resolution urging the municipal government of Buenos Aires to regulate the local meat trade through the acquisition of a meatpacking plant, reorganization of the stockyards, and price control.[42]

Significantly enough, Guido's introduction of these projects was couched in the language of traditional anti-imperialism. Even as a city-living lawyer and a Radical, he took great pains to point out that the country's "mother industry," as he and others called it, was the property not of a leisurely aristocracy but of valiant middle- and lower-class groups. At stake was more

[42] Diputados, 1922, VII (April 5, 1923), 57–70.

than the fate of a landed elite: it was the welfare, heritage, and independence of the nation. This "democratic" sector of production had fallen upon bad times, Guido continued, due to the avaricious manipulations of the foreign-owned packing-house pool. The problem lay not in excess supply, but in the lack of competition. Protection from the State was badly needed, specifically as envisioned in the program of the Special Committee. Passage of these bills would open the road to economic independence.[43]

While many Deputies supported the Committee's view, some Progressive Democrats from Santa Fe did not agree. Lisandro de la Torre—the party's leader, a presidential aspirant and later an outstanding figure in the politics of beef—mixed resentment of the packinghouse "trust" with an assault upon the ranchers. The meatpacking pool doubtless sought to strangle the market, he said, but its mere existence was the fault of Argentina's stockmen. Content to breed and fatten cattle, they had voluntarily left the overseas trade in the hands of foreign imperialists. As a further result of their social and economic myopia, cattle production was still based upon the latifundia system and its inequitable corollaries, land tenancy and absentee ownership. To some extent, as we shall see below, this argument expressed the attitudes held by Santa Fe's wheat farmers. Nevertheless, De la Torre paid deference to the ranchers; in their behalf, he proposed a State-controlled monopoly over the slaughter of cattle.[44]

Despite additional objections from the packers, the Chamber of Deputies began formal consideration of the various bills in mid-April 1923. A good deal of jockeying had already taken place behind the scenes. Because the President could specify the agenda during extra sessions of Congress, such as these, the

[43] *Ibid.*, 86–105; (April 6), 109–40. Trying to stress the multi-class and "democratic" character of cattle production, Guido claimed that there were 112,000 economically active stockmen in the country: *Ibid.* (April 5), 87–89. But as we have estimated in Chapter II, on the basis of the 1937 Livestock Census, only about 25,000 took much part in the urban and overseas beef trade and had a direct and permanent interest in this issue.

[44] Diputados, 1922, VII (April 14, 1923), 329–35; and see the remarks by Luciano F. Molinas (April 12), 226–31.

Alvear administration could limit the range of debate. As a result, of some 30 different projects presented to Congress since the crisis began, only five were brought to the floor: the live-weight scheme, the plan to build a packinghouse in Buenos Aires, the control measures of both the Special Committee and the administration, and the Committee's plan for a regulatory commission. Four out of these five had been included, implicitly or explicitly, in the Alvear-Le Breton proposals made in January. By way of an institutional technicality, the Executive thus exerted power over Congress.

After the live-weight bill and the plan for a State-supported packinghouse in Buenos Aires were approved without much opposition,[45] debate over governmental supervision of the meat trade brought a direct confrontation between the Alvear administration and the Special Committee. The government won its victory in two stages. First, the Committee's bill was voted down by 52 to 38.[46] The Committee's support came mainly from livestock interests, as 80 per cent of its backers came from cattle-producing constituencies; against this nucleus, the administration forged a temporary alliance between ranching representatives who favored the government plan (of 25 such Deputies from pastoral areas, 20 were Radicals) and those who opposed any special treatment for stockmen (over half the negative votes, including those of Socialists from Buenos Aires, came from nonpastoral regions). Second, the President's control bill was approved without further discussion.[47] Although data on the vote are not available, it seems likely that the issue was now drawn between all ranching representatives and spokesmen for the consumers. If this assumption is correct, the outcome once again demonstrates the stockmen's superior political strength.

Following this debate, the Special Committee's plan for the creation of a regulatory commission brought outspoken opposition from consumer spokesmen. Juan B. Justo, the Socialist,

[45] Diputados, 1922, VII (April 14, 1923), 372–81; (April 16), 398–413.
[46] (April 17), 504. The outcome did not follow party lines: of 58 Radicals voting, 22 supported the Special Committee.
[47] (April 17), 507; detailed consideration of each clause appears on 507–46.

announced his refusal to support any legislation that would
favor stockmen at the expense of urban consumers. Having sat
on the Committee, he vigorously denounced most of its proposals—particularly the direct challenge to consumers in the
minimum-price bill—as made in the exclusive interests of "a
cattle-raising oligarchy." The plan to regulate the meat trade—
by the producers, at the potential expense of consumers—epitomized the over-all bias in favor of the rural elite. In explanation
of his views, Justo took sarcastic note of the persistent references to stockraising as the country's "mother industry." Perhaps, he said, it could be called "the mother industry; but I
would rather call it the great-grandmother industry, the industry of dotage, which does not carry the country forward; a stag-
nant industry, an industry which paralyzes the nation's march
toward the future. . . ." Ranching perpetrated social injustice:
the glittering society of the cattle barons in grotesque contrast
to the downtrodden lives of rural peons.[48] This broadside assault on the aristocracy not only clarifies Justo's own position
on the issue; it also illustrates the tenuous nature of the consumer-cattleman alliance against the trusts. It further suggests
that, at this time, attacks on the aristocracy came mainly not
from the Radicals but from Socialists, who usually spoke for
the urban lower class.

Despite support from the Rural Society and other ranching
organizations,[49] the bill for a regulatory commission was never
brought to a vote. In all probability, its disappearance does not
reflect any growth in power for the Socialists or the consumers,
who had been badly beaten on other occasions. More likely, the
Alvear administration, which shied away from excessive governmental "regulation," quietly took the measure off the agenda.

The three bills passed by the Chamber of Deputies, in general accord with the President's original proposals, had clear
sailing in the Senate.[50] The rancher representatives in the upper
chamber turned to the need for intensified efforts. As Juan

48 (April 20), 607–40; and see (April 16), 416–23.
49 (April 25), 765.
50 Senadores, 1923, I (July 19), 255–64; (July 23), 277–303.

Ramón Vidal complained, the Executive program was altogether "incomplete." What he and others wanted was a minimum-price bill, particularly since the Special Committee's sliding-tax proposal had never reached the floor for debate. Vidal introduced one scheme for a minimum price, and a group of Radicals—curiously enough, all from outside major pastoral zones—introduced another. Ricardo Caballero, Radical from Santa Fe, took the side of consumers and promoted a maximum price for the retail sales of beef.[51]

Senate debate on the issue began in September 1923, when the Committee on Agriculture presented a bill authorizing the President to place a minimum price on cattle whose meat would be used for export and, acceding to Caballero's demand, a maximum price on retail beef. Advising the Executive on prices would be a six-man board composed of three representatives for the ranchers, one for the national government, one for the city of Buenos Aires, and one for the "corporation of packinghouses situated in the country." Le Breton doubted such a plan could ever work and, as Minister of Agriculture, publicly expressed his disapproval. Though several Senators expressed reservations about the plan, only one—a Socialist from Buenos Aires—actually voted against it.[52]

In the Chamber of Deputies, the Special Committee on Livestock Affairs recommended passage of the bill. Several spokesmen supported the plan: Mora y Araujo, the original proponent of a price floor, Sánchez Sorondo, and some Radicals from Santa Fe. Yet consumer representatives claimed the bill was a cruel hoax, despite its provision for a maximum price on meat. Juan B. Justo called the whole proposal "an oligarchic law," and Manuel Pinto, Radical from Buenos Aires, suggested land reform instead of price regulation as a means of resolving the crisis. Even so, the bill was approved by 65 to 19.[53] Once again, the producers defeated the consumers. Furthermore, they had overcome the objections of the government, despite the Radical

[51] *Ibid.* (July 23), 282–86; (July 17), 232–33; (July 19), 252–53.
[52] (September 18), 523–51.
[53] Diputados, 1923, VI (September 26), 680–714; (September 28), 834–48.

majorities; as in other instances, party loyalty or discipline was not maintained.[54]

After months of parliamentary give-and-take, the Argentine Congress passed four laws in response to the cattle market crisis. They provided for: (1) the construction of a State-run packing-house in the city of Buenos Aires; (2) governmental inspection and supervision of the beef trade; (3) the sale of cattle on a live-weight basis; and (4) a minimum price on the sale of cattle for export, and a maximum price on the local sale of meat. All but the price-fixing plan had the explicit approval of the Alvear administration. None was supported by the packers, whose campaign to prevent the passage of legislation ended in total defeat.

BATTLE OVER THE MINIMUM PRICE

Despite these promising developments, ranchers could not yet claim a total triumph. On October 3, 1923, less than a week after congressional approval of the minimum-price bill, Le Breton issued invitations to all pertinent groups, including the packinghouse "corporation," for a meeting of the advisory council. The packers refused to attend. In written answers, virtually all of them cited the same two counts: first, no such "corporation" existed; second, the law violated their constitutional freedom of trade. When the packers failed to send a spokesman to a second meeting, the council went ahead with a minimum-price recommendation. That same day, October 15, Alvear signed a decree fixing moderate prices on cattle sales, effective until the end of November: 27 centavos per live-weight kilo for chillers, 24 centavos for freezers, 19 centavos for lower-grade "continentals." [55]

The packers responded with decision and precision. As threatened in their public statements, they stopped purchasing steers. Suddenly, by common consent among the members of the pack-

[54] In fact Le Breton offered Alvear his resignation, but the President rejected it. *Review of the River Plate*, September 28, 1923, 733; and P.R.O., F.O. 371/8418, Alston to Curzon, October 23, 1923.

[55] Ministerio de Agricultura, *Comercio de carnes: el precio mínimo para la compra de carne bovina de exportación* (Buenos Aires, 1923), pp. 130–68.

inghouse pool, commerce in cattle for the export of beef was brought to a halt.[56]

This action clearly reflected the packers' desire to bring their conflict with the ranchers back into the economic system—and then transform their economic power into political power. Soundly defeated within the political sphere, on the congressional level, they sought to compensate for that setback by a spectacular assertion of economic strength. Apparently, the plan was intended to frustrate large-scale ranchers and the fatteners, anxious to get their grass-fed stock to market; if the economic hardship were sufficient, they might come out against the law, which was supported mainly by breeders.[57] This way, the packers could use economic pressure in order to gain indirect political representation.

When the advisory council met again on October 25, the law's proponents began to retreat. José Tomás Sojo, Pagés' colleague from the Rural Society and leader of the National Committee for the Defense of Production, proposed several concessions to make the minimum price acceptable to the packers. Possibly encouraged by complaints about the stoppage from some cattlemen, the packers rejected Sojo's offer.[58]

After the reception of these notes, a meeting of the advisory council broke into open conflict. When one speaker recommended suspension of the law, its advocates stood firm. Since the packers would try to exploit cattle ranchers anyway, they argued, the State might as well take its stand now. Yet letters and petitions continued to call for suspension or derogation of the law. Almost all the memorandums came from large-scale stockmen, including a number of fatteners.[59] The packers' strategy was working.

[56] Yet the packers kept slaughtering steers purchased in advance from a few of their favorite clients: Watson, *Los criollos y los gringos,* p. 103.

[57] For a retrospective definition of this conflict see *Anales,* LVIII, no. 2 (January 15, 1924), 87–89; also the statement by Pagés, *Ibid.,* LVII, no. 14 (July 15, 1923), 539–40.

[58] *El precio mínimo,* pp. 173–202.

[59] *Ibid.,* pp. 207–41. Juan E. Richelet later remarked that "Many of those who had been fervent supporters of the law were amongst the first to demand its abolition when they saw its prejudicial effects." "The Argentine Meat Trade," in A. Chadwick et al., *The Meat Trade* (London, 1934), III, 195.

It was not long before the government gave in. On November 7, only three weeks after signing the price-fixing decree, Alvear suspended application of the law for a period of six months. Apparently prepared by Le Breton, the President's statement noted that the law only authorized (but did not compel) the government to carry out its provisions and that market conditions were improving. The most remarkable comment implicitly promised that the measure would not be re-applied: given the state of the market, Alvear looked confidently forward to price increases that would make such intervention by the State "unnecessary in the future." [60] Never again, throughout his years in office, did Alvear try to implement the law for a minimum price.

Its defendants were furious. In the Senate, Juan Ramón Vidal heaped scorn upon the government and Le Breton for not upholding the law.[61] Rosario's leading daily newspaper, *La Capital*, scored the "unstatesmanlike" procedures which allowed the packers to ride roughshod over the law as blatantly as "some Juan Manuel de Rosas or other." Bartolomé Vasallo, president of the breeder assembly at Gualeguaychú, claimed that the measure failed because of Le Breton's incompetence and negligence. Pedro Pagés, president of the Rural Society, seconded these charges.[62]

But all such recriminations proved to be futile. The packers and their allies were triumphant. This outcome was partly dependent upon the usage of political institutions. In gaining passage of the law, the small-scale ranchers and breeders pressed their cause through Congress. In objecting to the law, the wealthy stockmen and fatteners turned to the Executive—and gained the final victory. One part of the government could thus be used to offset decisions that were made by another part of the government, and the law's opponents ultimately demonstrated greater *effective* political power than its advocates.

There is another significant point. The maximum-price

60 *El precio mínimo*, pp. 242–44.
61 Senadores, 1923, II (November 22), 475–79.
62 *Anales*, LVII, no. 22 (November 15, 1923), 859; LVII, no. 23 (December 1, 1923), 887–89.

clause intended to protect the consumers was never applied or even once tried. Though it appeared that consumers had won a legislative concession of sorts, the illusion was promptly dispelled outside the halls of Congress. If some ranchers and breeders had been beaten, they at least had had the chance to fight; the consumers, on the other hand, were never really able to step inside the ring.

Ultimately, the packers and their profit-making allies won such a complete victory that most of the other laws were not applied either. The project for a packinghouse in Buenos Aires was never carried out, leaving the municipality to construct its own (with more limited resources) at a later date. Though some minor fees were collected, the provision for State supervision of the meat trade was only nominally applied: the packers never surrendered their books, and no litigation was brought against them during the entire decade of the 'twenties. The only law put into effect was the live-weight measure, and that was the most innocuous of all. Efforts to regulate the cattle and meat market thus ended in practical failure.

THE USES OF IDEOLOGY

The postwar battles for control of the Argentine beef industry were also fought on ideological fronts. In the pursuit of their interests, the competing groups propounded more or less systematic sets (or at least suggestive seeds) of economic doctrine. The ideologies varied in purpose and tone, but they all paid some deference to nationalism and, in this atmosphere of crisis, they all had to face one fundamental question: Should the State attempt to regulate the beef trade?

The packers replied in the negative. Invoking the long-standing syndrome of laissez-faire economics, they sought to prevent governmental action. For the Americans, this position was consistent with their stand in 1913. For the British and Argentine firms, however, it represented a complete about-face. Ten years before, during the packinghouse competition, the Anglo-Argentines had formally requested intervention by the

State; now they ardently subscribed to laissez-faire. The conflict had changed and their interest had changed; ideology was altered as well.

Although the foreign packers used the "internationalist" features of economic liberalism to justify their presence and importance, they also sought to identify with the Argentine nation. To some degree, their untiring appeals to the Constitution banked upon popular pride in the country's political heritage. They often referred to their plants as investments in the national future. They even expressed faith in the "true" Argentina by distinguishing between livestock speculators and ranchers whose ancestors built up the nation. In one public memorandum, spokesmen for Swift & Company deftly asserted that demands for State intervention came from uncouth *arrivistes:*

it is highly significant that the present campaign [against the packers] should be headed by precisely those people who, having purchased their animals at times when the prices for cattle were reaching their maximum level, did not own land on which to fatten them. . . .

The fundamental element [among the stockmen] . . . , the men of stability and tradition, those who did not speculate wildly in livestock . . . undoubtedly suffer from the grave consequences of this terrible and unfortunate crisis, but they do not offend anyone, nor do they pretend to find a solution to this economic problem in blind attacks upon the Companies which have brought them so much benefit. . . .[63]

In fact, this effort to split the ranks of the opposition between "new" and "old" ranchers fell wide of the mark; Pagés and his friends in the Rural Society could hardly be considered transient speculators. At that, the inaccuracy of the charge shows how anxious the packers were to claim allegiance to Argentina's national heritage.

There were stockmen who shared the commitment to liberal doctrine. Large-scale producers and fatteners who could profit from the postwar trade stoutly upheld the sanctity of laissez-faire. For them, as for the packers, liberal ideology inveighed against political action; and once the issues reached Congress,

[63] Swift, *La industria frigorífica,* p. 53; also see p. 10.

it discouraged outside sectors from participating in the conflicts over beef. In effect, the contention that the livestock crisis resulted from the natural interplay of market forces also maintained that the crisis could be resolved only by those same forces. Since political action would be useless, if not downright harmful, other groups might as well ignore the problem; it would have to take care of itself. This way, the dominant economic groups promoted an ideology that served to restrict the scope of conflict.

On the other hand, ranchers who suffered from the crisis, particularly small stockmen and breeders, took up another kind of ideology: traditional anti-imperialism. The propagation of this doctrine demanded a close identification of stockraising with the rural essence and tradition of the nation. As a result, cattle-breeding was referred to as the "mother industry" of Argentina, and legislative action was repeatedly portrayed as an effort to protect "the economic independence of the nation" —now gravely endangered by the avaricious ambitions of alien meatpackers.[64] The issue was thus redefined. At stake was no longer the prosperity of an economic group, but a pillar of the national past and a symbol of Argentine sovereignty.

The fundamental purpose of this anti-imperialist argument was to justify State action in behalf of aggrieved ranchers. In one highly emotional appeal, Sánchez Sorondo stated the case for intervention:

Here we deal with the fate of thousands and thousands of producers, large and small, small above all, brought to ruin by the work that ought to sustain them at the least; here we deal with the great Argentine wealth, converted by the work of strange and foreign elements into a source of national poverty; here we deal with the economic life or death of a numerous class, the people in fact, which has committed no other sin than that of working from sunup to dusk . . . accepting the rigor of inclemency and the chances of time as a condition of their hard existence, trusting . . . in the support and protection of the law. Here we deal, fellow Deputies, with saying to these men: calmly continue your work, the base and foundation of our collective prosperity; we are aware of the

[64] For example see the statement by Pagés in *Anales*, LVII, no. 4 (February 15, 1923), 143.

maneuvers that strip you bare and destroy you; we will defend you, because it is our duty as political men in charge of the public welfare, our duty to justice, our duty as Argentines, and, I might add, to our own advantage. Or rather, to say to them: keep on, keep on in the present conditions; we cannot do anything for you; we cannot do anything against the law of supply and demand, nor against the packinghouses; they are your masters and ours, and if we are today obliged to give them the key to livestock production, tomorrow we will give them the honor of the government, the attribution of sovereignty, the keys to our very own houses.[65]

To protect the rural soul of the nation, its heritage from the past and its independence in the future, the State must decisively act.

Though traditional anti-imperialism sought to make the rancher-packer struggle a matter of public concern, and thus to widen the conflict, it did not tend to stimulate the active participation of outside groups. Its function instead was to elicit their passive sympathy. At a time when it was abundantly clear that the stockmen had enough political power to get some kind of legislation, this ideology merely sought general approval for their *de facto* strength. It provided only a justification (the historical role of the rancher) for their own political action, it did not invite others to take up the cause. We have the power, the doctrine seemed to say, but we have earned it and deserve it; just let us use it alone.

This ideology was employed by large numbers of stockmen and their spokesmen, many of whom had probably espoused different beliefs in 1913. Before, as prices soared because of the packinghouse competition, most ranchers (including breeders) stood stoutly in favor of laissez-faire; now, as prices dipped, many called for intervention by the State. But regardless of how many made it, this switch was not sheer hypocrisy. It was a rational response to economic interests. Furthermore, the change from laissez-faire to traditional anti-imperialism could be limited to the question of State action and responsibility; it was not necessary to revise one's basic values. Thus many cattlemen, many of whom probably held eclectic combinations

[65] Diputados, 1922, VII (April 12, 1923), 232.

of the two creeds anyway, could make the change without ideological or moral discomfort.

When in disagreement with the producers, consumer representatives offered counter-ideologies of their own. Their overall purpose was to prevent the approval of laws that would favor the stockmen at the expense of beef buyers. In pursuit of this aim, Manuel Pinto answered traditional anti-imperialism in terms of laissez-faire, scoring the "mercantilist" aspects of governmental regulation as economic heresies.[66] Taking a different tack, Juan B. Justo's assault on "oligarchic" law-making and the socio-economic "backwardness" of cattle production implied that defense of the ranchers would retard the progress and ultimate independence of the Argentine nation.[67] In vague and only partial form, his complaint about economic stagnation revealed traces of modern anti-imperialism. It could almost be said that Justo, in behalf of the consumers, was responding to one kind of nationalism with the ingredients of another.[68]

NON-PARTICIPANT OBSERVERS

The desires of all the major participant groups to limit the scope of these conflicts appear to have been satisfied. Industrialists ignored the crisis completely.[69] The *Boletín* of the Argentine Industrial Union, led by the colorful Luis Colombo, maintained absolute silence on the subject—just as it had during the debates of 1913 and afterward. While some businessmen

[66] *Ibid.*, 1922, VII (April 24, 1923), 734–40; 1923, VI (September 28), 821.

[67] *Ibid.*, 1922, VII (April 21), esp. 639.

[68] The parliamentary debate over the propriety of State action in the economy provides one instance in which one might imagine a generational split—the younger bloods rejecting the tenets of nineteenth-century liberalism—but the hypothesis does not seem to hold. For the only available sample, the average age of the pro-interventionists was 50, that of the noninterventionists 45: the dogged opponents to governmental action were, if anything, a bit younger than their rivals.

[69] The Confederation of Commerce, Industry, and Production, a heterogeneous organization that was led by one of the country's leading cattlemen, supported the Anchorena-Bosch position of laissez-faire. When Pagés took over the Rural Society, he explicitly shirked the Confederation's support and went his own way. *Anales*, LV, no. 15 (August 1, 1921), 587–88; Swift, *La industria frigorífica*, p. 51; *Anales*, LVII, no. 12 (June 15, 1923), 461–62.

might have voiced individual opinions on this matter,[70] it is clear that the industrial community, as a whole, did not express collective attitudes or take any positive action. They neither allied themselves with the ranchers nor challenged the rural aristocracy. Arch-representatives of the rising urban middle sectors, they stood on the sidelines and hardly acknowledged the fray.

The wheat farmers did not take active part in the conflict either—but they watched its progress closely. On the one hand, they expressed disapproval of the packinghouse pool, possibly because of its commercial resemblance to the (Argentine-owned) grain houses which exploited the farmers of Santa Fe. But farmers also resented the ranchers. During the parliamentary debates, *La Tierra* of the farmers' Agrarian Federation [71] drew a scathing picture of the cattlemen:

The stockmen are members and assiduous attendants of the aristocratic clubs of Buenos Aires, friends and relatives of the ministers, partygoers in all places of social amusement. We are the men of work, crude and badly bred, who do not know how to play roulette or to finance pretty operations at the cost of the nation or the province. Between them, cultured and refined, and us, honest and coarse, there can be no room for doubt. . . . When we ask something we do it with an ugly face, invoking sentiments of justice. They smile and talk in low voices; sometimes they look at their pockets.[72]

Such odious creatures hardly deserved special aid from the government. If the State was going to help someone, it ought to be the farmers.[73]

This resentment came from several sources. One concerned competition between the ranchers and the wheat farmers, still shaken from a crisis of their own, for the favor of the government: official time spent on the livestock problem was official

[70] See the comment by Mora y Araujo, Diputados, 1922, VII (April 14, 1923), 325.

[71] For background on the Agrarian Federation see Lázaro Nemirovsky, *Estructura económica y orientación política de la agricultura en la República Argentina* (Buenos Aires, 1933), pp. 215–41.

[72] April 12, 1923.

[73] *Ibid.*, April 7 and November 3, 1923.

time lost on the question of grains.[74] Another concerned the ranchers' practice of renting their land to wheat growers for a time, then turning it back to pasture again: their relationship was proprietor vs. tenant. In this context, *La Tierra* focused on two specific issues: the inequitable distribution of land, which made it difficult for tenants to acquire property of their own; and the way that stockmen threw farmers off their land during the boom times of the war, so as to raise cattle instead of wheat.[75] In 1912, the farmers' plight provoked a rebellion called the *Grito de Alcorta;* now their bitterness smoldered, not quite breaking into flames.[76]

Though the Federation went so far as to suggest State control of international transactions in beef and other goods,[77] its leaders never petitioned the Congress or the Ministry of Agriculture in specific connection with the politics of meat. While De la Torre's statement in the Chamber coincided with their views, they do not seem to have prompted or encouraged it. Wheat growers were quick to forge attitudes about the cattle crisis, but did not inject themselves into the conflict. Their opinion of the producer-packer struggle was definite—a plague on both your houses—but the distaste for both contestants also discouraged them from taking either side.

The postwar politics of beef concerned mainly the packers and the producers; both groups were led by members of the upper class, though the ranchers co-opted some spokesmen from the middle class. The consumers' participation was marginal, defensive, and largely ineffective. Industrialists and wheat farmers did not intervene in the conflicts. The struggles were expanded insofar as they were introduced into the political sys-

[74] Stockmen were also aware of this rivalry: *Review of the River Plate,* July 1, 1921, 19.

[75] *La Tierra,* May 8 and June 30, 1923.

[76] It is particularly regrettable that issues of *La Tierra* for the period of the 1913 debates on the beef industry could not be found anywhere in Argentina; an educated guess would suppose that the farmers resented the ranchers' prosperity, but I cannot demonstrate this point.

[77] *La Tierra,* November 10, 1923.

tem; once there, they were fought by upper-class groups with immediate interests in the rural economy.

WHOSE VICTORY?

The conflicts arising from the postwar cattle crisis were exceedingly complex. The struggle was multi-cornered—involving packers, divided groups of ranchers, and consumers—and fought in multiple stages. By way of summary, an effort to dissect the dynamics of the process should yield some insight into the usage, allocation, and nature of power in Argentina at the time.

Round One: Advocates of governmental intervention, mostly breeders and spokesmen for small-scale ranchers, won control of the Rural Society in regular elections. While this was a substantial victory over the Anchorena-Bosch group, it appears to have been based upon surprise as well as sheer strength. Later on, as we shall see, the large-scale ranchers and fatteners regained control of the institution.

Round Two: In the fight between cattlemen and the packers, the stockmen drew first blood. Over the strenuous objections of the packers, they managed to make a public issue out of a private grievance and gain the passage of protective legislation, including a minimum-price law. With the aid of anti-imperialism, they successfully transferred the conflict from the marketplace to the Congress.

Round Three: The actual passage of the bills revealed tight control over the Congress by the Executive branch. An open struggle over different bills for control of the trade resulted in triumph for the administration—as well as a victory for the ranchers over the consumers. Although defeated on the minimum-price question, the President still held command.

Round Four: The ranchers' legislative victory over the packers, particularly the minimum-price law, was promptly reversed when the packers stopped buying cattle. Responding to a political challenge with economic strength, they brought the conflict back into the economic arena.

Round Five: The packers' tactic forced leading stockmen, including fatteners, into a political struggle with smaller producers and breeders. Suspension of the minimum price represented total victory for the law's opponents, who used their influence with the Executive to offset power in the Congress. This was a triumph for the packers, who had employed their economic strength to gain indirect political strength.

Round Six: Consumer demands for inclusion of a retail price ceiling found expression in legislation, but not in practice. Their effective political power, like their economic power, was virtually nil; as a lower-class urban group, they could not mount a meaningful challenge to upper-class rural interests.

Round Seven: The victory of the packers and their allies in the campaign for governmental noninterference was augmented by the nonapplication of most of the other laws. In every practical sense of the term, they could continue to operate in an unregulated market. Theirs was the ultimate triumph.

In sum, those who eventually won out in the political sphere were the ones with superior economic power. The packers defeated the stockmen; richer ranchers and fatteners defeated smaller ranchers and breeders; and the cattlemen, as a group, defeated the hapless consumers. Political power could not be used to rectify economic imbalances. Though it is dangerous to generalize, it appears that economic power involved more effective sanctions than did political power in the postwar politics of Argentine beef.

V

The Era of the Meat War

AFTER the Argentine beef industry recovered from the post-war crisis, it was rocked by two major developments in the latter 1920s. First, the packers abandoned their pool for a period of unrestricted competition known ever since as the "Meat War." Second, the British reduced their consumption of foreign beef and began flirting with imperial protection. Caught in between these contradictory trends, Argentine ranchers again turned to their government, still in the hands of the Radicals. Yet the Alvear administration had completely broken with Yrigoyen and his followers, dividing the party into the "Anti-Personalist" and the "Personalist" Radicals, sup-posedly because the Alvear group refused to submit to *El Caudillo's* demands. When the senile Yrigoyen won the presi-dency in 1928, he was openly opposed by Anti-Personalists. In any case, Radicals (of one kind or another) continued to control the State.

SUSPENSION OF THE POOL

The prelude to the Meat War began in January 1925, when the British-owned Smithfield & Argentine firm announced the mod-ernization and enlargement of its plant and demanded a two-thirds increase in its quota (from 5.65 per cent to 8.50 per cent). The room for the change had been provided by Sansinena's withdrawal from the pool—as an Argentine company, it feared violation of the anti-trust law [1]—but the bigger packers forced

1 Watson, *Los criollos y los gringos*, pp. [49]–50.

the break. Swift was building a new plant at Rosario; the Vesteys of Britain were constructing an immense freezing-works at Buenos Aires' South Dock. When Swift requested a quota increase for its new plant up the river, Vestey proposed that both their factories take added portions at the other companies' expense. Smithfield & Argentine refused, as probably expected, so Swift and Vestey began preparing for a showdown. In April 1925 the Meat War broke out.[2]

The small companies could not take the competition. Within a month English & Dutch, a new firm which had purchased one of the Vestey plants, closed its doors. The River Plate, British & Continental cut its shipments down to almost nothing. Although it no longer belonged to the pool, Sansinena temporarily withdrew from the export trade, restricting its efforts to the domestic market until the others came to an agreement.

The British and American giants continued to clutch at each other's throats. Swift faced a powerful rival in Vestey, which had completely integrated all its economic operations: Vestey packed beef in its own plants, shipped cargo in its own boats, insured voyages through its own company, deposited meat in its own cold storage rooms and sold it to the public through its own butchers. Despite financial losses for competing firms,[3] the battle continued for more than two years. Finally, in October 1927, the packers reached a settlement: Americans, 54.9 per cent; British, 35.1 per cent; Argentines, only 10 per cent. The big companies—mainly Swift, Armour, and Vestey— took a large share of business away from their smaller rivals. And more than ever before, the Argentine beef trade was controlled by foreign interests.[4]

For the cattlemen, the Meat War introduced a paradoxical era. Recalling the packinghouse struggle of 1911–14, with its

[2] Hanson, *Argentine Meat*, pp. 242–51.

[3] See Ministerio de Agricultura, *Los frigoríficos*, graph between pp. 20–21.

[4] Watson, *Los criollos y los gringos*, p. 53; J. A. Brewster, "The South American Meat Trade," in Frank Gerrard, ed., *The Book of the Meat Trade* (London, 1949), II, 218–19.

inflated shipments and soaring cattle prices, Argentine ranchers might well have looked forward to another bonanza. This would bring a fitting sequel to the crisis of 1921–23, they might have guessed; the losses and low profits of the postwar interim would now be compensated by strong demand, brisk sales, and climbing prices.

What happened was nothing of the kind. Whereas the volume and value of trade had greatly increased after the break in 1911, this time—after a temporary boost—it actually declined. A comparison of data for the last 15 months of the pool and the 27-month period of competition shows that the packers actually reduced cattle purchases from a monthly average over 322,000 head to less than 260,000. They picked the prices up a bit, from a monthly average of 24.5 centavos per kilo to 27.5 centavos, but not enough to overcome the loss in volume. All in all, the average monthly value of cattle sales decreased by more than 10 per cent; though these figures might be slightly distorted by seasonal variations, they still represent a sizable drop. In brief, the packers made the ranchers pay part of the costs of the Meat War; as a result, some stockmen took financial losses.[5] (See Figure 5.1.)

One reason the packers limited their exports was because the foreign market was contracting, especially in all-important Britain. The steady weakening of the British pound automatically restricted imports; while home livestock output expanded, demographic changes reduced per capita demand for meat; labor problems, including a major crisis in the coal mines, cut down lower-class purchasing power.[6] In the meantime the Dominions, particularly the meat-producing places like New Zealand and Australia, were asking for economic preference. Within the United Kingdom, Conservatives picked up the call for imperial protection; though temporarily halted by the 1924

---

[5] Averages computed from *Anuario de la Sociedad Rural Argentina,* pp. 250 and 265. Also see N.A., D.A., Foreign Agricultural Relations: Reports, Argentina, Livestock-Marketing, file "Livestock, 1918–1929," Cable to Secretary of State, June 29, 1927. Throughout this period the cost-of-living index held reasonably steady: Junta Nacional de Carnes, *Estadísticas básicas,* p. 14.

[6] Ashworth, *Economic History of England,* pp. [305]–76.

Figure 5.1. *Indexes for Volume and Prices, 1924–1927*
(Based on Quarterly Averages)

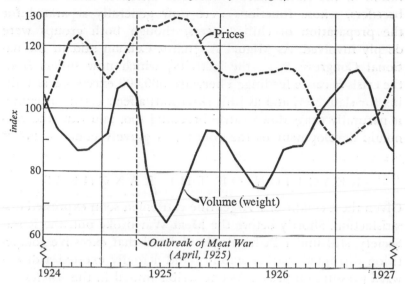

Source: Sociedad Rural Argentina, *El pool de frigoríficos: necesidad de intervención del Estado* (Buenos Aires, 1927), Gráfico 1.

elections, Stanley Baldwin's pro-Empire group took office late the next year.[7] Before long, it was rumored that His Majesty's Government was contemplating a heavy import tax on goods from outside the Dominions.[8] If the packers flooded the Smithfield Market, as they had before the war, they might well antagonize the British.[9] Generally, the prospects were depressing; conditions would probably get worse before they got better.

[7] See *The Times* of London, esp. October–December 1924; and the "Report of the Imperial Economic Committee on Marketing and Preparing for Market of Foodstuffs Produced in the Overseas Parts of the Empire. Second Report—Meat," *Parliamentary Papers,* 1924–25 (Cd. 2499), XIII, 837–71.

[8] Juan E. Richelet, *Los frigoríficos y la conferencia de fletes marítimos* (Paris, 1929), pp. 17–18.

[9] Especially since the British were generally suspicious of the packers, as shown by Inter-Departmental Committee on Meat Supplies, "Report of Committee Appointed by the Board of Trade to Consider the Means of Securing Sufficient Meat Supplies for the United Kingdom," *Parliamentary Papers,* 1919 (Cd. 456), XXV, 435–64; "Interim Report on Meat, Prepared by a Sub-Committee Appointed by the Standing Committee on Trusts," *Ibid.,* 1920 (Cd. 1057), XXIII, 545–57; and "First Report of the Royal Commission on Food Prices, 1925," *Ibid.,* 1924–25 (Cd. 2390), XIII, 1–223, esp. 135–36.

It is apparent from contemporary comment that this deterioration of the cattle market hurt the fatteners more than the breeders, whose functions were now generally separated for the preparation of chiller steers, though both groups were deeply involved. As Miguel A. Juárez Celman said in the national Congress: ". . . the [activity] which now suffers from the crisis is cattle feeding. There are 500,000 excess steers waiting for slaughter, and as [this situation] affects cattle fattening, it naturally drags down cattle breeding too, and thus the economic development of the country is gravely endangered." [10]

REACTION OF THE RANCHERS

Given these conditions, Argentine cattlemen soon expressed dissatisfaction. Shortly before the Meat War broke out, the Rural Society, still under Pedro Pagés, claimed that excessive competition disrupted market stability and actually exerted a downward pressure on prices. As one writer mused in the *Anales,*

> we cannot forget that we lived peacefully in the best of all worlds before the great packers from Chicago brought us new methods of meat elaboration and market exploitation, inasmuch as exploitation is the subject at hand. Under the English system we had at least one advantage, price stability. With the progress brought from Chicago, confidence in the stability of the cattle-raising business has been lost and we have come to recollect with sweet nostalgia [the Portuguese term *"saudades"*] those times in which the business worked on a basis that permitted those who dedicated themselves to the noble labors of the country to make a little money.[11]

Thus identified with a mild form of traditional anti-imperialism, the erstwhile monopoly of the British was preferred to the competitive drive of the Americans. As long as the packinghouse rivalry failed to increase volume and push up prices, the Meat War would be regarded as a crass demonstration of alien (that is, American) materialism, selfishness, and greed.

Instead of dwelling upon the War, Argentine ranchers—

10 Diputados, 1926, VI (December 9), 828. Also see the comment by Diego Molinari on p. 827.
11 *Anales,* LIX, no. 6 (March 15, 1925), 271.

breeders and fatteners alike—turned their attention to contraction of the market. One measure they consistently advocated was the taking of a livestock census. In August 1925, Mario Guido introduced a census bill to the Chamber of Deputies, declaring that an accurate count of the livestock population was needed in order to handle alterations in the market with efficiency and foresight.[12] The Rural Society enthusiastically supported this proposal,[13] and the following year the Alvear administration presented a bill of its own.[14] Another year later, some Radicals insisted on the measure once again.[15] In September 1928 a census bill was whisked through the Chamber of Deputies,[16] and a year after that the Senate voted to approve the project.[17] Despite delays in Congress, there was no major opposition to the plan. The ranchers could count their cattle again.

A second measure which many stockmen favored was the construction of a national packinghouse. This idea was supported mainly by the breeders, and seems to have hung over from the crisis of 1921–23. At a meeting with the Minister of Agriculture in December 1924, Celedonio Pereda and other spokesmen from the Rural Society contended that a national packinghouse was needed to defend cattlemen from the manipulations of the foreign packers.[18] In July 1925, Rodolfo Moreno (h.) introduced a bill that called for government expropriation of a freezing-works.[19] Leaders of the Rural Society considered plans for a cooperative packinghouse, paid for by ranchers but—in view of the brutality of the Meat War—supported by the State.[20] In August 1927, a Radical Deputy from

[12] Diputados, 1925, III (August 21), 687–88.
[13] *Anales*, LIX, no. 18 (September 15, 1925), 887–88; LIX, no. 20 (October 15, 1925), 1135; and later on LXIII, no. 18 (September 15, 1929), 743–46.
[14] Diputados, 1926, IV (August 18), 141.
[15] *Ibid.*, 1927, II (July 14), 262–63.
[16] *Ibid.*, 1928, IV (September 20), 545; V (September 30), 892.
[17] Senadores, 1929, II (September 3), 46–57; Diputados, 1929, III (September 18), 577 and (September 19), 674.
[18] *Anales*, LIX, no. 1 (January 1, 1925), 24.
[19] Diputados, 1925, II (July 1), 406.
[20] *Anales*, LIX, no. 10 (May 15, 1925), 461–62; also see LIX, no. 20 (October 15, 1925), 1127–32.

Entre Ríos proposed the creation of a "semi-official" company that would be evenly supported by public and private funds.[21] A year after that, well after the resumption of the pool, Guillermo Martínez Guerrero—an aristocratic, cattle-raising Radical from the province of Buenos Aires—put forth a somewhat similar plan.[22] But Congress took no positive action. Even so, this failure does not seem to represent a major political defeat for the breeders who supported it. Though the project was often suggested, there is no real evidence that truly significant efforts were mounted in its behalf.

During the Meat War the Alvear administration also proposed that the consumption of cows in the city of Buenos Aires be prohibited for a period of three years so as to shore up the market for baby steers, normally used in chilled beef. The plan was promptly abandoned after Enrique Dickmann—an urban Socialist who usually stood for consumers—pointed out that this would favor the fatteners at the expense of the breeders, since the breeders (who had most of the cows that were used for domestic consumption) would be left with a smaller outlet for their animals.[23] He might have added that it would reduce the supply of consumer cattle and probably drive up the retail price of beef in Buenos Aires. Since the fatteners backed off from this tacit breeder-consumer alliance, the proposal did not give rise to conflict; in public, at least, the bill was never discussed or debated again.

HOOF-AND-MOUTH DISEASE?

Regardless of the Argentine ranchers' low-keyed attitude, the Meat War indirectly challenged their interests because it contributed to the contraction of the market. First, it caused a spreading conviction among British consumers that renewal of the pool would sooner or later drive beef prices up, as the

21 Diputados, 1927, III (August 10), 570–78.

22 Ibid., 1928, II (July 6), 87–89.

23 Ibid., 1926, VI (December 2), 755; (December 9), 819. And see Anales, LXI, no. 1 (January 1, 1927), 19–23.

packers would try to compensate for losses incurred under the competition. This suspicion naturally helped create hostility to Argentine beef and probably curtailed its retail sales.[24] Second, unrestricted competition in the United Kingdom meat market antagonized British cattle farmers and prompted them to complain that Argentine beef was infected with hoof-and-mouth disease.[25] In malignant form, the disease had ravaged English herds in the early 1920s. As British farmers argued that meat importation brought risks of foreign infection, their claim was reinforced in the United States: in 1926, Calvin Coolidge's Republican administration yielded to demands from cattle-producing constituents and prohibited fresh Argentine beef on the grounds that it might be infected.[26]

Parenthetically, one might note that the United States embargo on Argentine meat was directly opposed to the interests of the American packers in the Plate. Apparently Swift, Armour, and Wilson managers had long been seeking to export beef to the United States; before they had been blocked by wartime emergencies or tariffs, but now they were outlawed from it. Washington's decision could hardly have been taken with a view to making the Argentine economy dependent on the Colossus up North. If anything, as we shall shortly see, the embargo tended to reduce the American sphere of influence and tighten the longstanding bonds between Argentina and Great Britain.

[24] In a self-conscious effort to allay consumer fears about renewal of the pool, one trade journal argued that "in the meat trade it is as much a case of 'beat your neighbours out of doors' as anywhere else. Hence we see no danger to the security of cheap meat in Britain so far as importers are concerned. There is no slackening in the pace of competition, and neither side among the big contestants, so far as we can see, is pulling away from the other in this race." *Cold Storage and Produce Review*, XXX, no. 350 (May 19, 1927), 164. And see the comment by J. H. Martínez in Diputados, 1928, II (July 5), 32.

[25] The farmers' reaction to the Meat War was expressed by A. M. Williamson in the House of Commons, *Parliamentary Debates*, 5th ser., vol. 220 (July 19, 1928), 612.

[26] For complete correspondence on this Bureau of Animal Industry Order no. 298 see N.A., Corr. Am. Emb., 1926, VI, 650. Also see Harold F. Peterson, *Argentina and the United States 1810–1960* (New York, 1964), pp. 352–54. For a statement on the political outlook of American ranchers see Arthur Capper, "The Middle West Looks Abroad," *Foreign Affairs*, V, no. 4 (July, 1927), 535–36.

In any case, the possible results of the hoof-and-mouth accusations were serious indeed. The loss of the United Kingdom market would spell disaster for the Argentine beef industry. In early 1928 Lord Bledisloe, parliamentary secretary to the British Minister of Agriculture, made an inspection tour of Argentina. He noted the mildness of the disease where it existed and recommended several measures for its control; these the cattlemen promised to carry out. The Bledisloe visit was encouraging, but it was also inconclusive.[27] More would have to be done.

In July 1928 José M. Bustillo, a future president of the Rural Society, proposed that the Chamber of Deputies invite some British Members of Parliament to check on Argentina's sanitary precautions. Though supported by some of Bustillo's fellow Conservatives, the resolution was voted down after some Radicals charged that such a gesture would compromise the nation's dignity; no one from another country, they claimed, should be invited to pass judgment on the practices of the Argentine government.[28] Undaunted by this argument, the Rural Society invited some M.P.'s itself. The visit took place in November 1928, when the guests were treated to a splendid tour of the country's leading ranches.[29] They could not help but be impressed.

The Argentine campaign against the charge of hoof-and-mouth disease was pressed on diplomatic levels as well. Juan E. Richelet, agricultural attaché at the Embassy in London, produced a flood of learned propaganda. In 1929 he came out with a long and persuasive polemic entitled *A Defence of Argentine Meat.*[30] Another book, published the same year, openly announced its intention "to refute the numerous attacks which have been made recently against the chilled and frozen meat trade." Refute them Richelet did, in his able and articulate

27 *Anales,* LXII, no. 3 (February 1, 1928), 155–64; *Annual Review of the Chilled and Frozen Meat Trade, 1927* (W. Weddel & Co., Ltd., London [1928]), 14.
28 Diputados, 1928, II (July 5), 20–42.
29 *Anales,* LXIII, no. 7 (April 1, 1929), *passim.*
30 London, 1929.

way, incidentally pointing out that British investments in Argentina would be gravely imperiled by restrictions on the trade in beef.[31]

Partly as a result of these multiple efforts, and possibly due to consumer complaints about the potential reduction of meat supplies,[32] the British government never yielded to the anti-Argentine argument on the question of cattle disease. The fact that the British could tighten regulations for inspection [33] and continue to import beef from the Plate points up the character of this controversy. Argentine meat was clearly suitable for importation. The issue, in Great Britain, concerned demands from local farmers and, to a lesser extent, those of the Dominions. In the United States, the fresh-meat embargo responded to pressures from the West and Middle West.[34] The problem derived from conflicts of interests rather than technical questions of hygiene. It is worth noting, incidentally, that the American restriction on fresh meat imports has continued to constitute a major stumbling block in relations between the two countries. Ever since the mid-1920s, ranchers and other Argentines have maintained some feeling of antagonism toward the United States because of the embargo.[35]

[31] *The Argentine Meat Trade,* p. vii. The determination of the Yrigoyen government to safeguard the international reputation of Argentine beef is also discussed in the *Review of the River Plate,* October 26, 1928, 7.

[32] Consumer interests were forcefully represented by members of the Labour Party: for example see House of Commons, *Parliamentary Debates,* 5th ser., vol. 196 (June 17, 1926), 2455.

[33] The arrangements for regulation were described by Walter Guinness, Baldwin's Minister of Agriculture, in the House of Commons, *Parliamentary Debates,* 5th ser., vol. 214 (February 27, 1928), 26–27 and vol. 217 (May 10, 1928), 404; and see Department of Overseas Trade, *Economic and Financial Conditions in the Argentine Republic* [by H. O. Chalkley] (London, 1928), 57–58.

[34] Voting on meat tariffs in the Fordney-McCumber debates of 1922 generally followed party lines—Republicans in favor, Democrats against—but all Senators from cattle-raising states (including Democrats) supported high tariffs. From roll calls in the United States *Congressional Record,* 67th Cong., 2nd sess. (June 28, 1922), 9543, 9558.

[35] For a classic expression of the ranchers' resentment see Carlos García Mata, *The Problem of Beef in United States-Argentine Relations* (Cambridge, Mass., 1941). Also see Peterson, *Argentina and the United States,* pp. 363–65; and E. Louise Peffer, "Foot-and-Mouth Disease in United States Policy," *Food Research Institute Studies,* III, no. 2 (May, 1962), [141]–180.

THE PACKINGHOUSE POOL AND
STATE INTERVENTION

During the course of the Meat War, the Rural Society changed leadership. In the institution's sharply contested elections of 1926, Pedro Pagés and his pro-breeder colleagues were beaten by a team under Luis F. Duhau, one of the wealthiest fatteners in the province of Buenos Aires. Although the tensions between breeder and fattener interests seemed to be muted at the time, this turnover at the top of the Rural Society brought some basic changes in its policy.

Duhau was a vigorous president, setting up a number of committees to investigate trends in agriculture and stockraising. In June 1927, as the Meat War continued, the Society's Subcommission on the Meat Export Trade came out with a mild-mannered report on the pool and its disruption. Noting the theory that the War was started by Americans in hopeful anticipation of a market in the United States, the commission thought this was legitimate; Americans would naturally know how to sell their goods to other Americans, just as the British could deal with the British. In opposition to the breeder-inspired scheme for a national packinghouse, the group warned Argentines to stay out of the business because they would not know how to handle either market. Regardless of the pool, the only sensible demand ranchers could make was for reasonable competition among the packers in order to assure a fair return on cattle production.[36]

Later that year, after the renewal of the pool, the Society produced one of the most important and controversial documents on the beef industry that was ever to appear: *El pool de frigoríficos: necesidad de intervención del Estado*. Drafted by an up-and-coming young economist named Raúl Prebisch, the report was submitted to the Minister of Agriculture in December 1927 and published promptly afterward. Impressively buttressed with statistics, the memorandum made two central points. First, de-

---

36 Subcomisión del Comercio Exterior de Carnes de la Sociedad Rural Argentina, *Comercio exterior de carnes* (Buenos Aires, 1927).

spite the packers' claims, the pool had never been able to co-ordinate supply and demand, as shown by continuous oscillations in volume and price. Second, the pool tended to suppress the free interplay of supply and demand, "that is, the essential condition . . . of free competition." As a result, the packers made "excessive profits" at the expense of the producers. The only possible solution to this situation was intervention by the State.[37]

The Society's idea of State intervention, however, could hardly be called radical. The report merely called for inspection of the companies' books by an independent board appointed by the government. "We are not even thinking of the possibility that the State, by construction, purchase, or nationalization of freezing establishments should become directly involved in the economic management of the firms, convinced [as we are] of the superiority of individual initiative which, in this case, has shown itself in the admirable development of the meatpacking industry in this country. It could well be . . . that the destruction of wealth brought by official management would exceed the harm which the monopolistic combinations could cause to us rural producers."[38] Though Duhau and the fatteners now expressed resentment of the pool, they would not go so far as to support the breeders' demands for a national packinghouse.

The difference between the Duhau and Pagés policies was highlighted a couple of weeks later, when the Board of Directors—apparently taken aback by critics who regarded the report as an attack on the packers—hastily explained itself. Transparently insulting the Pagés group, the Board declared its departure from "the streetcorner oratory" of its predecessors and asserted that, in contrast to previous demagoguery, this report resulted from patient and impartial research.[39] While the conflict in views was spelled out, it is revealing that Pagés and Duhau were both Conservatives, both aristocrats, and both from the province of Buenos Aires. Neither seemed to be charismatic.

[37] (Buenos Aires, 1927), pp. 14–17.
[38] *Ibid.*, p. 17.
[39] *Anales*, LXII, no. 1 (January 1, 1928), 9–10.

One was a breeder, another was a fattener. What separated them, essentially, was economic interest.

The renewal of the packinghouse pool stimulated debate within the national Congress as well as within the Rural Society. In August 1928 Víctor Juan Guillot, a middle-class lawyer and Yrigoyen Radical, interpellated Alvear's Minister of Agriculture, Emilio Mihura, on the condition of the cattle and meat markets. In the course of his comments the Minister, a well-known cattleman and member of the Rural Society, expressed no doubt that a pool existed but claimed that it did no harm to Argentine ranchers. The agreement kept supply in accord with demand, avoided gluts, and kept a market open for cattle at all times. Challenging Mihura's statement, Guillot cited the Rural Society's report on the pool and argued that the "entente" enabled the packers to regulate cattle prices at will.[40] This view was supported by several leading ranchers, who seemed to take a common stance: if market conditions were not good, the packers were at fault.

This debate over the packinghouses revealed another kind of intergroup rivalry. As José Heriberto Martínez said, the mediocrity of the livestock market led many landowners to use their pastures for wheat-growing instead of cattle-raising, usually under contract with tenant farmers. One result was a general decline in the country's cattle population; another was a hardening of the enmity between the pastoral and agricultural sectors, especially when—in Martínez' Conservative opinion— the Radical administration was "so closely linked to agrarian interests." [41] In defense of wheat farmers, Rogelio Araya blamed the ranchers' shortsightedness for the power of the pool, denounced their laziness and leisure, and called for land colonization and property redistribution. Such reforms would diversify production, increase over-all output, secure the country's economic independence, and also strike a blow for social equity.[42]

40 Diputados, 1928, II (August 1), 835–58, esp. 837; III (August 2), 41–69.

41 Ibid., III (August 8), 118–19; II (July 5), 24. And see Hanson, Argentine Meat, p. 255.

42 Diputados, 1928, III (August 9), 194–213.

Aside from this brief meat-wheat rivalry, the renewal of the packinghouse pool neither caused nor revealed any major group conflicts. Resentment of the pool was evident but not especially intense: despite the protests of the Rural Society and a couple of Deputies, no practical action was taken. Nor did the packers' agreement bring out significant opposition between cattle breeders and fatteners. Though control of the Rural Society passed from one group to the other, the fatteners' criticism of the pool brought them closer to the breeders' anti-imperialist position than at any recent time. When the fatteners denounced all schemes for a national packinghouse, the breeders did not retaliate perceptibly through politics. While the reaction to the resumption of the packinghouse pool showed the differences between these groups, in short, it did not lead to head-on conflict.

COMMERCIAL POLICY: "BUY FROM THOSE WHO BUY FROM US"

As clearly seen above, the central concern of Argentine ranchers during this period was not so much the Meat War as the sagging state of the international market for beef, particularly in Great Britain. Rumors that the United Kingdom might place taxes on beef that came from non-British packinghouses, or that imports from Argentina might be restricted by a quota system, provoked the widespread fear that cattlemen might lose their most profitable market.[43] Confronted by this problem, rancher spokesmen gradually shaped a new solution: the reorientation of Argentina's policy on international trade.

Ever since the founding of the Republic, Argentina had traditionally maintained an open door. All of its commercial treaties, beginning with the Anglo-Argentine pact of 1825, had included a "most-favored-nation" clause. Customs barriers had never been particularly high, and were usually erected for fiscal rather than protective purposes. Exports accounted for one of the country's most important—perhaps the most important—

[43] Richelet, Los frigoríficos, pp. 17–18.

economic activities. In general, Argentina had always been ready to trade with anyone at any time at any place.

In the late 1920s the ranchers—longtime beneficiaries and supporters of the open-door policy—started to question the wisdom of this tradition. While still president of the Rural Society, Pedro Pagés publicly suggested the reconsideration of all "most-favored-nation" stipulations.[44] His successor, Luis Duhau, launched a vigorous campaign against prevailing policy under a new commercial slogan: "Buy from those who buy from us." Stamped on the letterhead of all his Rural Society correspondence, it soon became one of the institution's official mottoes. As explained in the *Anales,* economic conditions made such a stance inevitable; distribution, as well as production, must now be a major concern. In a special meeting with the Minister of Agriculture, Duhau formally proposed the reorientation of economic policy along these lines.[45]

Ideologically speaking, there was a grain of nationalism in this whole idea. According to Duhau, the "most-favored-nation" policy stripped Argentina of her inalienable right to pick and choose among her trading partners. The result was over-dependence on the whimsies of the international market: if societies like Argentina "are politically sovereign, economically they are not." [46] But in practical terms, the motto meant that Argentina should tie her economy to the United Kingdom. Britain was by far the leading importer of Argentine products, particularly beef, and exported large amounts of manufactured goods to the Plate. The *Anales* drew the connection: "The less we buy from them, the less they will buy from us." [47] In spite of its homage to national feeling, this policy was consciously intended to make Argentina a sort of economic colony of Britain. Dependence was thus promoted in the name of independence.

The turning to Britain implicit in the reciprocal trade slogan was derived partly from the desire to stave off negative conse-

44 *Anales,* LX, no. 18 (September 15, 1926), 839–40.
45 *Ibid.,* LXI, no. 1 (January 1, 1927), 7–8; and see Luis Duhau, *Política económica internacional: "Comprar a quien nos compra"* (Buenos Aires, 1927).
46 *Anales,* LXI, no. 1 (January 1, 1927), 8.
47 *Ibid.,* LXI, no. 2 (January 15, 1927), 59–61.

quences of the hoof-and-mouth scare.[48] By the same token, resentment of the United States was deeply rooted in the motto's
meaning. As the ranchers' fears about the world market multi-
plied, the American embargo robbed them of a large and long-
desired market. While Argentina imported more and more
goods from up north, American imports from the Plate were
dropping off, and stockmen were understandably embittered.[49]

In its innocuous way, "Buy from those who buy from us"
seemed to reflect the interests of breeders and fatteners alike,
since a reduction in the volume of beef exports would naturally
bring harm to both. But in long-range terms, it tended to speak
for the fatteners—like Duhau—and a few wealthy breeders,
rather than for the breeders at large. The slogan demanded
economic reciprocity with Britain: Britain, one must remember, was almost the only buyer of chilled beef. So the Rural
Society's new motto promoted commerce not only in beef, but
specifically chilled beef taken from specially fattened steers.
Though the breeders did not protest against this implication
at the time, its significance should not be overlooked.[50]

In the meantime, "Buy from those who buy from us" was
avidly promoted by the packers. Company managers had several times addressed the Minister of Agriculture about the
market contraction,[51] and were delighted to take up the Society's slogan: after all, chilled beef was their biggest business
too. Duhau took proud note of this alliance and publicly acknowledged the packers' support of his stand.[52] The adoption

[48] See the statement by E. G. Drabble, vice-president of the Society, in
Anales, LXII, no. 9 (May 1, 1928), 555–56.

[49] Ibid., LXI, no. 2 (January 15, 1927), 59–61; and see LXI, no. 1 (January 1,
1927), 9–10, 17–18. American diplomats were acutely conscious of this trend
and accused the British Ambassador, Sir Malcolm Robertson, of fomenting
anti-American sentiment: for example see N.A., D.S., 635.1112/38, Cable to
Secretary of State, January 10, 1927; 635.4115/16, Bliss to Secretary of State,
May 9, 1928; 711.35/53, Bliss to Secretary of State, January 26, 1928.

[50] In the early 1940s some breeders countered with a slogan of their own,
"Sell the whole world over," but their campaign was muted by the practical
necessity of shipping meat to Britain during World War II. Olariaga, El
ruralismo argentino, pp. 377–92.

[51] Richelet, Los frigoríficos, p. 43.

[52] Anales, LXII, no. 8 (April 15, 1928), 491–92. Before the middle 1920s the
American packers might not have approved of this policy, since they ap-

of this ideology did not provoke any conflict between the cattlemen, especially fatteners, and the meatpackers. On the contrary, it tended to unite the two groups.

It was not long before the Rural Society's steady pressure for
change in Argentina's commercial policy reached the political
arena. At Duhau's insistence, President Alvear included a reference to reciprocal trade in his congressional message of 1927.[53]
That June Gabriel Chiossone, a sugar-cane grower and Radical,
proposed the revision of all international trade agreements in
accord with the Society's slogan.[54] A few months later Daniel
Amadeo y Videla, a Conservative rancher from the province of
Buenos Aires, suggested a 6 per cent tax on all imports from
the United States in order to promote reciprocal exchange.[55]
The next year, closely following the Duhau logic, José Heriberto Martínez presented a bill to renounce all existing commercial treaties and provide a preferential tariff for British
goods.[56]

After Yrigoyen resumed the presidency in 1928, practical
steps to implement this policy were taken on the Executive
level. Informal discussions with the United Kingdom were undertaken in 1929, and late that year agreement was reached
on the D'Abernon Pact, named after Britain's chief negotiator.
The document called for mutual credits of 100 million pesos,
with the understanding that Argentina would obtain railroad
equipment for the State-run lines while the British would use
their credit for cereals and other products (presumably meat).
The governments, it should be noted, would make the acquisi-
tions; in a sense, this barter-type agreement stood in direct
anticipation of the State control over international transactions later practiced by Perón.[57]

parently hoped to gain access to the United States market. After the American
embargo was imposed on fresh meat, though, they supported the notion of
"Buy from those who buy from us."

[53] N.A., D.S., 635.1111/2, Cable to Secretary of State, May 30, 1927.

[54] Diputados, 1927, II (June 24), 54–57.

[55] Ibid., 1927, V (September 21), 19–24.

[56] Ibid., 1928, II (August 1), 815–16; III (August 8), 124–25.

[57] The text and presidential message are in Diputados, 1929, IV (December 4),
249–51. Also see Anales, LXIII, no. 20 (October 15, 1929), 807.

At any rate, the D'Abernon Pact drew high praise from British trading interests [58] and the Argentine Rural Society. In spite of constitutional criticism that the President could not make any such agreement without the consent of the Senate, in spite of its apparent violation of Argentine commercial law, and in spite of the advantages it yielded to Great Britain, the Society upheld its moral force: it was, in every sense, "Buy from those who buy from us" incarnate.[59] Though the agreement was never put into effect,[60] the Rural Society was still getting its way under Yrigoyen's administration.[61]

THE RADICALS IN RETROSPECT

The D'Abernon agreement was the last major measure taken in behalf of livestock producers during the period of Radical rule that stretched from 1916 to 1930. As such, it brought an era to a close, and provides an excellent vantage point for reviewing and assessing the performance of the Radicals, often considered the leaders of an urban middle-class challenge to the rural upper class. Without assuming that they operated as a monolithic unit, our present purpose is to see how the Radicals used their political power with respect to the beef industry, the principal source of wealth for the landed aristocracy and a key element in the country's export-import economic structure.[62]

From the start, it should be understood that the Conservatives were the most forthright spokesmen for ranching interests. They responded with greater vigor and speed to the crisis of

[58] See, for instance, the *Review of the River Plate*, September 13, 1929, 13.

[59] *Anales*, LXIII, no. 20 (October 15, 1929), 807–8.

[60] The pact was soon sanctioned by the British government and, perhaps in deference to legal criticism, submitted to the Argentine Congress. It gained approval from the Deputies, but failed to pass the Senate before Congress was suspended by the revolution of 1930. See *Review of the River Plate*, September 20, 1929, 19–21; Diputados, 1929, IV (December 12–13), 439–74.

[61] Despite the Minister of Agriculture's promise not to be unduly influenced by the Society: N.A., D.S., 611.353/17, White to Secretary of State, March 14, 1929.

[62] The following argument has been fully spelled out in my article on "Los radicales argentinos y la defensa de los intereses ganaderos, 1916–1930," *Desarrollo económico*, VII, no. 25 (abril–junio 1967), [795]–829.

1922–1923, and Matías Sánchez Sorondo and others sometimes complained about the negligence of the Yrigoyen and Alvear administrations. The Yrigoyen government took no really decisive measures against the sag in cattle prices. The Le Breton recovery plan was undeniably less sweeping than that of the Conservatives, and the Alvear leadership flatly opposed the application of a minimum price.

Even so, it seems fair to say that the Radicals gave strong support to cattlemen throughout their period of rule. Yrigoyen started by crushing a movement of the packinghouse workers, in line with—though perhaps not as a direct result of—the wishes of the Rural Society. He failed to take much positive action to offset the cattle crisis of 1922–1923, but that was partly because his term expired before the issue came to a head; he stepped down in October 1922, and not even Sánchez Sorondo introduced his plan until December of that year. Then the Alvear government took prompt action after coming to power, proposing and pushing through a series of bills in behalf of the stockmen. The only serious disagreement concerned the matter of the minimum price, and even this exception helps prove the rule: the scheme was first proposed by Manuel Mora y Araujo, a member of the Radical Party.

The extent to which Radicals stood up for the cattle-producing interests is clearly demonstrated in the table below, which represents the political (party) origin of all the major initiatives put forth in behalf of the stockmen in the Congress between 1916 and 1930.[63] The figures are somewhat surprising: the Radicals proposed *fully 60 per cent* of the total number of measures, twice as many as the Conservatives. The Socialists, almost all of whose positive participation concerned the general anti-trust bill, and the Progressive Democrats fell far behind. Despite the inevitable imperfections in calculations of this kind,

[63] "Initiatives" include bills, resolutions, interpellations, and demands for debate, and deal, where relevant, with general commercial and anti-trust policy as well as with stockraising itself. Multi-partisan measures have been divided on a proportional basis: if two Radicals and two Conservatives collaborated on a proposal, each party is credited with one-half of one initiative.

there can be absolutely no doubt that the Radicals, as a group, were deeply concerned with the fate of the cattle producers.

Table 5.1. *Party Origin of Pro-Rancher Initiatives, 1916–1930*

Period	Number of Initiatives	Radical %	Conservative %	P.D.P. %	Socialist %
1916–22	25	70	18	8	4
1922–28	52	52	38	4	6
1928–30	13	75	17	–	8
Totals	90	60	29	5	6

Roughly three-quarters of all the proposals put forth by Radical Senators or Deputies [64] came from delegates of mainly rural areas, outside the city of Buenos Aires. Alone, the province of Buenos Aires accounted for more than a third of all the Radical initiatives; together, the stockraising provinces to the north (Córdoba, Santa Fe, Entre Ríos, and Corrientes) contributed another third. Geographically speaking, it is clear that the Radical Party provided ample representation for its cattle-producing constituencies.

Many of these measures came directly from livestock owners. By a conservative estimate, about 20 per cent of the Radical proposals came from congressmen who belonged to the Argentine Rural Society; in all likelihood, another 20 per cent came from men who had relatives in the Society.[65] Despite the prevalence of the aristocratic Rural Society, approximately 60 per cent of the Radical measures from rural areas came from members of the middle class. Presumably, these were men on the way up, directly or indirectly tied to the promotion of rural activities (or at least the interests of rural constituencies). In

[64] Initiatives by the Executive branch were included in Table 5.1 but have been omitted from these subsequent calculations because of the difficulties of attributing regional, social, or occupational characteristics to projects that might have been designed by differing groups in the Cabinet.

[65] With some exceptions for exceedingly common surnames (e.g. García), it is assumed that a Senator or Deputy whose family name appears on the membership list of the Rural Society probably had a relative who did belong to it.

particular, these spokesmen from the middle class accounted for many of the pro-rancher measures sponsored by areas to the north and along the upper Littoral.

Strictly speaking, the scarcity of data makes it extremely difficult to isolate the number of proposals put forth by "urban" congressmen. Whether or not representatives from Entre Ríos or Córdoba came from municipal backgrounds is extraordinarily hard to find out. Given this problem, it is necessary to limit the discussion of "urban" participation in beef politics to the city of Buenos Aires, whose delegates contributed about one-quarter of all the Radical initiatives intended to protect the livestock producers. Of these measures, about 40 per cent came from city-living aristocrats, and 60 per cent came from members of the middle and upper-middle classes.

On the whole, this information strongly suggests that Radical leaders, recruited from both the upper class and the middle sectors, identified their interests with those of the landed aristocracy. They did not pose, at this time, a middle-class urban challenge to the lordly barons of beef. They did not promote, in any significant way, the interests of laborers or consumers in opposition to those of the producers. They did not claim that over-dependence on exports or the crisis in prices proved a need for indigenous industrialization. They did not kick the cattle industry when it was down, but sprang to its defense. In short, the Radicals did not introduce an era of urban-rural class conflict.

Nor did the Radicals do much to influence or alter the distribution of power within the ranching sector. It is possible that Yrigoyen hoped to strengthen the breeders and smaller-scale ranchers,[66] but he failed to fight hard for this goal. Throughout this period, the fatteners maintained their economic and political supremacy over the breeders. In the most straightforward confrontation between the two groups, the battle over the minimum price, the fatteners won a decisive victory with the

[66] The British Minister, at least, thought Yrigoyen proposed one bill reducing rural rents in the belief "that he can afford to antagonize the conservative and land owning interests if he secures the votes of the numerous agricultural tenant class." P.R.O., F.O. 371/7172, Macleay to Curzon, February 6, 1922.

help of the Alvear administration. Years later, the implicitly pro-fattener idea of "Buy from those who buy from us" was first mentioned by Alvear, then applied by Yrigoyen.

As an explanation of the Radicals' behavior, it cannot be satisfactorily argued that the Party was always acting to protect the nation from plunder by foreign enterprise. Alvear's capitulation to the packer-fattener alliance on the question of the minimum price could hardly be called an expression of militant anti-imperialism; nor could the statement made by his Minister of Agriculture that the packinghouse pool posed no threat to the ranchers' welfare. Other governmental measures, ranging from Yrigoyen's intervention in the strike of 1917 to his efforts to enact the principle of "Buy from those who buy from us," actively promoted the interests of the foreign packers. Though the Radicals' support of the stockmen often included opposition to the packers, their actions do not seem to have been governed by an unshakable commitment to nationalistic ideology.

It has been suggested that the rapid growth of the Argentine economy in the postwar years deterred the Radicals from tampering with a "tried-and-true" process of development through expression of their middle-class desires for industrialization.[67] Protection of livestock interests would be regarded as a singular example of statesmanship, according to this theory, rather than as a manifestation of fundamental goals or aspirations. Though this argument cannot be totally disproved, it does not stand alone. In the meat market, at least, there was more than enough conflict, crisis, and contraction to have justified (or rationalized) a major departure in governmental policy.

The most promising explanation of Radical behavior lies in the Party's socio-economic composition. It is important to remember that Radical leadership contained a fairly large number of stockmen, some of patrician background: Marcelo T. de Alvear, Tomás Le Breton, and many others came from prominent families and belonged to the Rural Society. Not all of the Party's direction was either urban or middle-class. To a very

[67] Whitaker, *Argentina*, p. 73.

real degree, there was a sharp social distinction between upper-class elements in the effective party leadership and the largely middle-class rank and file of their followers. Thus it might be surmised that Radical participation in the politics of beef can best be understood through the immediate interests of the leaders.

Yet it is also apparent that middle-class Radicals did not regard aristocrats as enemies. First, particularly as shown in the composition of the Cabinets, they recruited (or at least accepted) much of their leadership from the traditional upper class. Second, they actively promoted aristocratic interests. When faced with a choice, the Radicals, even Yrigoyen, supported the ranchers instead of urban lower-class groups.

These actions of middle-sector members of the Radical Party can be explained largely by their backgrounds and activities. On one level, as Ezequiel Gallo (h.) and Silvia Sigal have argued, the bulk of the movement's support came from groups which had been mobilized by the development of the export-import economy, typically as merchants or lawyers.[68] In the politics of beef, the high participation of middle-class Radicals from the provinces outside Buenos Aires, especially those along the Littoral, corroborates the Gallo-Sigal thesis. Activated by the growth of the rural economy, most Radicals had a stake in its progress and improvement. Thus their behavior was not a betrayal of middle-class ideals, but a rational pursuit of their interests.

On another level, the behavior of upper middle-class Radicals, especially those of urban background, was liable to be influenced by their social aspirations. In a relatively mobile society, these were men on the rise. What many seem to have wanted was admission to the circles of the oligarchy. These considerations might have been secondary to the coincidence of economic interests, and were probably conditioned by it, but nevertheless were important. As an example of this impulse, the Argentine Industrial Union was recruited mostly from the rising middle sectors and, because of its emphasis on

[68] "La formación," in Di Tella et al., *Argentina, sociedad de masas,* cited above.

manufacturing, stood in hypothetical economic rivalry to the stockmen; yet in 1925, the industrialists granted honorary membership in their organization to the Argentine Rural Society.[69]

Because of these multiple factors, there was no perceptible difference between the actions of the Personalist and the Anti-Personalist Radicals.[70] Alvear's wing was probably more patrician than that of Yrigoyen, to be sure, and took most of the definite measures in defense of the cattlemen. On the other hand, no open dispute broke out between the two on livestock matters. Except for Alvear's suspension of the minimum price, both administrations consistently acceded to demands from the Argentine Rural Society. And during Yrigoyen's term of leadership the Party was strongly outspoken in favor of ranchers; according to Table 5.1, relative concern (as measured by the percentages) was even greater than during the Alvear presidency. Though for slightly different reasons, Yrigoyen and the Party's urban elements seem to have supported ranchers in the same way, if not always to the same degree, as Alvear and the rural aristocrats.

Alone, the conflicts over the meat industry do not provide a conclusive test of the Radicals' political behavior. For one thing, only about 15 per cent of all the Party members in Congress took overt initiatives in defense of livestock producers.[71] For another, their actions on separate issues would naturally have to be considered before any general conclusions are drawn.

[69] *Boletín,* XXXVIII, no. 678 (June, 1925), 75–76. Even this action could be interpreted as a rational pursuit of economic interest, since most of Argentina's industry at the time provided services and technology which supported the export-import economy.

[70] Generalization on this question is hampered by the fact that the *formal* split between Personalists and Anti-Personalists does not appear in the available election returns until 1926, though the break began as soon as Alvear stepped into the presidency, so it has been difficult to trace the political allegiance of Radicals *within* the party.

[71] Based on figures for the Chamber of Deputies. There were about 303 Radicals in the Chamber between 1916 and 1930, not counting three Anti-Personalists; about 44 actively helped defend ranching interests in one way or another. Many others also voted in favor of pro-livestock measures, though the Party was sometimes divided. Unfortunately a complete study of party politics and Radical behavior—which might best be accomplished by statistical roll-call analysis—lies outside the bounds of this book.

What this analysis indicates, though, is that any straightforward identification of the Radical Party with reform-minded or industry-oriented middle sectors is simplistic and misleading.

The active participation of middle-class elements in the politics of beef also provides some clues about Argentina's over-all pattern of modernization. As described in Chapter I, rapid changes in the economic and social areas were combining to produce an urban proletariat. Simultaneous developments were taking place in politics—particularly the "professionalization" of interest representation and the increasing utility of the national Congress. The political system thus expanded to allow meaningful participation for members of the *middle* class, who posed little threat to the established order—but it did not give the *lower* class an effective opportunity. Throughout this entire period, consumers and laborers showed no significant power in politics; at that, they did not make many demands on the system. But as we shall see in Chapter IX, the accumulation of socio-economic pressure would issue a far-reaching challenge to Argentina's political leaders within the coming decade.

VI

Reaction to the Depression

THE worldwide Depression of the 1930s not only disrupted the Argentine beef trade, but also contributed to revolution. On September 6, 1930 the Yrigoyen government was toppled by a military coup, engineered by a small coterie of officers but supported by large numbers of people. The overthrow, and its popularity, derived from several sources: the aristocracy's desire for direct control of politics, increasing restiveness within the armed forces, Yrigoyen's personal senility, and the over-all incompetence of his administration. Another cause was no doubt the Depression itself, as many Argentines blamed Yrigoyen for the collapse and sought economic recovery through the military seizure of the State. For all these reasons, Argentina's 68-year reign of constitutional stability suddenly came to an end.

As leader of the revolution, the patrician General José F. Uriburu promptly set up a Provisional Government. Of his eight original Cabinet officers, four belonged to the Rural Society; two were military men; the other two were aristocratic civilians, including Matías G. Sánchez Sorondo. All the ministers, except for the armed forces professionals, came from the traditional upper class. Whereas the last Yrigoyen administration drew most of its leadership from the urban middle classes, this new regime was based on a clear-cut alliance between the aristocracy and the military.

With the government's official blessing, General Agustín P. Justo won the next year's presidential elections and took office in February 1932. An Anti-Personalist, a member of the Rural

Society, and a military leader, Justo recruited his Cabinet mainly from the aristocracy and the armed forces.[1] But its political complexion was mottled. Charged with a delicate balancing act, Justo tried to even the Conservatives off against the Anti-Personalists, and gave two key posts—first Agriculture, later the Treasury—to Independent Socialists, moderate ex-members of the Socialist Party founded by Juan B. Justo.

It is particularly significant that the new President turned the Ministry of Agriculture over to Antonio de Tomaso, a brilliant lawyer, first-class politician, Independent Socialist, and self-made son of an urban bricklayer. He had probably never even visited the Rural Society, much less belonged to it. Although it is an isolated example, his appointment accentuates the increasing "professionalization" in the politics of beef. It suggests that the aristocracy was seeking to co-opt able spokesmen from lower- and middle-class ranks. It implies a certain amount of upward social mobility. Finally, De Tomaso's acceptance of the post indicates that men of urban lower-class origin could come to identify themselves with the rural upper class.

The Justo regime started its term with firm control of power. In party politics, the government drew staunch support from a coalition or "Concordancia" between the old-time Conservatives, now known as National Democrats; the Anti-Personalist Radicals; and the Independent Socialists. Opposition came from the regular Socialists and the Progressive Democrats, still led by Lisandro de la Torre, but the largest opposition group—the Personalist Radicals—abstained from all elections in protest against notorious fraud. As a result, both houses of Congress were dominated by pro-administration forces: in 1933, the Concordancia accounted for roughly 63 per cent of the Deputies and 87 per cent of the Senators.[2] By means of revolution, the cattle barons reasserted and augmented their awesome political strength.

[1] Justo's first Cabinet contained six traditional aristocrats, three of whom belonged to the Rural Society; one middle-class Admiral; and a lower-class Minister of Agriculture whose appointment is discussed in the following paragraph.

[2] La Prensa and La Nación, February 20, 1932; Zalduendo, Geografía electoral, pp. 226–27.

Figure 6.1.   *Monthly Prices for Cattle Bought on Ranches, 1929–1933*

Source: Junta Nacional de Carnes, *Informe de la labor realizada desde 1935 hasta 1937*, pp. 17–18.

CATTLE PRODUCTION IN DEPRESSION

Though the economic consequences of the Depression took a couple of years to reach the ranchers,[3] the reduction in foreign purchasing power eventually brought a severe contraction in demand for Argentine beef. The volume of overseas exports dropped by more than 25 per cent between 1929 and 1932; though the domestic trade took up some of the slack, annual slaughters in 1931 and 1932 were about 15 per cent smaller than in 1929.[4] As volume declined, prices fell too. As shown in Figure 6.1, the average price for all steers bought on ranches plunged from over 34 centavos per live kilo in November 1929 to less than 17 centavos in January 1933. According to the available figures, the total value of cattle sales dropped more than 40 per cent between 1929 and 1932.[5]

[3] See the comment in *Anales*, LXV, no. 12 (December 1, 1931), 691.
[4] Junta Nacional de Carnes, *Estadísticas básicas*, p. 8.
[5] This figure has been obtained by computing the average annual prices for

In some contrast to the situation of 1922–23, this crisis hurt the fatteners as well as the breeders. Average prices for heavy chiller steers followed almost exactly the same curve as the one above.[6] Yet prices for newly bred cattle held relatively firm, since the demand for lighter stock (and smaller cuts of beef) remained comparatively strong. Therefore the fatteners had less outlet for their finished cattle, but had to bid for new steers at competitive rates. Caught in this cost-price squeeze, shown in Figure 6.2, the fatteners suffered as they rarely had before. They were not the only ones to feel the impact of the crisis; but this time, they might want to do something about it.

As though these market conditions were not distressing enough, Argentine cattlemen—and the packers—were also threatened by an artificial limitation on sales to Great Britain. In mid-1932, as nations all over the world were struggling for economic survival and the Beaverbrook press was demanding imperial protection,[7] spokesmen from Britain and her dependencies met at the Ottawa Conference. Responding to the interests of agricultural producers in the United Kingdom and the Dominions, they made a series of agreements designed to promote the economic unity of the Empire. As far as Argentina was concerned, the most significant provisions related to commerce in meat. To Australia and New Zealand, Great Britain promised that the importation of extra-imperial chilled beef would be held to the level of imports during the year ending June 30, 1932—when Argentine exports reached one of the

1929 and 1932 from the data in Junta Nacional de Carnes, *Informe de la labor realizada desde 1935 hasta 1937*, p. 17, then multiplying them by the total volume figures in Junta Nacional de Carnes, *Estadísticas básicas*, p. 8. The overall drop in business comes out at 43 per cent—but might have been as high as 50 per cent, since these price figures concern purchases on ranches and do not include transactions at Liniers, where prices probably declined more rapidly. During this same period the cost-of-living index declined by only 20 per cent, so the reduction in real cattle values was sharp indeed: Junta Nacional de Carnes, *Estadísticas básicas*, p. 14.

[6] *Anales*, LXXII, no. 1 (January, 1938), between 32–33.

[7] For background on the British viewpoints see Lord Beaverbrook (William M. Aitken), *Empire Free Trade: The New Policy for Prosperity* (London, 1929); Beaverbrook, *My Case for Empire Free Trade* (London, 1930); and the response by Sir Herbert Samuel, *Empire Free Trade? An Examination of Lord Beaverbrook's Proposal* (London, 1930).

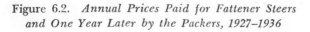

Figure 6.2. *Annual Prices Paid for Fattener Steers
and One Year Later by the Packers, 1927–1936*

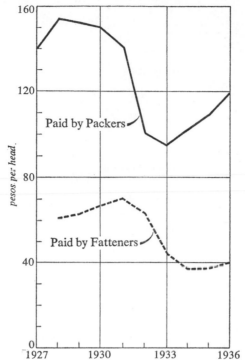

Source: Ministerio de Agricultura, *Informe del Comité Mixto Investigador del
Comercio de Carnes Anglo-Argentino* (London, 1938), Apéndice V, Gráfico B.

lowest points in nearly a decade. Restrictions on frozen beef,
which was produced by the Dominions, were even tighter: with
regard to the same base year, imports would be reduced in six
quarterly stages to only 65 per cent of their previous level. (A
similar provision was made for mutton and lamb; there was
no special quota for the trade in canned beef.) [8] It looked as
though Argentine ranchers, both breeders and fatteners, might
be losing their most valuable clients.

It should be clear that the packers could not have created

[8] Secretary of State for Dominion Affairs, "Imperial Economic Conference at
Ottawa, 1932: Summary of Proceedings and Copies of Trade Agreements,"
Parliamentary Papers, 1931–32 (Cd. 4174), X, 701–95.

this entire crisis. The decreasing volume of meat and cattle sales can be better explained by reduced consumer demand than by conspiratorial restraint of trade. Furthermore, the Ottawa Conference and the British quotas on Argentine meat threatened the interests of the packers as well as the ranchers, and company spokesmen frequently declared their opposition to imperial protection.[9] But because of their economic power, the packers could pass any consequent drop in prices along to the cattlemen and thus maintain their profits. As shown by Table 6.1, they continued to take average earnings of 10 to 15 per cent, while the producers made almost nothing.[10] Understandably, the packinghouse pool became a focal point of rancher resentment.

Table 6.1. *Profits of Major Ranches and Packinghouses, 1929–1934*

	Ranches %	Packinghouses %
1929	8.49	10.80
1930	4.91	13.65
1931	2.29	13.13
1932	0.65	12.22
1933	1.15	11.46
1934	1.91	14.12

Source: (British) Board of Trade, *Report of the Joint Committee of Enquiry into the Anglo-Argentine Meat Trade* (London, 1938), pp. 59, 136.

THE ROCA-RUNCIMAN PACT

The Argentine Rural Society, now led by Horacio N. Bruzone, regarded these various trends in the cattle and beef markets with mounting alarm. It was not long before the Society began to press the Justo government for diplomatic action. At least a partial solution to the general crisis, argued the Society's

[9] See the comments by Lord Vestey to the British Parliament in *Ottawa y la "preferencia imperial"* (Buenos Aires, n.d.) and in the *Review of the River Plate*, July 22, 1932, 11–15.

[10] The data are taken from a sample of 30 to 40 ranches "engaged in breeding and fattening beef cattle" and the packers' earnings "as disclosed in published accounts."

directors, could be obtained through the application of "Buy from those who buy from us." [11] The D'Abernon Pact was clearly inadequate for problems of this size; a new kind of effort was needed. In response to these demands, Justo eventually sent off a top-level negotiating team to bargain with the British, under no less a figure than Julio A. Roca, Vice-President of the Republic, son of a former President, prominent aristocrat, and member of the Rural Society. The mission's ostensible purpose was social—to repay a visit by the Prince of Wales—but its ultimate purpose was clear.[12] The aristocrats were on the move.

Apparently Roca had two main instructions. First, he was to help Argentine cattle ranchers by increasing their share in the United Kingdom market; second, he was to wrest control of the export trade away from the Anglo-American packinghouse pool. The British, represented by Walter Runciman as president of the Board of Trade, had a varied mixture of motives. They were short of pounds sterling, and sought to "unfreeze" about £11 million worth of pesos which had been blocked by Argentine exchange controls since October 1931. They hoped to expand foreign markets for their manufactured goods.[13] And they wanted to keep protecting British cattle farmers. After months of strenuous bargaining an agreement was finally reached, and the Roca-Runciman Pact (also known as the Treaty of London) was signed on May 1, 1933.[14]

Scheduled to last for three years, the compact met the demands of Argentine ranchers in conditional terms. "Fully recognizing the importance of the *chilled* beef industry to the

[11] *Anales*, LXVI, no. 11 (November, 1932), 815–16; LXVII, no. 2 (February, 1933), 61–62.

[12] See the London *Times*, esp. February 2, 11, and 16, 1933.

[13] Frederic Benham, *Great Britain under Protection* (New York, 1941), pp. 129, 135.

[14] For some details on the negotiations see Ministerio de Relaciones Exteriores y Culto, *Memoria presentada al Honorable Congreso Nacional, correspondiente al período 1933–1934* (Buenos Aires, 1934), pp. [351]–482; and N.A., D.S., 641.3515/1–29. For the official texts of the treaty see Secretary of State for Foreign Affairs, "Convention between the Government of the United Kingdom and the Government of the Argentine Republic Relating to Trade and Commerce, with Protocol, London, May 1, 1933," *Parliamentary Papers*, 1932–33 (Cd. 4310), XXVII, 1–15.

economic life of Argentina," [15] Britain promised to maintain the quotas permitted by the Ottawa accords—unless, for the sake of cattle farmers at home and in the Empire, reductions became necessary "to secure a remunerative level of prices in the United Kingdom market." If "unforeseen circumstances" ever compelled Britain to reduce chilled imports by more than 10 per cent, she pledged to cut imports of Dominion beef by the portion in excess of 10 per cent. For frozen beef, mutton, and lamb, Runciman agreed not to reduce the quotas outlined at Ottawa—which called for an eventual decrease of 35 per cent—unless restrictions were placed on the Dominions. In addition, the British consented to take part in an official joint investigation of the Anglo-Argentine meat trade "with particular reference to the means to be adopted to ensure a reasonable return to the cattle producers."

According to another stipulation, the United Kingdom would provide a 15 per cent quota for any non-profit meat-packing enterprise supported by the Argentine government with the intention of improving cattle prices "on the understanding that any such shipments are efficiently marketed through normal channels"—presumably, in British hulls. Since two existing plants were included in this quota, the portion available to any new enterprise would actually be just under 11 per cent. This was an ambivalent clause. It would greatly increase Argentina's share in the meatpacking business, as regulated by import licenses from the Board of Trade, but would also limit her future participation. The provision represented a failure for Roca, since the Argentine government formally renounced the right to control the distribution of meat exports. Through the influence of British diplomacy, it appeared, the foreign-owned packinghouses were guaranteed continuing predominance in the Anglo-Argentine meat trade.

In the absence of documentary proof, it is difficult to say whether this 85-15 clause was intended to keep the trade in the "imperialist" grip of British investors. Undoubtedly the "normal channels" stipulation would protect the English ship-

15 My italics.

pers; as one Labourite quipped, "Lord Vestey must count for something." [16] But this theory would not explain Runciman's failure to reduce the share of the American packers, so often opposed to the British and the most powerful group in the business.[17] A more convincing interpretation of this clause, I think, might focus on the National Government's policy of compromise—this time, with the United Kingdom's consumers. First, the 85-15 provision would help assure a regular flow of beef to Britain, in the experienced hands of the packinghouse pool and the shipping lines, and tend to stabilize prices at Smithfield. Second, it ruled out any possible "producers' monopoly" which might seize control of the trade and push up prices for meat. In these ways, both the volume and the value of imported beef could be kept at acceptable levels. Of course the clause would incidentally help some British investors; but it might well have been designed for the consumers.[18]

While making these arrangements, Runciman drove a hard bargain. First, he got control of the peso pound exchange rate. Essentially, Argentina promised to use sterling acquired through sales to the United Kingdom to make cash payments on British-owned peso accounts. To help Argentina pay debts outside the Commonwealth, Britain offered (in a separate agreement) a loan of £10 million in paper pesos, but insisted that decisions on the priority of outside debts be made by both governments together. Second, Runciman persuaded the Argentines not to place tariffs on duty-free goods, especially coal, and to reduce the tariffs on all other British goods to their 1930 level: in effect, this meant preferential treatment. Third, he exacted a promise that the Argentine government would give

[16] House of Commons, *Parliamentary Debates*, 5th ser., vol. 277 (May 10, 1933), 1558.

[17] In practice, the Board of Trade let the Anglo-American packers distribute shares in the trade by themselves. N.A., D.S., 641.3515/18, Bliss to Secretary of State, March 3, 1933.

[18] As one government official said, "If the British people [wish] to win their way back to prosperity they must eat more meat." London *Times*, April 11, 1933. And see Imperial Economic Committee, *Cattle and Beef Survey: A Survey of Production and Trade in British Empire and Foreign Countries* (London, 1934).

"benevolent treatment" to British capital invested in private and public enterprises, notably railroad and tramway companies.

From the moment it was signed, the Roca-Runciman Pact became a subject of heated debate. Reactions were mixed in the United Kingdom. In apoplectic tones, Lord Beaverbrook's *Daily Express* deplored "the great meat muddle," bemoaned the "betrayal of the farmers," and expressed sorrow that British negotiators had fallen into "the Argentine trap." [19] Stating Labour's view, Clement Attlee argued that the pact would make British consumers pay "remunerative" prices to Argentine ranchers so they, in turn, could pay back English *rentiers:* "I call that a pretty cold-blooded scheme. . . ." [20] Nevertheless the treaty drew general support, even from the farmers.[21] As explained in the *Daily Mail,* it showed the advantages of Britain's tariffs: "For the first time in the last seventy years, *British statesmen have been able to negotiate with foreign powers upon even terms."* [22]

In Argentina, most groups connected with beef production approved of the pact. With some reservations about Britain's control of the export quotas, the Rural Society pronounced its satisfaction with market stabilization and commercial reciprocity.[23] Despite the pro-fattener implications of the special concern for chilled beef, breeders backed the agreement.[24] The packers, who naturally had a high stake in the trade and might have appreciated the 85-15 clause, also supported the treaty.[25] The only vocal group that stood to lose from the pact con-

[19] *Daily Express,* April 24, May 1, and May 3, 1933.

[20] House of Commons, *Parliamentary Debates,* 5th ser., vol. 277 (May 10, 1933), 1653–55.

[21] See London *Times,* May 3 and 12, 1933; and the *Argentine Review,* II, no. 14 (June, 1933), 4–5.

[22] Quoted in Rennie, *Argentine Republic,* p. 237.

[23] *Anales,* LXVII, no. 5 (May, 1933), 199–201.

[24] See the petition of the Confederation of Rural Societies of the Littoral in Diputados, 1932, VI (September 20), 190, and the statement in Olariaga, *El ruralismo argentino,* pp. [273]–88.

[25] [Empresas Frigoríficas], *Presentación de las empresas frigoríficas ante el Congreso de la Nación* (Buenos Aires, 1933), pp. 21–23. Also see the remarks in the *Buenos Aires Herald,* May 3 and July 29, 1933.

sisted of urban consumers, since most of the treaty's provisions would tend to push up local retail prices.

CONGRESS AND COMMERCIAL POLICY

The Argentine Chamber of Deputies began to consider the Roca-Runciman Pact in mid-July 1933. As requested by the Justo administration, the joint committees on finance and foreign relations recommended sanction of the treaty. But the majority was slim—only 11 to 9—and broke down along party lines: the Concordancia in favor, the Socialists and Progressive Democrats in dissent.[26] It looked as though commercial policy was becoming a partisan issue.

Spokesman for the majority was Adrian Escobar, upper-class cattleman and National Democrat, who contended that reciprocal trade must protect the country's rural activities. Premature industrialization, he said, would only lead to higher costs. "Our problem is agricultural-pastoral and is resolved this way: by the greater purchase of our products [abroad], by the greater acquisition of foreign commodities. Increasing the volume of our transactions, we generate labor and prosperity." As for the treaty itself, Escobar argued that the 85-15 clause gave Argentina a larger portion of the trade than at any recent time, and dismissed the question of export control because "we have unfortunately never had it" anyway. Given the worldwide fight for economic survival, the exchange agreement was remarkably fair. In conclusion, he paid rhetorical deference to Anglo-Argentine amity and exhorted his colleagues to uphold the administration's "active economic policy." [27]

Vociferous opposition to the treaty came from Nicolás Repetto, Socialist from Buenos Aires. He assaulted the 85-15 clause for its abandonment of national dignity, its violation of anti-trust laws, and its stipulation that participant Argentine firms must be "non-profit" organizations. He predicted the

[26] Diputados, 1933, I (June 7), 403–7; II (July 18), 264.
[27] Ibid., II (July 18), 269–85.

£10 million loan would become an impossible financial burden during the Depression. He said the preferential tariffs for British goods would discourage trade with other countries, and threatened Argentina's embryonic industry. And in sweeping terms, he struck at the whole notion of reciprocal trade: "the essential thing for a country like ours," Repetto maintained, "is to keep our doors wide open and to demand open doors from the rest of the world." Protection only pushed up retail prices, and in this case catered to the short-term needs of the aristocracy and not to the permanent interests of urban consumers.[28]

As the session continued, debate on the treaty divided along partisan lines: the Concordancia and the opposition. Perhaps because of their cattle-producing constituents, however, the Progressive Democrats ultimately voted for the agreement. So in the final analysis, it was the producers against the consumers. In accordance with this split, the Roca-Runciman Pact was approved by 61 to 41.[29] Though the poll was not taken by name, it is almost certain that the negative ballots were cast by the Socialists—since there were exactly 41 members of the Party in the Chamber that day. The consumers lost again.

A somewhat different scene took place in the Senate, where Lisandro de la Torre challenged the treaty's effectiveness—but not its general purpose of protecting ranchers. Twice-beaten presidential candidate and Progressive Democrat, he claimed that the agreement would solve nothing. "If we were at Great Britain's mercy after the Ottawa agreements, we remain at Great Britain's mercy after the Treaty of London." Under the "unforeseen circumstances" clause, charged De la Torre, there was no limit to eventual British reductions in the importation of Argentine chilled beef. The "non-profit" requirement for national firms in the 85-15 clause would effectively postpone Argentine participation in the trade, for the locally owned (profit-seeking) Sansinena Company could easily handle the 15

28 Ibid., 285–301. Repetto made no explicit effort to reconcile the paradox between his concern for native industry and his insistence on free trade.
29 Ibid. (July 19), 379.

per cent by itself. "This is called subordinating the interests of Argentine livestock production to the interests of the foreign meatpacking companies. . . ." While Britain obtained protection for the railroads, preferential tariffs, and the release of frozen funds, the Senator continued, she made notably meager concessions: a pledge of good will, a promise not to raise the already-high duties on wheat, a loan of £10 million. Argentina reached neither of her major goals, higher meat quotas and control of export distribution. As a result, claimed De la Torre, the Roca-Runciman Pact constituted "a total failure: a diplomatic failure, and a commercial failure." In openly partisan fashion, he blamed this outcome on the ineptitude of the administration—particularly the Foreign Minister, Carlos Saavedra Lamas.[30] To some degree the Senator was playing politics.

After Saavedra Lamas and other governmental officials spoke in self-defense, the Senate promptly approved the pact.[31] Data on the vote are not available, but—given the overwhelming predominance of the Concordancia—there is little doubt that the margin of favor was wide. The cattlemen wanted the treaty and they got it.[32]

In general, the debates over the Treaty of London reveal a mixed clash between economic interests and political allegiances. Most ranchers and their representatives favored the treaty, though some found it inadequate. (There is no particular reason to believe that this conflict pitted the fatteners against the breeders.) Then came the consumers. In the Chamber of Deputies, the consumers and the anti-government rancher spokesmen formed a rhetorical alliance along party lines, but in the final vote a functional split divided the producers from the consumers. Debate in the Senate was largely partisan, as pro-administration ranchers and anti-administration ranchers

[30] Senadores, 1933, I (July 27), 568–81 and (July 28), 605–11; also in [Lisandro de la Torre], *Obras de Lisandro de la Torre,* ed. Raúl Larra, 3rd ed., II (Buenos Aires, 1958), 10–49. And see the similar remarks by J. A. Noble, another Progressive Democrat, in Diputados, 1933, II (July 19), 332–45.

[31] Senadores, 1933, I (July 28), 584–98, 615–16.

[32] For the debates on a subsequent protocol to the treaty concerning specific tariff measures, see Diputados, 1933, V (September 26–27), 411–12; VI (September 29–30), 141–42, 146–65. And Senadores, 1933, II (September 30), 881–82.

quarreled over means and not ends. Even so, there was never much doubt about the outcome, and the pact was readily approved.

RURAL SOCIETY: CAMPAIGN
FOR LEGISLATION

Despite its importance, the Roca-Runciman Pact formed only part of Argentina's answer to the post-Depression cattle crisis. For the declared purpose of protecting ranchers from the money-grubbing tactics of the packinghouse pool, the Rural Society began campaigning for a new and sweeping legislative program. Apparently, the Society launched this effort because the crisis hurt fatteners as well as breeders; and the institution's Board of Directors, under Horacio Bruzone, was made up mainly of fatteners. Breeders from within and without the Society joined in the campaign, since they also suffered some setbacks, and were eager for protection from the State. Both groups favored a law: the only issue between them was what the law should be like.[33]

In a series of public announcements and memorandums to the government between December 1931 and May 1932, the Society defined its "organic plan" for the defense of livestock production.[34] Its general features included: (1) the creation of an eight-man National Commission for Control of the Meat Trade, with five representatives from the Rural Society and three appointed by the President; (2) joint action with Uruguay and Brazil for inspection and control of overseas commerce;

[33] Early in this campaign the Rural Society persuaded the government to impose fines on the packers, for the first time ever, under the control and inspection law of 1923. *Anales*, LXVI, no. 1 (January, 1932), 57; LXVII, no. 4 (April, 1933), 151–52, 155–56. Ministerio de Agricultura, *Carnes—granos—elevadores de granos—colonización—petróleo: año 1932* (Buenos Aires, 1933), pp. [52]–57. For texts of the briefs filed by the packers and the government during the ensuing litigation, which the government won, see Abelardo M. Barrios et al., *Las empresas de frigoríficos en juicio contencioso con el gobierno de la Nación sobre la interpretación y constitucionalidad de la ley 11.226: demandas, alegatos, memoriales y antecedentes* (Buenos Aires, 1934).

[34] Sociedad Rural Argentina, *Plan orgánico de defensa ganadera*, Boletín de Divulgación No. 5 (Buenos Aires, 1932). And see *Anales*, LXVI, no. 1 (January, 1932), 7–12; no. 5 (May, 1932), 263–66; and no. 6 (June, 1932), 395–96.

(3) direct intervention by cattlemen in the domestic market, by turning the Municipal Packinghouse of the City of Buenos Aires into a mixed enterprise supported by the national government and the country's stockmen; [35] (4) and finally, in the future, rancher participation in the international beef trade. The priority on these last two points was clear: intervention in the local trade, according to the Society, should by all means precede intervention in the international trade.

In May 1932 the Justo administration responded to these demands with the appointment of a National Meat Commission to advise the government on pastoral matters, supervise the application of pertinent laws, study price movements, promote the sale of Argentine beef abroad, and propose new legislation —in particular, the feasible means by which ranchers might take part in meatpacking for the local and (later on) the foreign markets.[36] Except for the idea of joint action with Uruguay and Brazil, apparently given up by general consent,[37] the Commission was charged with virtual fulfillment of the "organic plan." The Society's influence also showed in the Commission's composition. Although the presidential decree said only five of the 15 members would have to come from the Society, eight of the seats were held by the current Directors—and three quarters of all the designates belonged to the institution. To no one's evident surprise, the Commission soon adopted the Society's "organic plan" and recommended it to the President.[38]

[35] This proposal was originally promoted by Rómulo Naón, Mayor of the city of Buenos Aires; his explanation appears in Concejo Deliberante, 1932, III (September 9), 2495. A new city slaughterhouse had begun operations in 1930.

[36] Sociedad Rural Argentina, *Plan orgánico,* pp. 35–38. *Anales,* LXVI, no. 6 (June, 1932), 351–56.

[37] One tripartite meeting was held, but no specific action was taken. *Anales,* LXVI, no. 3 (March, 1932), 135–37; Sociedad Rural Argentina, *Plan orgánico,* pp. 26–31.

[38] *Anales,* LXVII, no. 5 (May, 1932), 209–10; no. 8 (August, 1932), 543. For the protest of a breeder and member of the Rural Society who thought that Bruzone's Board of Directors had acted in a highhanded manner, see [Octavio Augusto Mariño], *Observaciones al proyecto de ley de "defensa ganadera" del Poder Ejecutivo de la Nación* (Buenos Aires, 1932), pp. 3–4. For other instances in which the Commission followed the Society's advice see Ministerio de Agricultura, *Carnes,* pp. [9]–12, and *Anales,* LXVI, no. 8 (August, 1932), 495–500.

A few weeks later Justo and De Tomaso, the Minister of Agriculture, sent a bill to Congress establishing a National Meat Board (*Junta Nacional de Carnes*) "as an autonomous entity, pertaining to the Ministry of Agriculture," responsible for supervision of the meat trade and all laws relevant to it.[39] The Board would be composed of ten members: four would be named at the President's discretion, while the other six would be selected from a list of candidates submitted by the Rural Society. All the Society's nominees would have to be "livestock producers," that is, persons who had worked for at least five years "at the breeding or the fattening of cattle." No member of the Board would receive any pay for his services, or be allowed to have any personal connection with the packinghouses.

The Board's most significant function would be to set up a cooperative type of packinghouse "for the defense of national livestock production and to lower the price of [retail] products. . . ." This was the organization anticipated in the Roca-Runciman Pact, and its main purpose would be to utilize the 11 per cent quota made available for such an enterprise. Once established, this packinghouse would become "totally independent" of the Board, though still subject to the general regulations of the trade.

The Meat Board was supposed to protect the ranchers in other ways too. In an effort to discourage discriminatory buying by the packers, it would lay down official rules for the classification and grading of Argentine beef. To prevent the post-purchase upgrading of meat (buying cattle at freezer prices, for instance, and selling the meat in chilled form), it would set up procedural norms for beef exportation. With regard to anti-trust action, its role was somewhat uncertain: the Board would find out if the packinghouse pool violated the law, but would not apply the law itself.

According to this bill, the over-all program of the Meat Board was to be supported by fines, private donations, and especially an automatic "contribution by those who sell cattle to the meat-processing firms." Twenty per cent of these funds

[39] For text see Diputados, 1932, IV (July 27), 420–25.

would be used to cover the Board's operating expenses; the rest was assigned to the producers' meatpacking organization. Here was the catch: shares in the new enterprise would be distributed according to each man's "contribution," though no person would have more than one vote in assemblies or elections. And since the contribution covered cattle sales from the fatteners to the packers, but not from the breeders to the fatteners, it meant that the fatteners would gain economic control over the cattlemen's packinghouse.

As a complementary measure, Justo and De Tomaso introduced another bill in September 1932 for nationalization of the Buenos Aires packinghouse.[40] Under these provisions, the city plant would become a mixed enterprise, run jointly by the municipality and the Meat Board—in other words, by both consumers and producers—with the Meat Board in the majority. The project's purpose was dual, not to say ambiguous: to help raise the price of livestock, and also to lower the retail price of beef. But its basic significance was clear: ranchers would take over the city slaughterhouse. With this proposal and the Meat Board bill, the Justo administration was following the Rural Society's "organic plan" almost to the letter.[41]

CHALLENGE BY THE BREEDERS

As the fatteners in the Rural Society pressed their campaign for legislation, the breeders began to unite. The process took place in the early 1930s, throughout the stockraising areas, when a number of associations was established: the Confederation of Rural Societies of the Littoral, the Confederation of Rural Societies of the Middle and Western Littoral, and another group for Patagonian sheepmen. The most vital and vocal of the breeder organizations, however, was the Confederation of Rural Associations of the Province of Buenos Aires and

40 *Ibid.*, V (September 2), 329–32.
41 It even appears that Horacio Bruzone, president of the Society, drafted the bills himself. Tomás Patricio Ryan, "El festín de los buitres," unpubl. manuscript given to me by the author (Buenos Aires, n.d.), p. 19.

the Territory of La Pampa, known from its Spanish initials as CARBAP and founded in 1932.[42]

CARBAP's mood was militant. At first, while recommending some additional measures, its member groups supported the Rural Society's "organic plan." [43] But it did not take long for the breeders to fight with the fatteners. At a meeting in Nueve de Julio, just after the Justo administration presented its bill for the National Meat Board, the first confrontation emerged. On one side were the breeders, represented by most members of the fledgling CARBAP; on the other were the fatteners, represented by Horacio Bruzone and the Rural Society's Board of Directors. Exchanges were heated and frequently bitter.

The breeders expressed a number of major complaints. First, they resolved that the producer-supported packinghouse should be entirely independent of the Meat Board and, as such, should be established by a separate law. Similarly, they objected to the possibility of "interference" in the conduct of the Meat Board by the Ministry of Agriculture, claiming that the Board should have "great autonomy." In effect, the breeders were demanding institutional independence from the political influence of the Rural Society. Second, breeder spokesmen maintained that the Board should be empowered to apply the general anti-trust law, not merely inquire about its violation; to a greater extent than the fatteners, they wanted to attack the packinghouse pool. Third, they pointed out that rules for the "contribution" on cattle sales would give credit (and shares in the cooperative meatpacking firm) to the fatteners and not to themselves, who would probably bear the ultimate brunt of this expense anyway.[44]

After this stormy convention, CARBAP turned to Congress. In a written recitation of their grievances,[45] the breeders proposed a change in the "contribution" procedure and also ques-

[42] Confederación de Asociaciones Rurales de Buenos Aires y La Pampa (CARBAP), *Recopilación de las deliberaciones de los congresos rurales, 1932 a 1942* (Buenos Aires, 1946), pp. 3–6.

[43] *Ibid.*, pp. 229–30.

[44] *Ibid.*, pp. 230–31.

[45] Diputados, 1932, VI (September 27–28), 683–90.

tioned the composition of the Meat Board. Instead of six men from the Rural Society and four appointed by the President, CARBAP contended, the distribution should be different: three designated by the President, three by the Rural Society, and four by legally constituted "Confederations of Rural Societies." In addition, there should be salaries for members of the Board to prevent economic losses for men of the interior. Cattle merchants (*consignatarios*) and anyone connected with the packinghouses or transportation companies (railroads or shipping lines) should be automatically excluded from the Board.

Striking off on a new tangent, CARBAP attacked the plan to nationalize the municipal packinghouse, partly because of its supposedly inadequate equipment. Furthermore, CARBAP challenged the Rural Society's high priority on participation in the domestic market. Intervention in the local trade would throw the stockmen into open and expensive conflict with the masses of urban consumers, whereas an attempt to enter the export trade would bring on battle with the foreign packers— a battle in which Argentine ranchers could probably count on the support of the British government and British consumers. Besides, the price level in the export market was of vital importance to the breeders, while the fatteners could usually maintain profits by passing along price reductions. In any case, the breeders wanted to take part in the export trade as soon as possible.[46]

Thus the breeders issued their challenge to the fatteners and the Rural Society. CARBAP's protests were echoed by other associations,[47] and the breeder movement continued to gather momentum. In 1932 CARBAP started with only ten charter member groups, including the Rural Society; by mid-1935 there were 19 member groups and over 3,800 individual followers, already more than the Rural Society; by 1939, after the Rural Society finally withdrew, there were 29 local societies in

46 *Ibid.*, 688–89. A plan for participation in the export trade had been promoted by Octavio Augusto Mariño and approved by a cattlemen's conference at La Plata in June 1932. See Mariño, *Proyecto de Asociación Cooperativa Nacional* (Buenos Aires [?], 1932).
47 See Mariño, *Observaciones*.

RBAP.[48] As a remarkable sign of political modernization thin the rural sector, the breeders pursued their conflict with the fatteners by means of institutional organization. This process naturally involved the mobilization of many middle-class breeders; even so, the movement drew most of its leadership from the aristocracy.

THE PACKERS' SELF-DEFENSE

While the breeders were battling the fatteners for control of the livestock defense campaign, the packers were seeking to prevent legislation. As in 1921–23, they wanted to restrict the conflict to the economic and not the political arena. They delayed their response until the middle of 1933, when the Justo-De Tomaso proposals came up for consideration in the Congress, then stated their position. Throughout the ensuing debate, the packers expressed surprise that the Roca-Runciman Pact had not warded off irrational demands for "legislative panaceas" and reminded the ranchers of the 1923 fiasco over the minimum price. If offensive laws were passed, it was hinted, the packers might have to stop business again.[49]

Firmly denying repeated allegations about their excess profits, the packers went on to predict the disastrous results of the government's proposals. Nationalization of the municipal packing-house would involve expensive renovation of the plant, and State intervention in the domestic trade would eventually fall prey to politics. The price of meat would undoubtedly go up. They also contended that the producers' meatpacking concern would have unfair access to the private packers' commercial secrets through its linkage with the Ministry of Agriculture, and frighten foreign capital out of the country. This was particularly possible, they said, because of the projected "preponderance" of ranchers on the Meat Board; in their own view,

[48] CARBAP, *Recopilación*, pp. ix–xiv. *Buenos Aires y La Pampa*, I, no. 1 (April, 1935), 5.

[49] See their *Presentación*, pp. 21–23, [41]–47; and N.A., D.S., 835.6582/63, Bliss to Secretary of State, May 19, 1932, and 835.6582/75, memo by J. C. Shillock, October 28, 1932.

the packers should have as many representatives as the cattle-men.[50]

Conceding that the Meat Board might play a useful role in the domestic market—where it would not bother the pool—the packers also declared that the projected "contribution" on cattle sales was unconstitutional. They further noted some complaints among ranchers that the tax would be "almost confiscatory," and doubted that stockmen really wanted to pay it. In support of this argument, the packers dared the Rural Society to take a plebiscite among ranchers on its plan to levy the tax.[51] Their object was obvious: to open a rift in the ranks of the producers and thereby weaken the opposition.

The tactic failed. The Rural Society vehemently claimed support for the scheme and cited some resolutions by CARBAP to back up its point.[52] Though the packers responded with a petition opposing the tax from some ranchers,[53] they were unable to gain the lasting allegiance of any major interest group. The fatteners' intense desire for protective legislation ruled out the immediate possibility of an alliance with them. Nor did the militant breeders look like promising allies. Almost all ranchers wanted a law.

As implied by their reliance on an issue as weak as the tax, the packers did not have many strategic alternatives at their disposal. In particular, they could not exert the economic pressure—by stopping cattle purchases—that had worked so well in 1923. Such action might only have angered the ranchers. Furthermore, there was the question of the British quota. The Roca-Runciman Pact had not yet gone into effect. If the packers stopped all operations at this time, they ran a sizable risk of having their share in the United Kingdom market reduced even more by the British government, which wanted a steady beef supply for its consumers. Under these circumstances, the packers were stuck.

At a later stage in the debate, the packers turned to a totally

[50] *Presentación*, pp. 27–28, 30.
[51] *Ibid.*, pp. 28–29, [iii].
[52] Diputados, 1933, II (July 7), 254–57.
[53] *Presentación*, pp. [35]–38.

different group: the urban consumers. More forcefully than before, company representatives argued that State intervention in the meat trade would cause a rise in the retail price of beef. A producers' packinghouse would be unable to operate on the economics of scale; smaller quotas would increase unit costs for all the packers, and this would push up butchers' prices. In the end, consumers would have to pay for this waste. What they should do, the packers suggested, was to establish a cooperative of their own.[54]

With these arguments, the members of the meatpacking pool sought to defend themselves from legislation. To some their logic was doubtless persuasive, and the pro-British press, especially the *Review of the River Plate,* repeatedly sided with the packers.[55] But the fundamental problem still remained: stockmen could not be divided at the moment, since both breeders and fatteners wanted a law of some kind. The packers' only hope was to approach the consumers, the weakest of all the participant groups, in search of political support. Unable to gain significant indirect representation in the Argentine political system, the packers could only proclaim their innocence and opposition to legislation—to anyone who would listen.

PASSAGE OF THE MEAT LAW

In spite of an intensive effort by the Rural Society and other ranching associations to have the bills on the Meat Board and the municipal packinghouse brought up in extra sessions of the 1932 Congress, the Justo administration, because of an "acuerdo"-type agreement with the packers, decided to wait until the completion of some litigation over application of the 1923 control law.[56] In July 1933, the projects were presented

54 Senadores, 1933, II (September 29), 808–9. This is also in *Presentación,* pp. [9]–17.

55 *Review of the River Plate,* September 2, 1932, 7–9; September 9, 1932, 7; September 16, 1932, 7–11; November 11, 1932, 7; March 17, 1933, 5–7; June 30, 1933, 11–13, 48–49; July 7, 1933, 7; September 1, 1933, 5–7.

56 Diputados, 1932, VI (September 21), 267; (September 26–27), 564; (September 28), 854. División de Archivo, Museo, y Publicaciones of the Biblioteca del Congreso Nacional, Buenos Aires: 1932, Caja 1299, Expedientes 944, 946.5, 985;

to the Chamber of Deputies in combined form (hereafter known as the Meat Law bill) with the 11-to-3 approval of the joint committee on agriculture, industry, and commerce.[57] Supporting the recommendation were men of the Concordancia, plus two Progressive Democrats; in opposition were three Socialists from Buenos Aires. The division was not so much political as functional: once again, the producers against the consumers.

This conflict dominated the preliminary debate. Introducing the bill, Benjamín Palacio, National Democrat from Córdoba, explained the need to defend Argentine ranchers from the rapacity of the foreign packers; this could be done only by restoring competition to the trade, which could be partly achieved by nationalization of the city packinghouse.[58] Sharply attacking this argument, Nicolás Repetto, Buenos Aires Socialist, called the scheme an attempt "to establish a monopoly on internal meat consumption" that would eventually lead to higher retail prices. Instead of such extravagant measures, he suggested plans for a stockmen's cooperative and agrarian reform in behalf of rural peons.[59] Palacio's view found strong support among other rancher representatives, however, and the Meat Law bill won general approval from the Deputies.[60] Though the *Diario de Sesiones* gives no data on the vote itself, the onesidedness of the debate suggests that the margin was wide.

After general passage of the bill, the conflict realigned itself. Instead of producers vs. consumers, it now involved the breeders and the fatteners. The issue concerned the composition of the Meat Board. As revised by the joint committee, the Meat Law proposal called for "an autonomous entity" presided over by the Minister of Agriculture. Three members would be appointed by the President, three by the Rural Society, one by the nationalized packinghouse. The most striking change in-

Caja 1300, Expediente 998. For comments on the government's bargain with the packers see N.A., D.S., 835.6582/75, memo by J. C. Shillock, October 28, 1932. Also see note 33 above.

[57] Diputados, 1933, II (July 26), 589–99.
[58] *Ibid.* (July 26), 600–11, and (July 27), 672–82.
[59] *Ibid.*, 682–701. And see the speech by Demetrio Buirá (August 2), 784–96.
[60] Diputados, 1933, III (August 11), 113.

volved the packers: private, foreign, and resented as they were, they were given one seat on the Board. This fell far short of their demand for as much representation as the ranchers,[61] but still signified a major concession; at least, it meant that the Board could never take surprise or secret action against the pool. It is unclear how this decision was reached. Perhaps the stockmen reasoned that the packers' commercial experience would be helpful to the Board; perhaps they expected to control policy anyway; perhaps, by giving the packers one seat, they hoped to avoid unchecked strife in the future. Whatever the case, Congress appears to have reached a cloakroom consensus. Remarkably enough, the ensuing debate barely touched on this issue.

Instead of fighting the packers, ranchers fought among themselves. Breeder spokesmen insisted that the Board should include members from outside the Rural Society. Some suggested there should be two from the Society and one from the organizations of the interior, including CARBAP. Others suggested there should be one from the Society and two from the interior. Luis Duhau, ex-president of the Society, proposed a compromise: two from each. Eduardo Bruchou, cattle breeder from Corrientes, declared that all fatteners should be excluded from the Board because of their commercial connections with the packers; the idea was voted down, but by the astonishingly close margin of 44 to 41. Enrique Dickmann, Socialist from Buenos Aires, dismissed the breeder-fattener controversy as "a minor dispute," demanded full representation for urban consumers, and denied that foreign packers should have any seat on the Board.[62]

As debate on this subject drew to a close, Palacio, speaking in behalf of the joint committee, accepted Duhau's compromise. There would be two delegates from the Rural Society and two

[61] According to one official at the American Embassy, "The packers greatly object to their minority representation on the commission." N.A., D.S., 835.6582/80, memo by J. C. Pool, September 1, 1933.

[62] Diputados, 1933, III (August 11), 113–35. Also see the petition from the Asociación de Ganaderos: Biblioteca del Congreso, División de Archivo, Museo, y Publicaciones, 1932, Caja 1295, Expediente 644.

from the interior, with fatteners eligible for representation. Palacio also agreed that the Board should be completely separate from the Ministry of Agriculture. The packers would still have one delegate. The consumers would not have any. Despite breeder objections, it was decided that no member of the Meat Board (except its president) would receive any salary.[63]

As indicated by the vote on Bruchou's proposal and Table 6.2, this outcome represents a partial triumph for the breeders. They did not get everything they wanted but, through organization and congressional participation, they wrung some notable concessions out of the fatteners, the Rural Society, and the Justo administration.

Table 6.2. *Proposals and Results on Meat Board Composition*

	Executive/ Rural Soc.	CARBAP	Joint Comm.	Dickmann	Result
Min. of Agr.	–	–	1	–	–
President	4	3	3	3	3
Rural Society	6	3	3	} 3	2
Interior	–	4	–	}	2
Packers	–	–	1	–	1
Nationalized Packinghouse	–	–	1	.	1
Consumers	–	–	–	3	–
Totals	10	10	9	9	9

At least on the congressional level, there is no indication that this breeder-fattener conflict had clearly defined social, partisan, or personalistic overtones. Archetypical spokesman for the fatteners was Luis Duhau, aristocratic National Democrat from the province of Buenos Aires. Of the six major spokesmen for the breeders, four belonged to the upper class; five supported the Concordancia, three as National Democrats; two came from the province of Buenos Aires. Neither side had charismatic leaders. Though there were some regional distinctions, this was essentially an intraclass struggle over economic interests.

[63] Diputados, 1933, III (August 11), 129–36; (August 16), 208.

Later in the debate, a different kind of conflict erupted over the plan for nationalization of the city packinghouse. Once again, the consumers took on the producers. Led by Nicolás Repetto, Socialists argued that producer control of the plant would bring a rise in retail prices.[64] Daniel Amadeo y Videla, National Democrat from Buenos Aires province, sought to set the record straight. He cried,

> No! There is no plundering of the municipality or any monopoly of the business of meat sales [in this plan]. What it concerns is the imperative necessity of saving not rancher A, B, or C but the entire country, since it has been established that this country cannot move forward if livestock production and agriculture do not receive . . . the remuneration required to cover the costs of production . . . because the basic sources of our prosperity are livestock production and agriculture.[65]

The clause was finally brought to a vote and approved by 63 to 44.[66] At bottom, it was a fight between producers and consumers. Thirty-five of the votes for nationalization were cast by delegates from cattle-producing constituencies, including many members of the Rural Society. The opposition was sparked by consumers; 21 negative votes were cast by Socialists from Buenos Aires. Yet this conflict took on partisan meaning too. All the support for the scheme came from the parties of the Concordancia; the dissent came from 40 Socialists and three Progressive Democrats—the standard opposition parties—and one lone Radical. Nevertheless, the relative closeness of the vote should not be construed as a sign of the government's weakness. On the contrary it shows that, for all their party discipline and parliamentary efforts, consumer spokesmen still were far from gaining power.[67]

It is significant that available, but limited, data reveal a perceptible class dimension to the fight between producers and consumers, between the Concordancia and the opposition. As shown in Table 6.3, congressmen who came from the upper

[64] *Ibid.*, III (August 17), 272–77, 279–87; (August 18), 319–39, 345–49.
[65] *Ibid.* (August 17), 289.
[66] *Ibid.* (August 18), 340–41.
[67] The Socialists mustered 40 of their 43 Deputies up for the occasion; the Concordancia had only two-thirds of its men on hand—still more than enough to win.

class voted to nationalize the city packinghouse; those from the lower class voted against the plan; the middle classes split. Of course the processes of cooptation and professionalization have demonstrated that social origin does not provide a definite index to social attitudes; but the data are suggestive. As we shall see later on, battles between producers and consumers came to be waged on multiple fronts.

Table 6.3. *Class Origin of Deputies For and Against Nationalization of the City Packinghouse*

Class	For	Against
Upper	15	–
Upper Middle	4	–
Lower Middle	–	8
Lower	–	7
Totals	19	15

When the bill for the Meat Law got to the Senate, it was approved practically without debate. There were quite a few petitions, including one from CARBAP,[68] but no one spoke up in dissent. On September 29, 1933 the bill was brought to the floor and introduced by Benjamín Villafañe—an industrialist from Jujuy, of all people—and passed that same afternoon.[69] At long last, the ranchers had a comprehensive Meat Law.

While approval of the bill marked a major triumph for the stockmen, it should not be taken out of context. Cattleowners were not the only ones to obtain aid from the Justo administration. In keeping with its "corporativist" outlook, the government also put through bills for a National Grain Board and a National Wine Board. Ranchers got special consideration, as shown by Justo's assiduous cooperation with the Rural Society and by the stockmen's substantial control of their board.[70] Even so, it is important to remember that the creation of the Meat

68 Senadores, 1933, III (September 29), 806–13.
69 *Ibid.*, 746–55.
70 The vintners and farmers received much smaller representation: see Diputados, 1933, VI ("Leyes sancionadas"), 396–98; 1934, IX ("Leyes sancionadas"), 460–61.

Board was consistent with a general government policy of increasing State control over the economy, and not an exception to it.[71]

NATIONALISM AND RHETORICAL
RESTRAINT

These political fights over the meat industry also took place on an ideological level. As in 1923, the packers were opposed to any legislation that might threaten their superiority within the economic sphere. Accordingly, they continued to sustain the sanctity of laissez-faire. Political action could never offset the forces of the market; as one manifesto argued, "The inflexible law of supply and demand does not tolerate artificial barriers that might detain or paralyze its free play." [72] By obstructing competition, governmental interference would only hold back progress. Needless to say, it would also endanger the packers' position of power.

Cattlemen and their spokesmen, on the other hand, resorted to traditional anti-imperialism. As on previous occasions, they made repeated rhetorical allusions to the historic role of the ranchers in the making of the nation-state, salutes to the necessity of economic independence, calculations of packinghouse profits, and accusations against the monopolistic actions of the pool. The picture was by now familiar: the hard-working men of the country, subject to ruthless exploitation by money-mongers from abroad.

Julio and Rodolfo Irazusta, two brothers from a cattle-owning clan in Entre Ríos, gave undiluted expression to this view in a well-known book called *La Argentina y el imperialismo británico*. Their thesis had a double edge. First, the Roca-Runciman Pact revealed Great Britain's longstanding plan to make Argentina into an "economic colony." Second, by tacit cooperation with this plan, Argentina's ruling aristocracy sold out the nation's independence. According to the Irazustas, Anglo-Argentine trade had always amounted to economic bondage—under

71 See Ministerios de Hacienda y Agricultura, *El plan de acción económica nacional* (Buenos Aires, 1934).
72 [Empresas Frigoríficas], *Presentación*, pp. 47–48.

the guise of liberal doctrine, consecrated in the 1825 treaty, or under the governmental direction of the Roca-Runciman Pact. Sarmiento, Roca, and now their descendants abandoned the true Argentina for empty foreign models: they tried "to systematize anti-patriotism, to change completely the country, its temper, its customs, its ideas, its religion, its character. No Latin-Spanish traditionalism; no Catholicism." To save its identity, the country must revive its sacred historical values and indigenous institutions, typified by the authoritarian leadership of Juan Manuel de Rosas.[73]

While the Irazustas stated their case in moralistic and ideological terms, most ranchers adjusted their use of traditional anti-imperialism to the pragmatic demands of the moment. Their political leaders, at least, were careful to avoid gross exaggeration. There is no question that the ranchers deeply resented the packers.[74] Nevertheless, they did not find anti-imperialism so necessary or so useful as on other occasions.

One of the central functions of this ideology, particularly as observed in Chapter IV, was to justify the transferral of conflict from the economic to the political sphere. But in the early 1930s, there was no doubt that cattlemen could turn their complaints into political issues. Pro-rancher delegations possessed great influence in the Congress, as well as in the Cabinet; the Justo administration took up their cause with precious little prompting. Nationalism was not needed for this purpose.

Nor was it necessary to unite the ranchers in a symbolic struggle against the alien forces of modernism, materialism, and decay. The breeders and the fatteners sometimes disagreed, but held one view in common: the State should take decisive action. Both groups blamed their trouble on the packinghouse pool. Under these circumstances, there was little to gain from the rhetorical evocation of an ideological enemy.

Given the diplomatic realities of the moment, in fact, there might well have been something to lose. Most Argentine ranchers were shocked by the Ottawa Conference, and by no means eager to alienate the British and provide excuses for even tighter

[73] (Buenos Aires, 1934); the quote is on p. 149.
[74] See Ministerio de Agricultura, *Carnes*, pp. 44–46; and *La Res*, I, no. 1 (February, 1933), 4–6.

restrictions on trade. In all likelihood, the negotiation and consideration of the Roca-Runciman Pact deterred some angry cattlemen from berating the evils of British private investment. At a time like this, unrestrained anti-imperialism could have easily backfired.

These limited political functions of traditional anti-imperialism help account for its cautious quality. Most of the time it was not needed. If the ideology had any main purpose at all, it was probably to allay any doubts among outside sectors that ranchers would act in ultimate behalf of the nation and its economic independence. This would ward off the potential participation of other groups and assure the stockmen of continuing superiority. Clearly, the ranchers had great political strength, and did not want anyone else to interfere in the process that eventually led to the passage of the Meat Law.

OUTSIDE SECTORS

In accordance with these wishes, though not necessarily in response to them, groups outside the meat industry failed to take active part in the politics of beef. The official bulletin of the newly established labor organization, the C.G.T., never once referred to the Meat Law or the Roca-Runciman Pact. Presumably preoccupied with problems of its own, the C.G.T. did not seem to regard these conflicts as relevant to the laborers. Not a word was printed about the whole crisis.

The manufacturers also guarded a discreet silence. In spite of its own apparently antithetical campaign for tariff protection,[75] the Argentine Industrial Union accepted the Roca-Runciman Pact without protest—possibly because it might discourage competition from the United States. With respect to the Meat Law, the Union seems to have acquiesced in the idea of pro-rancher legislation as long as it did not hurt the manufacturers.[76] On the whole, their attitude was one of passive consent. Whatever their feelings, the industrialists took no definite action.

[75] *Boletin*, XLIV, no. 746 (February, 1931), 23–25.
[76] See the interview with Bruzone in *Ibid.*, XLVI, no. 775 (July, 1933), 32.

The wheat farmers, in the meantime, were undergoing a crisis of their own. The Agrarian Federation came out in open support of the Roca-Runciman Pact because it included a British promise not to raise duties on wheat, as well as all the provisions concerning beef.[77] Even more significant was *La Tierra*'s stand on pastoral legislation, which identified the fate of the farmers with that of the ranchers: "The farmers, the cattlemen, all of us who dedicate our activities to the labor of the land, conscious of the obligations that we have to the community at large, are meeting them with courage, bravery, and despite everything." The least that both groups deserved was legislative protection. The Federation later noted passage of the Meat Law with approval, interpreting it as part of the government's overall plan to defend and sustain the twin pillars of the national economy.[78]

Thus the Agrarian Federation discarded its formerly hostile attitude toward cattle ranchers. The main reason for this change appears to have been that both groups were in economic crisis, and State aid to one implied at least the possibility of State aid to the other. Furthermore, the ranchers' extraordinary influence with the Justo administration might have cowed some farmers into compliant cooperation with the pro-livestock plans. Whatever inherent resentment the Agrarian Federation bore for stockmen and the Rural Society was temporarily suppressed by this community of economic and political interests. Even so, the wheat farmers' organization took no positive steps to support the cattlemen's campaign for legislation. As at other times, the politics of beef belonged to those who were directly connected with it.

THE WINNERS AND THE LOSERS

This intricate pattern of intergroup conflict yielded no single or clearly cut winner. Virtually all the victories were partial, almost none was absolute.

[77] *La Tierra*, February 13, April 30, and July 30, 1933.
[78] *Ibid.*, June 30, August 13, and August 20, 1933.

Round One: The Roca-Runciman Pact had the avid support of the fatteners, the packers, and even the breeders—who at least did not complain about the restrictive implications of reciprocal trade. The only Argentine group that lost on this issue consisted of urban consumers. Lisandro de la Torre's political appeal against the treaty also proved to be fruitless.

Round Two: The passage of the Meat Law represented a major triumph for the cattlemen, breeders and fatteners alike, over the packers. The ranchers successfully managed to transfer the conflict to the political system on both the Executive and the congressional levels, where the law was first drawn up and then approved.

Round Three: This victory was partly neutralized by the packers' acquisition of a seat on the Meat Board. Though the packers had asked for more representation, this concession still meant that the Board would never be able to take surprise action against the pool. How the packers achieved this much remains something of a political mystery.

Round Four: The most direct confrontation between CARBAP and the fatteners of the Rural Society concerned the composition of the Meat Board. Through its influence with the Justo administration, the Rural Society was first slated to dominate the new organization. But by applying pressure on the Congress, the breeders gained equal representation. Thus CARBAP won a major moral victory. In some measure, this outcome seems to indicate that conflicts within the upper class could be affected by political action.

Round Five: On other issues, however, CARBAP was solidly beaten by the Rural Society. There was no separate law for the State-supported packinghouse, the domestic trade retained top priority for ranchers' intervention in the meatpacking business, members of the Meat Board would not receive any salaries. In general, the final form of the Meat Law represents a triumph of the fatteners over the breeders.

Round Six: The producer-consumer clash over the plan to nationalize the municipal packinghouse resulted in total victory for the stockmen. Without exerting maximum political strength, they won easy approval for the scheme. Nor were consumer spokesmen able to gain representation on the Meat Board. At every turn, this lower-class urban group was soundly defeated by its upper-class rural opponents.

For the most part, political power still corresponded to economic power. Being foreign, the packers might be excepted from this generalization—although it could be argued that their relative lack of political influence derived from their inability to apply economic pressure as they had in 1923. At any rate, within the Argentine political system, the correlation continued: the fatteners beat the breeders and, together, they repeatedly crushed the consumers. As on previous occasions, groups with grievances in the economic system were unable to gain much effective retribution through recourse to the political system.

economic groups and political power

VII

The Great Debate

THE most sensational conflict that ever erupted in the politics of beef took place in the Argentine Senate of 1935, where Lisandro de la Torre denounced the meat trade as a national scandal. The ensuing debate was one of the most significant political events in the Concordancia decade, and has since become a symbol for the Argentina of today. At present, De la Torre is commonly remembered as the country's first statesman with the temerity and wit to reveal the evils of foreign imperialism and stand up for genuine economic independence.[1] The myth is based partly upon the drama of the debate, and draws its principal sustenance from the widespread intensity of anti-imperialism. Despite some dissent from parts of the left, whose members claim that his defense of cattle ranchers amounted to support of the prevailing socio-economic structure,[2] De la Torre is generally taken to be the original advocate of economic sovereignty.

We have already seen that De la Torre was by no means the

[1] See B. González Arrili, *Vida de Lisandro de la Torre* (Buenos Aires, 1940); Juan Lazarte, *Lisandro de la Torre: reformador social americano*, 2nd ed. (Buenos Aires, 1955); Raúl Larra, *Lisandro de la Torre: el solitario de Pinas*, 6th ed. (Buenos Aires, 1956); and Rennie, *Argentine Republic*. The publication of De la Torre's *Obras* has helped perpetuate the myth, and even Juan Perón has paid homage to De la Torre in *Los vendepatria: las pruebas de una traición* (Buenos Aires, 1958), esp. p. 90.

[2] See H. García Ledesma, *Lisandro de la Torre y la pampa gringa* (Buenos Aires, 1954); Juan José Hernández Arregui, *La formación de la conciencia nacional (1930–1960)* (Buenos Aires, 1960), pp. 157–64; and Jorge Abelardo Ramos, *Revolución y contrarrevolución en Argentina: las masas en nuestra historia* (Buenos Aires, 1957), pp. 362–68.

first politician to resort to anti-imperialism. The brothers Carlés made appeals of this kind as early as 1909, and rancher representatives employed nationalistic rhetoric on numerous other occasions. But what matters is not so much the timing of De la Torre's declaration as whether or not he put anti-imperialism to any unique or novel uses. In order to explore such aspects of the myth, as well as to assess the contemporary impact of the debate, it will be necessary to examine the arguments in some detail.

COMMITTEE INVESTIGATION AND MAJORITY REPORT

The scene for the confrontation was set in 1934, when De la Torre, Progressive Democrat from Santa Fe, proposed the appointment of a three-man committee to investigate the Argentine meat industry. Regardless of the Meat Law, he said, livestock producers were still exploited by the packinghouse "monopoly," which paid far less money for Argentine cattle than the current prices in Australia.[3] Despite some debate on this point,[4] the Senate established a commission to determine: (1) whether prices paid for Argentine stock bore any relation to the prices paid for meat in foreign markets; (2) what portion of the increase in the peso value of meat sold abroad, brought about by an official devaluation of the peso, was being passed along to ranchers;[5] (3) whether Australian cattle prices were actually higher than those in Argentina; and (4) how large the profits of the packinghouses were. Appointed for the job, along with De la Torre, were Laureano Landaburu of San Luis and Carlos Serrey of Salta. Both these men were

---

[3] Senadores, 1934, II (September 1), 10–19; Obras, II, 50–69. Whenever possible, citations will be made from both these sources.

[4] Senadores, 1934, II (September 8), 88–122.

[5] New exchange regulations had been established in November 1933. The British pound was consequently worth more pesos—but because the regulations were so complex, no one knew exactly how much more. See Ministerios de Hacienda y Agricultura, El plan de acción económica, pp. 65–121; and (British) Department of Overseas Trade, Economic Conditions in the Argentine Republic [by Stanley G. Irving] (London, 1935), pp. 41–48.

aristocrats and National Democrats—but, as a further suggestion
of political professionalization, neither one owned cattle. After
nearly a year of research, testimony, and interrogation, the commission prepared to make its report in June 1935.

The majority report, issued by Landaburu and Serrey, flatly
accused the packinghouse managers of unfairly dominating the
Argentine beef industry.[6] They declared that the pool gave the
packers a virtual monopoly over 80 per cent of the country's
meat exports, reducing the price for cattle even when the price
of meat at Smithfield rose; except for the era of the Meat War,
there was no correlation at all between British meat prices and
local cattle prices. In disagreement with the Minister of Agriculture, who claimed that livestock prices had gone up more than
the peso value of the English pound, they also maintained that
Argentine ranchers received less than half the increase in the
commercial value of meat. As a result of these factors, wrote the
majority, the profits of the packers were "considerable . . . and
at times really exorbitant." [7]

The Senators also complained about the packers' refusal to
cooperate with the investigation. The managers had used irreg-
ular accounting procedures, they had tried to hide their books,
and one of them (Richard Tootell of Anglo) displayed such
adamance that he was thrown briefly into jail. The most startling episode followed the Anglo firm's denial that copies of
cost-estimate papers were kept in Buenos Aires. Acting on a
night-time tip from two deckhands, the committee then in-
spected the hold of a ship called the *Norman Star:* there, crated
as "Corned Beef" and ready for shipment to Britain, were stacks
of cost-estimate papers from the Frigorífico Anglo! Partly with
this memory in mind, Landaburu asserted that the packinghouses should be held subject to penalties under the general
law against trusts.

At the same time, the majority argued that cattle prices were
no higher in Australia than in Argentina. On the export side,
Argentine stock was superior in quality and fetched justly

---

[6] The majority report appears in Senadores, 1935, I (June 11), 148–51;
Landaburu's oral introduction is on 158–82. Only verbatim quotations will be
cited below.
[7] *Ibid.,* 151.

higher prices. The confusion seemed to concern the domestic market, since Australia's top-grade cattle were used for internal consumption and received higher bids than the relatively low-grade stock sold for local use in Argentina. Things were no better Down Under; on this point, they insisted, De la Torre had been wrong.

In view of these varied observations, Landaburu and Serrey made several recommendations. The exchange regulations, which allowed the major packers to submit their own estimates of the export (F.O.B.) value of their products, badly needed readjustment. As long as the Roca-Runciman Pact stayed in effect, Argentina's 11 per cent quota should be given to some entity that was "apart from any monopolistic combination" [8]— not leased to private packers on a temporary basis, as the government had done. Further, public authorities should seek to eliminate all barriers to the exportation of beef and to open as many new markets as possible.

Despite their attack on the packers, the Senators closed their report by introducing two relatively innocuous bills. The first would impose strict accounting regulations upon the packing-houses; the second would put the purchase of cattle on a beef-yield basis, thus revoking the live-weight law of 1923. They frankly acknowledged the limitations of the proposals, but insisted they were being realistic. "The majority of the commission," concluded Landaburu in his oral statement, "does not believe in seeking nonexistent panaceas to solve the varied and multiple problems offered by our meat trade. We merely present, as a modest collaboration, these two bills, with which we seek to resolve difficulties, problems, and arbitrary situations found by the commission and which are repeated daily in our meat trade." [9]

ATTACK BY DE LA TORRE

Then De la Torre rose to speak. At 67 years of age he made an impressive figure, with clear blue eyes and white hair and

[8] *Ibid.*, 151.
[9] *Ibid.*, 181.

beard. Still at the peak of his rhetorical powers, he was volatile, acid, impetuous, powerful, something of a political purist— "intransigent," as Argentines would say. One of Santa Fe's aristocrats and formerly a Radical, he had long since broken (and duelled) with Yrigoyen. As the presidential candidate of the Progressive Democrat Party in 1916, De la Torre was given a chance to bargain with the Conservatives and defeat Yrigoyen, but turned down the offer and took a seat in the Chamber of Deputies. He later left Congress to administer his cattle ranch in Córdoba, but re-entered the political arena after the 1930 revolution. This time he had an opportunity to make a deal with the Provisional Government and become the official candidate for President; again he refused, and led the campaign of the opposition. Hopelessly defeated by the fraud, De la Torre then joined the Senate. When it was announced that he would issue a dissenting report on the meat market problem, popular interest was generally mild. Little did the public realize that this would be one of the final, but most important, acts of his entire political career.

What De la Torre essentially contributed to this debate was an attack—not so much against the packers as against the Justo government.[10] The tone of his speech, which lasted through five whole sessions of the Senate, was set by his opening words. His own investigation into the beef trade revealed "a disconsolate scene. The livestock industry, the most genuine one on Argentine soil, stands in ruin because of two factors: the extortionate action of a foreign monopoly, and the complicity of a government which sometimes leaves it alone and at other times provides direct protection." [11] Contrary to much currently prevailing myth, the novelty of his charge did not lie in his accusation of the meatpackers, although he denounced them at length. What was new, shocking, and sensational was his claim that the Justo administration had cooperated with

10 De la Torre's speech is in Senadores, 1935, I (June 18), 187–212; (June 19), 216–47; (June 21), 248–76; (June 22), 289–310; (June 27), 356–86. And in *Obras*, II, 110–382. His written minority report is in Senadores, 1935, I (June 11), 151–58. Only the verbatim quotations will be cited below.

11 Senadores, 1935, I (June 18), 187; *Obras*, II, 110.

them, advancing alien interests at the expense of the country's
cattlemen and thereby dishonoring the Argentine nation.

The character of De la Torre's challenge appears to have
been mixed. To some extent he spoke in behalf of cattle
breeders, particularly the small- and middle-scale producers
from outside the province of Buenos Aires. When De la Torre
criticized the government, he frequently complained that its
policies unduly favored the fatteners. He also charged that
the packinghouse monopoly, permitted and protected by the
government, had been established "with the complicity of a
circle of cattlemen . . . principally the fatteners," [12] and particularly as represented by the Argentine Rural Society. The
conflict was drawn partly along functional lines; De la Torre,
a cattle raiser and ex-president of the Rural Society of Santa Fe,
was speaking for the breeders.

But the central issue was probably political. As the head of
the Progressive Democrat Party and former presidential candidate, De la Torre was the recognized leader of the P.D.P.-
Socialist alliance that posed outspoken opposition to the Concordancia. His previous objections to the Roca-Runciman Pact
had shown a plainly political bent, and how he had a specific
goal: key provincial elections in November, which could greatly
influence the congressional elections scheduled for March 1936.
(His detractors never tired of citing these political interests,
despite their irrelevance to the validity of his charges.) He was
not so much trying to rectify an imbalance in the economic
system through recourse to the political system, as stockmen
had done on previous occasions; rather, he was seeking to rectify
an imbalance in the political system by seizing upon and pub-
licizing the plight of an economic group, that is, the breeders.

As an illustration of this point, the following piece of content analysis shows how much space (by the number of lines)
De la Torre devoted to the major themes of his five-day speech.
Though it is difficult to maintain consistent working distinctions between the various categories, the analysis indicates

[12] Senadores, 1935, I (June 18), 192; *Obras*, II, 120. And see Senadores, 1935,
I (June 19), 228; *Obras*, II, 182.

that he was more concerned with the government than with
the packers, fatteners, Rural Society, or any policy proposals.

Figure 7.1. *Distribution of Emphasis in De la Torre Exposé*

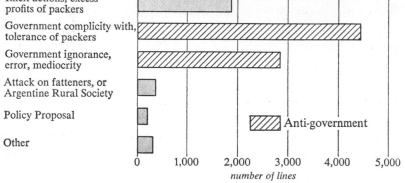

Source: [De la Torre], *Obras*, II, 110–382.

While De la Torre's attack on the government took diverse
and varied forms, most of his substantive arguments were related to three basic issues: (1) the personal complicity of the
Minister of Agriculture, Luis F. Duhau; (2) the usage of the 11
per cent quota granted to a State-supported packinghouse under the Roca-Runciman Pact; (3) taxes paid to the Argentine
government by the packers. Along with many lesser charges,
these points combined to buttress his central contention that
the Justo administration had complied with alien interests.

Although De la Torre opened his speech by disclaiming
rumors of personal dislike for Duhau—to hear him tell it, they
had barely met—he promptly launched the most sensational
charge of the entire investigation. He asserted that Duhau,
one of the most prominent fatteners in the province of Buenos
Aires, had been accepting consistently inflated prices for his
cattle from Swift & Company since entering the Cabinet, presumably in return for official favoritism. While cheating other
stockmen, packinghouse managers overpaid Duhau. Here was an
insult and a challenge to personal honor. It raised an air of
scandal, tension, and temper that hung over the debate like a
lowering cloud.

The charges about the 11 per cent export quota concerned Duhau's decision to lease the quota to foreign packinghouses, not Argentine firms, while the National Meat Board made arrangements for the establishment of a producer-supported packinghouse under the 1933 law. In defense of his action, Duhau had publicly explained that the quota was not given to the Frigorífico Gualeguaychú or the Grondona Company (both owned by Argentines, and located in Entre Ríos) because their inferior products would damage the prestige of Argentine beef abroad. De la Torre strongly defended the quality of their beef exports, expressing horror at Duhau's open criticism of Argentine enterprise and claiming that the Minister had refused to give them the "authorized" exporter status (permission to ship without specific clearance every time) that he had given to the members of the packinghouse pool.

In the same vein, De la Torre criticized the packinghouse that was finally set up by the National Meat Board, the Argentine Meat Producers' Corporation (*Corporación Argentina de Productores de Carne*, known from its initials as the CAP). This firm, which finally made its first shipment in the middle of 1935, had subcontracted its quota to the Sansinena and Smithfield & Argentine packinghouses. According to De la Torre, the CAP should never have dealt with Smithfield & Argentine because it belonged to the pool. He also hinted at a possible connection between the Sansinena contract and the position of Horacio V. Pereda, director of the CAP, on the Sansinena board of directors—in explicit violation of the Corporation's statutes. Under influence of this kind, De la Torre implied, the CAP had betrayed its original purpose.

This point about the quota's usage bore great significance for the breeder-fattener rivalry, since Duhau's insistence that the 11 per cent should be filled only by meat of the highest quality meant that it would be taken up by specially fattened stock. As the Senator snapped, "it amounts to reserving the quota for the exclusive benefit of the large-scale cattlemen." [13] Furthermore, the discrimination against the Gualeguaychú and Grondona companies signified discrimination against the breed-

---

[13] Senadores, 1935, I (June 11), 156.

ers around Entre Ríos, with whom these firms did much of their business. Governmental policy on the quota thus promoted the interests of a few wealthy breeders of high-grade stock and, more particularly, the fatteners.

On the question of taxes, De la Torre claimed to have discovered, without any cooperation from the government, that packinghouse payments were far less than they should have been. In 1933 alone, he declared, Swift & Company enterprises cheated the government by a total of 414,000 pesos. In a paradox of incredible proportions, the Frigorífico Anglo paid fewer taxes than the tiny Grondona firm, although it had fifty times the export quota. The only reason that foreign packers could get away with such grand larceny, the Senator said, was because the government let them. The Treasury had made little or no effort to check up on their returns, and permitted the international companies to compensate losses abroad with gains that were made in Argentina. (In practice, this meant that foreign beef industries could be supported by earnings made in the Plate; that is, Argentine ranchers were forced to subsidize their competitors.) In addition, the administration had sponsored a bill to eliminate a tax paid by the packinghouses under a 1923 law on the fraudulent grounds that, along with the Meat Law contribution, which was levied on the cattlemen, it constituted a double tax. "Could one want," inquired De la Torre, "more definite proof of exceptional favoritism?" [14]

In conclusion, the Senator suggested that the only conceivable solution to these manifold problems would be to establish a State monopoly over the Argentine beef industry, as he had proposed in 1923. Under this arrangement the State could either process meat by itself, or it could subcontract the packing operation to firms that promised to maintain a reasonable relationship between costs and prices—in other words, reasonable and not exorbitant profits. As De la Torre explained it, the plan would not amount to a "declaration of war to the death" against the packers; it would simply tighten controls on the

[14] *Ibid.* (June 21), 250; *Obras,* II, 227. For the Administration's bill to repeal the tax see Diputados, 1934, III (August 1), 744–54.

trade.[15] If the foreign monopoly were ever broken, it would have to be broken by the State.

REBUTTAL BY THE GOVERNMENT

Directly addressing the Congress, Duhau began his reply to De la Torre's attack by denying the charge that he had received special prices for his livestock. Offering to open his books to the public, he claimed that De la Torre had selected only 12 per cent of his total sales in 1934–35 as the basis of his accusation, ignoring the fact that he had been cheated and swindled as much as anyone else on the vast majority of transactions. Since he had accepted the portfolio of agriculture, the relative price of his cattle had actually gone down. Duhau displayed some figures to back up his contentions, then drew thundering applause with the outright assertion that the charge was "False! Absolutely false!" [16]

In further demonstration of his personal integrity, the Minister emphasized his long-standing concern with the packinghouse pool and its profits. As president of the Rural Society, he had supervised the publication of *El pool de frigoríficos* in 1927. As a Deputy, he had helped put through the Meat Law. As Minister of Agriculture, he was putting that law into practice and promoting the Anglo-Argentine investigation under the Roca-Runciman Pact (with which, he credulously remarked, the packinghouse managers had "unanimously promised to collaborate fully and openly").[17] At his direction, the government had made estimates of packinghouse profits that, after some adjustments, were entirely consistent with the data discovered aboard the *Norman Star*. De la Torre, on the other hand, had merely proposed one livestock bill in all the years preceding the Depression; and now the Senator was using the

---

[15] Senadores, 1935, I (June 18), 193; *Obras*, II, 122.

[16] Senadores, 1935, I (June 28), 390–94. Duhau's entire speech is given in Senadores, 1935, I (June 28), 388–404; (July 2), 406–19, 421–23; (July 4), 424–65; (July 5), 470–85; (July 11), 490–535. Only the verbatim quotations will be cited below.

[17] *Ibid.* (July 5), 480.

Norman Star episode as "just a lot of ballyhoo, to lure ingenuous customers into the electoral circus!" [18] The basic point was clear: Duhau was at least as opposed to the packinghouse pool as De la Torre had ever been.

Most of the Minister's speech, however, was devoted to the defense of government policy. With regard to the 11 per cent quota, Duhau confirmed his previous statement that protection of the prestige of Argentine beef abroad formed a cornerstone of administration policy. Particularly in view of increasing competition from South Africa and Brazil, he had therefore refused to give part of the quota to Gualeguaychú or Grondona. (Pressed for clarification, though, he admitted that "good" grade chilled, which came from Entre Ríos, would uphold the name of Argentine beef as well as the "exceptional" grade.) Besides, he said in something of a tautology, the 11 per cent could not be given to Gualeguaychú because the administration had always planned to reserve the quota for the CAP alone. After the CAP was finally established, Duhau claimed, the subcontracting of its quota kept down overhead costs and, as a matter of fact, responded to the principle involved in De la Torre's proposal for a State monopoly. Furthermore, Pereda's position at Sansinena violated only the letter of the law and not its spirit, since the post was nonremunerative and intended only to give him experience. In sum, Duhau contended, the 11 per cent had been used to maximum advantage and now rested in safe hands. Under its unspectacular but realistic "policy of understanding," [19] the Argentine government had met the cattle crisis of the 1930s with decision and strength.

De la Torre's charges about governmental complicity in the nonpayment of packinghouse taxes were answered by the quick-witted and brilliant Federico Pinedo, Minister of the Treasury and an Independent Socialist. After a biting attack on the reliability of De la Torre's chief accountant, Pinedo defended the administration's decision not to give packinghouse returns

18 *Ibid.* (July 2), 409.
19 Senadores, 1935, I (July 11), 508.

to the Senate investigators because the law demanded secrecy.
De la Torre's argument that tax records could be subpoenaed
might seem plausible, he conceded, but the government's view
was legally correct. Furthermore, the administration had been
checking on the packers' returns since 1933. Though the international juggling of profits was plainly illegal, a still incomplete investigation indicated that the Swift & Company accounts
were actually in "perfect" order.[20] On the other hand, the
government was suing the Frigorífico Anglo for under-payment
of taxes. According to Pinedo, De la Torre made the general
mistake of confusing the Treasury's approval of payments on
declared profits with indifference as to what the profits actually
were.

In a winding explanation of Argentine exchange regulations,
Pinedo denied that "authorized" exporter status had been refused to the Gualeguaychú or Grondona firms because of discrimination. Gualeguaychú had failed to include all the necessary documents in its application for authorization and did
not keep accounts in the city of Buenos Aires, where they could
be easily reached for inspection. Grondona had never even requested the privilege. He went on to say that the administration
relied on the "authorized" packers' own estimates of export
values (F.O.B.) as only a temporary measure; ultimately, as De
la Torre demanded, exchange transactions would be based on
the prices of meat in Britain (C.I.F.) minus transportation
and insurance costs as calculated by the Argentine government.

The tone of Pinedo's reply strongly suggested that whatever
problems might exist were rapidly moving toward solution.
Insisting that the Justo administration had fulfilled its obligations, the Minister drew prolonged applause from the galleries
and the benches with his confident conclusion. "We are not
sorry," he said, "that a man who sees everything as black, bad,
cloudy, shady, murky, has brought us to this fateful concert.

[20] *Ibid.* (July 16), 634. Pinedo's entire speech is in Senadores, 1935, I (July
12), 536–83; (July 15), 584–614; (July 16), 615–62; (July 17), 667–719; (July 18),
720–87. Only the verbatim quotations will be cited below.

We await the judgment of other men, and have no doubt that, with a knowledge of the facts, their judgment will be favorable to the work that we have done." [21]

DENOUEMENT

De la Torre promptly jumped to the counterattack.[22] He declared that the administration was trying to reduce the political impact of his charges by unnecessarily stretching out the debate (it took Duhau and Pinedo more than three weeks to answer a challenge that was made in just over one). He used Duhau's own data to confirm his claim about special treatment from the packers. Pereda's seat on the Sansinena board still stood in flagrant violation of the rules, and if the quality of cattle was so low in Entre Ríos—as Duhau had said—why was the CAP making its first purchases on the upper Littoral? Turning to the Treasury, De la Torre countered Pinedo's defense of the Swift accounts by quoting admissions of error made by company officials. The recent prosecution of Anglo was a transparent response to the Senate investigation, he maintained, while there continued to be enormous irregularities in the payment of taxes.

In the session of July 23, De la Torre returned to the matter of the *Norman Star*. Official statistics were not consistent with the papers there discovered, he said, and the president of the Meat Board had admitted as much. And even if the records were consistent, Anglo's devious attempt to hide its records deserved much more than Duhau's casual dismissal of the case. Recalling that Duhau had once accused De la Torre of hiding one of the *Norman Star* papers from the government, the Santafecino bluntly called the charge a lie. Duhau angrily slammed his fist down on his desk. Pinedo and De la Torre began to shout at one another. As the Treasury Minister spoke, De la Torre got up and started walking toward him:

21 *Ibid.* (July 18), 758–59.
22 Senadores, 1935, I (July 20), 824–43; (July 22), 847–76; II (July 23), 193–96. Or see *Obras*, II, 382–489.

Pinedo: "He calls me an insolent coward! Mister President, the Senator from Santa Fe is capable of challenging me to a duel because he knows I cannot fight, due to my convictions."

De la Torre, now standing next to Pinedo: "And you would not fight because you are a coward!"

Infuriated by such insults to his friend and colleague, Duhau gave De la Torre a shove that sent him sprawling in the aisle. The bell was vainly rung for order as spectators gasped in astonishment.[23] Then some shots rang out. Enzo Bordabehere, Senator-elect from Santa Fe who had sprung to De la Torre's aid, slumped to the floor. Mortally wounded, he died that same afternoon. Duhau also crashed to the ground in the confusion, shot through one hand and breaking some ribs in the fall. Police quickly apprehended the assassin, Ramón Valdez Cora, and took him off to jail. Though the Senate immediately launched an investigation of the murder, De la Torre dropped his discussion of the meat industry. For all intents and purposes, the Great Debate was over.[24]

DIGRESSION: PROS AND CONS

The Great Debate continues to be shrouded in mystery. Who possessed what motives? Which of the charges against whom were true? What inspired the killing of Bordabehere? None of these questions can be given final or definitive answers at this time. They have remained a source of controversy and dogmatic assertion ever since 1935, and I have not been able to resolve them through historical research. It should be plainly understood that the following comments represent my personal conjectures, based on circumstantial evidence and not the discovery of any new or conclusive facts.

[23] This much of the exchange is in *Senadores,* 1935, II (July 23), 201. It is widely rumored that De la Torre called Pinedo a cuckold; as González Arrili delicately phrased it, the Senator committed "the most brutal verbal aggression imaginable." *Vida de Lisandro de la Torre,* p. 228. The official version of the exchange was not released for a month and a half.

[24] Later on the two bills proposed by Landaburu and Serrey were approved by the Senate. *Senadores,* 1935, II (September 12–13), 274–77. However, they were never even considered in the Chamber of Deputies.

One point was quite clearly established: the foreign packing-houses had made a bad impression. It is impossible to know whether each of the charges made against them was correct. Taken at face value, the facts do not speak in their favor. Alone, the *Norman Star* incident suggests that some of the accusations must have been valid, and it seems fair to infer that the packers committed some of the sins decried by both the government and the opposition. At any rate, the packers' lack of cooperation with the investigation led everyone to think they had resorted to commercial malpractice—and this was bad business, if nothing else.

Among the Argentine contestants, neither side was entirely right. The dominant issues were too complex to yield a clear-cut triumph. On the nonpayment of packinghouse taxes, De la Torre made a strong case. It is probably true that the packers were not paying their full share of taxes, as Pinedo indirectly admitted, but this does not resolve the question of govern-mental complicity. There is not much doubt that the Justo administration could have taken earlier and more energetic action in this area. Yet the Concordancia alone could not be held responsible for this laxity. No other administration, in-cluding the Radical regimes, had made any strenuous efforts to collect these taxes—and this government was at least making an attempt. If the Concordancia was guilty, so was everyone else.

Arguments over the 11 per cent quota dealt mainly with matters of policy, rather than complicity. Duhau, and other members of the Justo administration, had the specific intention of filling the Argentine quota with the finest possible beef. In itself, this was no sacrifice of national dignity. At bottom, it was a question of economic interests. Fatteners no doubt sup-ported the policy, since it promoted the exportation of specially fed stock; so did the foreign packinghouse managers, who wanted to retain their share of the trade. Most breeders would naturally oppose the policy, since it tended to shut them out of the market. Here lay the roots of all the discussions about ex-porter "authorization," the quality of meat from Entre Ríos,

the merits of Gualeguaychú and Grondona, Duhau's cooperation with the packers and his unconcern with the *Norman
Star* affair.

There remains another fundamental question: whether it was
professionally ethical for Duhau to follow a policy that fur-
thered the interests of one group of ranchers, and a minority at
that. One would normally think not. Of course it should be
remembered that beef politics had often erupted in conflict—
and it was understandable, if not justifiable, for whichever
group had power to use it in its own interests. But generally
speaking, De la Torre scored some points on this issue.

This brings us to the most sensational of all the Senator's
charges, the accusation that Duhau accepted special prices for
his stock while serving in the government. Although the evidence is scanty, the subsequent Anglo-Argentine investigation
into the meat trade provided statistical data which make it possible to compare the profit percentage of "F. de Duhau y Cía."
with an average for leading Argentine ranches. Though they
probably deal with only one small portion of his total business,
the figures [25] show that Duhau's earnings consistently outstripped the general average by wide margins. The sheer mag-
nitude of profit seems to suggest that Duhau was getting special
treatment from the packers. This favoritism might well have
been for purely economic reasons; as shown in Chapter II, the
packers often flattered major clients. Duhau obtained substantial returns in 1929–30, when he did not hold public office,
though he doubtless exerted some influence as ex-president
of the Argentine Rural Society. More important is the fact
that he continued to make exceptional profits while sitting in
the Chamber of Deputies (1932–33) as well as during his tenure
in the Ministry of Agriculture (August 1933–December 1935).
The subsequent and sharp decline in earnings might also be
significant. Whether or not there was explicit collusion, however, it definitely appears that Duhau did not perceive any con-

[25] Compiled, interestingly enough, by Anselmo Viacava, whom De la Torre
regarded as an "invariable" ally of the packers. Senadores, 1935, I (June 22),
310; *Obras,* II, 320.

flict of interest between his private dealings and public service—
and De la Torre's exposure of the situation had thrown the
Minister into a highly embarrassing position. But would this
have supplied the motive for an attempt on De la Torre's life?

Table 7.1.   *Profit Percentages for F. de Duhau y Cía.*
and Leading Cattle Ranches

	Duhau %	Average %
1929	75.34	8.49
1930	34.67	4.91
1931	9.09	2.29
1932	27.04	0.65
1933	13.86	1.15
1934	29.97	1.91
1935	68.95	3.15
1936	6.80	3.61

Source: *Report of the Joint Committee,* pp. 130–36.

Ever since Bordabehere's death, wide currency has been given
to the notion that Ramón Valdez Cora was hired by Duhau to
kill De la Torre. According to this version, the Santafecino's
attacks had driven the Minister to utter desperation. Valdez
Cora was known to be an ardent National Democrat, a low-life
character, and, as De la Torre later charged, an acquaintance
of Duhau. He had gotten into the Senate chamber that day
through his connections with the Minister, and aimed his shots
at De la Torre; Bordabehere had moved in the way, and the
plot had thus been foiled.[26]
    Yet there is another way of viewing these events, even ac-
cepting the friendship between Duhau and the assassin. The
crucial point is Valdez Cora's claim that Bordabehere was
carrying a gun. It seems unlikely that he was, though witnesses
were just about evenly divided on this question at subsequent
hearings.[27] If Bordabehere did have a revolver in his hand, or

[26] Rennie, *Argentine Republic,* p. 257; and see De la Torre's comments in
Senadores, 1935, II (September 10), 151–64 or *Obras,* II, 489–514.
[27] Senadores, 1935, II (September 2), 6–43; (September 3), 50–76; (September

even if Valdez Cora merely thought so for an instant, the murder could be explained as an impulsive effort to protect a friend. All the witnesses agreed that Valdez Cora had taken his shots from only two or three meters away; it is hard to believe that, at this range, he could actually have missed De la Torre and hit Bordabehere by mistake. And if Duhau had known the murder was coming, why would he have fallen on the floor, near De la Torre, putting his hand in the way of a shot that apparently came from Valdez Cora's gun? [28] Besides, if Duhau had wanted to have De la Torre (or Bordabehere) killed, is it reasonable for him to have ordered the deed to take place in public? Wouldn't he have realized that such an act would amount to a confession of guilt? These questions can probably never be answered; they only serve to illustrate the complexity of the problem and the fragility of historical myth. With that in mind, let us turn to the political and ideological implications of the debate.

POLITICAL SIGNIFICANCE

The Great Debate bore tremendous political impact. With regard to the beef industry itself, De la Torre's investigation seems to have spurred the Justo administration to action. It has been persuasively argued that the government consciously accelerated application of the Meat Law after the Senator's call for an investigation in 1934, and that many subsequent decisions responded to the parliamentary pressure: the creation of the CAP, the distribution of the 11 per cent quota, the auditing of accounts, and the litigation against the Frigorífico Anglo.[29] Whether this occurred by coincidence or design is a matter of speculation, but De la Torre might well have forced the administration's hand on these specific measures.

The general implications of the Great Debate were not im-

4), 84–129; (September 5), 139–42; (September 10), 151–89. Also see the *Buenos Aires Herald*, August 21, September 4, and September 17, 1935.

[28] The ballistics report is mentioned in the *Buenos Aires Herald*, September 4, 1935.

[29] See Olariaga, *El ruralismo argentino*, pp. 268–69.

mediately clear. Dissension over the conduct (rather than the substance) of the debate threw the Justo Cabinet into a week-long crisis, Duhau and Pinedo each offering to resign no less than five times—once so that Pinedo, in violation of the law and his own proclaimed principles, could fight a harmless duel with De la Torre. But Justo eventually and publicly declared his confidence in both Pinedo and Duhau, who continued to serve in their ministries until the end of the year.[30] With the return of the (ex-Yrigoyen) Radicals to electoral politics in the campaign of 1936, opposition representation in the Chamber of Deputies increased from 57 to 71 seats, but the Concordancia still held firm control of Congress.[31] In the short run, the Great Debate did not stimulate any major perceptible change in the political situation.

However, the De la Torre debate was immensely important in the long run. The gravity of the accusations, the assassination of an elected official, and the subsequent stoppage of the debate not only dishonored the Senate and the Justo administration. *They also helped to discredit the entire political system.* According to the Argentine Constitution and prevailing practice, Congress was supposed to provide a national forum where groups and individuals could present and promote their demands; with this outlet for dissent, parliamentary action tended to justify the distribution of political power. But the leaders of the Concordancia ruled from the top. Controlled by electoral fraud and conservative elements, Congress became a puppet of the Executive branch, just as it had been during the old days of the "acuerdo." As seen in the figure below, total congressional activity, measured by the annual number of pages in the *Diario de Sesiones,* fell far downward during the Justo era.[32]

[30] See the *Buenos Aires Herald,* July 31–August 6, 1935.

[31] Zalduendo, *Geografía electoral,* pp. 226–27. Good accounts of the political infighting after the shooting can be found in N.A., D.S., 835.00/707–22.

[32] There was a temporary increase in congressional activity when Roberto Ortiz became President in 1938, as shown in Figure 1.4, but by then it was too late. The system had been discredited under Justo, and when Ramón Castillo assumed the role of Chief Executive around 1940 congressional activity declined again. Naturally this single measure does not provide a conclusive index to delegitimation, though it seems to be one of the most revealing; published

Figure 7.2. *Activity of the Argentine Congress, 1932–1937*

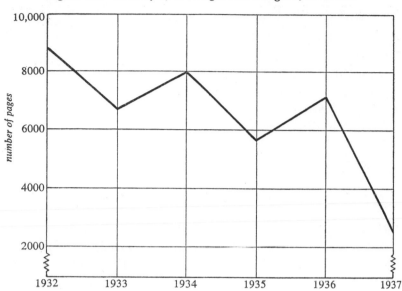

Without an effective parliament, aggrieved groups outside the Concordancia had nowhere to turn.

Of course, the Great Debate on the meat industry was not the only cause of the decline. Yet it certainly intensified the trend—and, more important, emphasized the uselessness of participation in the prevailing political system. De la Torre had started to talk with fire in his eye, but also with some well-reasoned arguments; the discussion ended in death. Many people were bound to conclude that parliamentary action was doomed to defeat. Perhaps De la Torre's own realization of the situation helps account for his subsequent despair, his retirement from the Senate, and his dramatic suicide in 1938—which promptly made him a martyr for democracy. Imbued with this significance, the Great Debate became a widely recognized symbol of governmental illegitimacy.

voter turnout figures are scanty and, for this particular purpose, probably too uncertain (see Germani, *Política y sociedad*, p. 225 n, and Table 9.1 below). It is to be hoped that other students will devise additional indices in order to analyze the structure and function of Argentina's political system during this critical period of the Concordancia.

THE STRATEGY OF RHETORIC

As in other instances, the rhetorical or ideological appeals in
the Great Debate responded to the interests of the two sides.
Administration spokesmen naturally wanted to give the debate
as little publicity as possible. They had nothing to gain from
widening the conflict. As members of the Concordancia, they
held firm control over the State; and as livestock fatteners, like
Duhau, they possessed a good deal of economic strength. Any
change in the imbalance of power could only work to their own
disadvantage. Any increase in the number of contestants could
only jeopardize the ruling group's supremacy.

Accordingly, government representatives adopted three main
forensic tactics. One was to stretch out the debate as long as
possible, taking up ten full congressional sessions to reply to
charges that were made in only five, evidently trying to bore
and disinterest the public at large.[33] Another device emphasized
the "political" character of De la Torre's aspirations, casting
doubt upon the validity of his accusations by casting doubt
upon the nobility of his motives. Thus the audience would be
dissuaded from participation: De la Torre's attack was merely
part of an electoral game, the rules of which were widely understood. Third, Duhau and Pinedo tried to picture the central
issue as one of policy rather than motivation. The government
had made its decisions and was carrying them out; one could
challenge the decisions, but not their ultimate purpose—which
was, of course, to promote the national welfare. An issue involving the interests of one group therefore had no particular bearing on the interests of another. In short, the audience should
not become involved in the politics of beef.

De la Torre stood in an entirely different position. Both
politically and economically, he was on the losing side. The
Concordancia far outweighed the opposition, the fatteners were
stronger than the breeders. De la Torre needed help from
other sectors.

[33] With some success, as shown by impatient editorials in the *Buenos Aires
Herald*, July 9 and 18, 1935.

First he had to call the conflict to the attention of the public. This much was accomplished largely by the sensational nature of his exposé. Scandal has popular appeal. In this sense, the charges against Duhau were not only accusations of personal guilt; rhetorically, they performed the vital function of shocking the audience into attention.

Once this had been achieved, De la Torre then had to define the issue in such a way as to include the interests of originally unaffected groups. On the level of leadership, his political and economic challenge involved essentially intraclass conflict; but in the pursuit of his goal, De la Torre sought to picture the fight as an anti-oligarchic class struggle. In an effort to identify his opposition as the upper class, he frequently framed his attack on the "large landowners" of the Argentine Rural Society and not just the fatteners of livestock. This socio-economic distinction not only restricted his immediate constituency to the less prosperous breeders—who formed the majority of cattle ranchers anyway—but also allowed him to address his appeal to middle- and lower-class groups of all kinds. Similarly, his complaints about working conditions in the packinghouses can be interpreted as a call to the urban laboring class. In this way the injection of class antagonism tended to broaden the meaning and attraction of De la Torre's struggle.

Yet the Santafecino's most persistent attempt to widen the conflict lay in the usage of anti-imperialism. Repeatedly, he charged or implied that the Justo government's pro-fattener policies posed a threat to the national sovereignty and therefore to all conscientious Argentines. The rhetorical difference in the debate is clearly shown in the following table. In his efforts to emphasize national interests and awaken the public at large, De la Torre constantly referred to the packinghouse pool as an instrument of alien domination. Though Concordancia spokesmen sometimes mentioned their attention to the general welfare, their desire to minimize public concern and participation led them to avoid all mention of "foreign imperialism." For those on the government's side, the pool was an economic

Table 7.2. *References to Packinghouses and Public Interest*

		Concordancia			
Type of Reference	*De la Torre*	*Landaburu*	*Duhau*	*Pinedo*	*Total*
Packinghouses only (no adjectives)	222	36	97	32	165
Packinghouse trust, monopoly, pool, etc.	107	17	18	5	40
Foreign-owned packinghouses	51	2	—	1	3
Foreign trust, pool, monopoly, etc.	24	—	—	—	—
Public, national, Argentine interest	47	3	24	7	34

Sample: For De la Torre, Senadores, 1935, I (June 18), 187–212; (June 19), 216–47; (June 21), 248–76; (June 22), 286–310; (June 27), 356–87; or see *Obras*, II, 110–382. For Landaburu, Senadores, 1935, I (June 11), 158–82. For Duhau, Senadores, 1935, I (June 28), 388–401; (July 20), 406–19; (July 4), 424–55. For Pinedo, Senadores, 1935, I (July 12), 536–68; (July 15), 584–602. The sample for De la Torre and the combined sample for all his opponents are practically equal in length.

obstacle; for De la Torre, it was a matter of national security and pride.

De la Torre's identification of the Justo administration with alien packinghouse interests put the government in an extremely awkward position. Silence would amount to a confession of guilt. But in order to defend itself, the administration would partly have to defend the packers—as in Pinedo's exculpation of Swift & Company on the matter of taxes—and this, in turn, would only reinforce the impression of official complicity with the packers. Playing adroitly upon this theme, De la Torre thus employed anti-imperialism for internal political purposes; his target was not so much the packers as it was the Concordancia.

It was in his particular usage of anti-imperialism that De la Torre made his special contribution to the ideology—not, as myth would hold, in the fact that he used it at all. Though other politicians had resorted to anti-imperialism in the politics of beef, none had employed it as part of a broadside attack on the aristocracy and the government in general. Despite strong traces of traditionalism, most notably in his pleas for rural livestock breeders, De la Torre considerably broadened the appeal of anti-imperialism by purporting to speak in behalf of middle- and lower-class groups throughout the entire country.

The scope of De la Torre's statements prevents his rhetoric from being neatly placed into the "traditional" or "modern" categories. Generally speaking, he tried to play both ends against the middle: as he sought to improve the lot of some stockmen, he also flirted with the swelling urban masses. And while his argument carried anti-oligarchic content, his concern for the livestock producers revealed no burning desire to overthrow the established system or stage a social revolution. It is precisely this ambiguity—the nonrevolutionary opposition to the aristocracy and foreign investment—that has recently frustrated and annoyed spokesmen for the Argentine left. Roughly since the middle 1940s, modern leftists, particularly urban-oriented Marxists, have tried to claim anti-imperialism as their exclusive ideological property. Yet De la Torre had shown that it could be used for the promotion of rural cattle-owning interests, and thus pre-empted much of their popular appeal.

Though De la Torre's usage of nationalism helped to mobilize lower-class groups in Argentina, it also contributed to their frustration. Awakened by the debate, as well as by other means, the masses were confronted with a closed political system that offered no access to power. With the elections betrayed by fraud, the Congress stripped of its functions, and the Executive controlled by aristocrats, there were no institutions through which these groups could press their grievances and demands. As we shall later see, the mobilization of the masses for the sake of intraclass conflict involved a risky game of political brinkmanship.

THE POPULAR RESPONSE

Despite the breadth of De la Torre's plea, there was little manifest reaction among institutionalized interest groups. The magazine *La Res*, concerned with matters of livestock production, asserted that De la Torre's accusations were grossly unfair to the packers.[34] The *Anales* of the Argentine Rural Society, itself under fire from the Senator, generally maintained a discreet and diplomatic silence.[35] Remarkably enough, CARBAP had nothing to say about the debate either. *Buenos Aires y La Pampa,* the association's monthly review, made only the vaguest passing reference to the Senate investigation.[36] The livestock breeders, in whose name De la Torre purported to speak, failed to recognize him as the champion of their own cause! Their silence can probably be explained by changes in the government's policy on beef, partly in response to De la Torre's needling, and by an improvement in their economic lot. While things were going well, as shown in the next chapter, they did not want to rock the boat.[37] Besides, their interests were not entirely the same as De la Torre's. He was fighting a largely political battle against the Concordancia; CARBAP was concerned with the economic welfare of the breeders.

Nor did outside sectors commit themselves on the debate. *La Tierra,* of the Agrarian Federation, deplored the death of Bordabehere but took no sides on the issues.[38] The C.G.T. and the Industrial Union ignored the entire affair. Given the weakness of the political opposition to the Concordancia, outside groups were not about to support attacks on the administration unless their own interests were at stake; nationalism, as preached by De la Torre, could not acquire their allegiance. In this sense, the government's effort to restrict the participation of the audience met with total success.

But De la Torre did manage to awaken some interest among the public at large. The debate was closely followed in the press, and editors freely expressed their opinions. Quite a few atti-

---

[34] III, no. 36 (July 5, 1935), 2221–22; no. 37 (July 20, 1935), 2271–72.

[35] The Society defended itself from the charges made by De la Torre in a meeting of the Board of Directors, but made no really public declaration. *Anales,* LXIX, no. 7 (July, 1935), 527.

[36] I, no. 3 (June, 1935), 7.

[37] Praise for De la Torre came later, when the breeders were locked in combat with the fatteners. See Olariaga, *El ruralismo argentino,* pp. [236]–69.

[38] July 26, 1935.

tudes were negative. The arch-conservative *La Fronda* upheld
the Concordancia argument and repeatedly slashed at De la
Torre.[39] The *Review of the River Plate*, prestigious and pro-
British, scored De la Torre's political aspirations and dismissed
his remarks for their "sour antagonism, unscrupulous, unrea-
soning acerbity, senile petulance, and self-centered susceptibil-
ity." [40] Nevertheless *La Prensa,* one of Buenos Aires' most re-
spectable dailies, caught an apparently general mood:

> We believe that we are in the presence of one of the most useful parlia-
> mentary labors ever realized until now in the country, and the fact that
> it has been beclouded by a crime that constitutes a great shame, does not
> detract from its importance. The Senate investigation has by several years
> advanced the solution, which cannot be simple, of the national livestock
> problem and its relationship to the domestic and foreign meat trade. . . .
> From today onward, neither the present administration nor its succes-
> sors will be able to remain impassive before the monopolistic procedures,
> legal transgressions, and tax evasions which have been demonstrated [in
> the debate] without the risk of incurring the most severe moral sanctions
> from public opinion.[41]

Through De la Torre's efforts and the sheer drama of the
affair, the politics of beef captured the popular imagination.
Yet it also contributed to popular frustration; open debate on
the issue was henceforth muted, and the decay of the political
system was exposed. As *La Prensa* foresaw, the public would
eventually respond with sanctions of its own.

[39] July 3, 1935. Almost every issue of *La Fronda* published during the month
of July 1935 carried some caustic remarks about De la Torre.
[40] July 5, 1935, 3; and see July 12, 1935, 5–7.
[41] July 31, 1935; and see *La Nación,* July 24, 1935.

VIII

The Struggle for Control

THE last major rural conflict in the Argentine beef industry involved bitter rivalry between cattle breeders and fatteners over control of the two institutions created by the 1933 Meat Law, the National Meat Board and the Argentine Meat Producers' Corporation (CAP). Paradoxically enough, a period of workable consensus followed the Great Debate of 1935; then, as the decade wore on, a series of skirmishes among the ranchers turned into political warfare. In contrast to previous struggles, these battles were fought mostly within and over semipublic institutions, and did not arouse much outside popular interest. Congressional and public concern for the beef industry declined, and intergroup issues were more often resolved by the Executive than by parliament.

As these struggles were developing, the national presidency passed from General Justo to Roberto M. Ortiz, another Anti-Personalist Radical, in 1938. The Concordancia continued to control Executive power under the new President, a civilian, and the ministerial appointments revealed a persisting alliance between the landed aristocracy and the armed forces. Even so, some slight but significant changes took place. Cattlemen obtained a bit less direct representation in the Cabinet than before, though Ortiz belonged to the Rural Society, and the Ministry of Agriculture was given to José Padilla, a sugar-cane grower from Tucumán. Increasing social mobility was also demonstrated by the rising prominence of the upper middle class, which held half the new portfolios. It also appears that Ortiz hoped to rehabilitate the decaying institutions of the State, especially the Congress. Whatever alterations Ortiz might have sought to make in the political system were nullified, however, when ill health later forced him to turn the presidency over to Ramón Castillo, ultraconservative aristocrat from Catamarca. Although the Personalist Radicals dropped their policy of electoral abstention in the mid-1930s and gained sizable representation in the Chamber of Deputies, the Concordancia still reigned supreme.

A PERIOD OF PEACE

As seen in the previous chapter, there was actually little breeder-fattener conflict at the time of the De la Torre investigation. The fatteners had every reason to be content. Their economic fortunes were improving, as their cost-price margins yielded solid profits (see Figure 6.2). They also maintained great political influence. They controlled the Rural Society, they were highly connected in the Justo administration, and, as will be described below, they had acquired strong representation on the Meat Board.

In the meantime, the breeders drew substantial satisfaction from the early operations of the Meat Board, which looked into local market conditions, sought new outlets abroad, and studied the problems of classification and grading. By far its most significant act was the creation of the CAP, "so as to assure reasonable returns to the ranchers." [1] Placed under the leadership of Horacio V. Pereda, an energetic breeder, the CAP immediately subcontracted its 11 per cent quota under the Roca-Runciman Pact to private packinghouses, principally the Sansinena and the Smithfield & Argentine; this way the packers could gain from the increase in volume while the CAP could enter the trade without delay and also get some experience. In the domestic market, the Corporation openly tried to favor "the small

[1] For a review of early Meat Board policy see Junta Nacional de Carnes, *Informe de la labor realizada desde el 1o de enero de 1934 hasta el 30 de septiembre de 1935* (Buenos Aires, 1935). The statutes of the Meat Producers' Corporation appear on pp. 7–16.

Figure 8.1.   *Chiller Prices at Liniers and on Ranches*

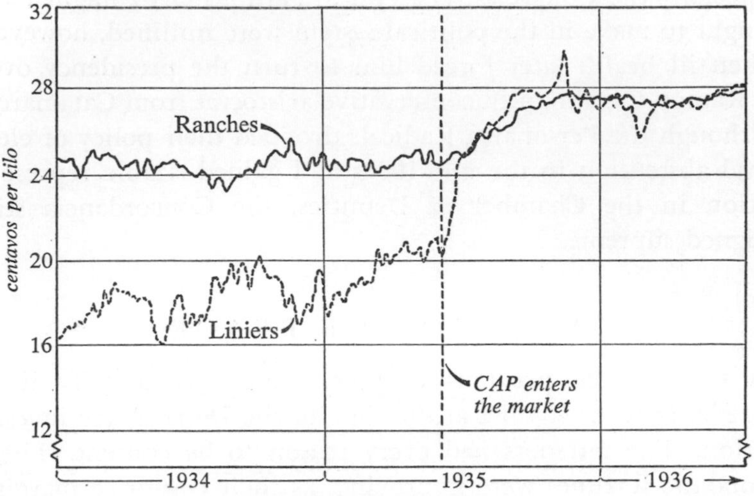

Source: Corporación Argentina de Productores de Carne, *Memoria y balance,*
VII (Buenos Aires, 1942), Gráfico no. 8, part 1.

producer" by purchasing stock at Liniers, rather than on
ranches,[2] and offering market information through a paper entitled *Acción Rural*. As the CAP became one of the country's
largest buyers of cattle, the volume of slaughters increased [3] and
prices also improved: there was a general upward trend, shown
in the figure above, while Liniers prices moved into line with
those on the ranches for the first time. Though some of these
developments were undoubtedly due to an over-all amelioration
of economic conditions, the Corporation was fulfilling its purposes with determination and success.

For a while it even looked as though this state of euphoria
would survive the renegotiation of the Roca-Runciman Pact in
1936. Under mounting pressure from cattle-raising constituents,
the British government announced its intention to place a heavy

[2] Corporación Argentina de Productores de Carne, *Memoria y balance,* II
(Buenos Aires, 1937), 7; also see the CAP's report on *La Corporación en el
mercado de Liniers: hacienda para consumo* (Buenos Aires, 1937). Breeder support
for the Liniers Market was demonstrated in a CARBAP resolution of November
1936: CARBAP, *Recopilación,* p. 260.
[3] Junta Nacional de Carnes, *Estadísticas básicas,* p. 8.

import duty on beef from the Plate as soon as the original treaty expired.[4] Argentina's ranchers were indignant: as *Buenos Aires y La Pampa* angrily advised, John Bull must learn "not to spit at the sky, because then he'll get hit in the face." [5] After months of strenuous bargaining a compromise was reached. In exchange for an import tax, reduced to roughly 20 per cent of the total sale price, His Majesty's Government agreed to recognize Argentine control over the distribution of meat export licenses and take this "into consideration" when setting up its import regulations.[6]

When ranching spokesmen wondered how these provisions might be applied,[7] they promptly got their answer. On December 30, 1936 Minister of Agriculture Miguel Ángel Cárcano made it clear that the Argentine government planned to use control over export licenses in order to sustain a minimum price. Any packinghouse that failed to pay "reasonable and equitable" prices for livestock, Cárcano announced, would have its license cancelled by the government.[8] Furthermore, the Justo administration decided to supplement this plan with a temporary subsidy for cattle prices.[9] For the first time since 1923, a minimum price had official support.

At this stage, governmental policy looked favorable to all Argentine stockmen, the breeders as well as the fatteners. In December 1936, CARBAP openly praised the "beneficent"

4 See official British statements on "The Livestock Situation," *Parliamentary Papers*, 1933–34 (Cd. 4651), XXI, 561–64; and "Import of Meat into the United Kingdom: Statement of the Views of His Majesty's Government in the United Kingdom," *Ibid.*, 1934–35 (Cd. 4828), XVII, 755–60.

5 II, no. 14 (May, 1936), 15. Also see the comments in *Anales*, XXX, no. 9 (September, 1936), 7–8; *La Res*, IV, no. 58 (June, 1936), 3389; and CARBAP, *Recopilación*, pp. 347–48.

6 A text of the 1936 treaty is in *Senadores*, 1936, III (December 29), 514–16.

7 *Buenos Aires y La Pampa*, II, no. 21 (December, 1936), 5–6, 32–34; *Anales*, LXX, no. 12 (December, 1936), 907–9; and *La Res*, IV, no. 71 (December, 1936), 4277.

8 Junta Nacional de Carnes, *Discursos pronunciados por el Excmo. Señor Presidente de la Nación, General Agustín P. Justo, Ministro de Agricultura de la Nación, Doctor Miguel A. Cárcano, y palabras del Señor Presidente de la Junta Nacional de Carnes, Doctor Horacio N. Bruzone, con motivo de la visita al local de la entidad, el día 30 de diciembre de 1936* (Buenos Aires, 1937), p. 11.

9 An original text of the decree is in the *Informe del Comité Mixto*, pp. 27–28.

action of the Meat Board.[10] The following year, the rancher consensus was clearly illustrated after a handful of fatteners, objecting to the compulsory contributions, challenged the constitutionality of the Meat Law—thereby implicating both the Meat Board and the CAP. Realizing the danger of this threat, the Argentine Rural Society called a meeting of livestock representatives at Buenos Aires' glittering Teatro Colón in December 1937. Breeders and fatteners alike rallied to the cause, applauding numerous speeches defending the law—including an address by President Justo himself.[11] This extraordinary display of solidarity serves to demonstrate one fundamental point: squabbles might develop over the interpretation, specifications, or application of the Meat Law, but there was never any doubt in the minds of most stockmen that the protection it provided was both desirable and necessary.

SEEDS OF DISCORD

Ironically enough, it was the Meat Board's application of its minimum-price policy, particularly the subsidy decree, that would ultimately begin to divide the ranks of Argentine cattlemen. Faced with the British import tax, the Board decided to adopt a policy of "solidary action" with the packers. Initiated in December 1936, this "Integral Plan for the Meat Trade" essentially stipulated that if the packers would pay a minimum price for chiller cattle (26 centavos per kilo at first) the Argentine government would not alter the distribution of export quotas, thus leaving the foreign-owned packinghouses with 85 per cent of the trade.[12] In a further effort to cooperate, the Meat Board announced its intention to use the subsidy program to split the 33-peso British import duty among the three interested

10 *Buenos Aires y La Pampa*, II, no. 21 (December, 1936), 32–34. For an earlier comment see II, no. 17 (August, 1936), 9.

11 See *Anales*, LXXII, no. 1 (January, 1938), 5–71. CARBAP support was pledged in November 1937: CARBAP, *Recopilación*, pp. 232–34. After years of litigation the law was ruled constitutional. See Junta Nacional de Carnes, *Constitucionalidad de la ley 11.747* (Buenos Aires, 1944).

12 A full explanation of the Integral Plan is given in Junta Nacional de Carnes, *Respuestas del Poder Ejecutivo Nacional a los pedidos de informes de las HH. CC. de Senadores y Diputados de la Nación, sobre cumplimiento de la ley 11.747* (Buenos Aires, n.d.), pp. 119–28.

parties—the Argentine government, the stockmen, and the packers—but supplied the subsidy *only for chilled beef* and not the lower grades of meat. The decision was apparently based on the idea that chilled beef suffered most from the British tax, and that chilled beef prices set the trends for other types as well.

In addition to this preferential treatment of chiller steers, the Meat Board took measures which restricted the operations of the CAP. Toward the middle of 1937, in alleged fulfillment of its obligations to urban consumers, the Board decreed that limits should be placed on the sale of meat by auction in the city of Buenos Aires. This would repress speculation, eliminate unnecessary intermediaries, and improve hygienic conditions.[13] Yet it would also reduce the commercial freedom of the CAP, which sold large quantities of meat in Buenos Aires through the auction procedure.

A more important policy decision concerned the disbursement of Meat Board funds. In April 1937, CAP president Pereda declared that it was "indispensable" for a truly independent Corporation to have its own packinghouse, instead of leasing its quota.[14] Soon after this statement, Horacio Bruzone, president of the Board, noted some unhygienic and uneconomical aspects of the Liniers Market and local distributing facilities. "The problem," as Bruzone saw it, "is one of cold storage rooms and not of packing plants." As a practical recommendation, the Meat Board proposed the establishment of a Livestock and Meat Market system (*Mercados de Haciendas y Carnes*) for the general purpose of constructing or acquiring cattle markets, meat markets, and cold storage space throughout the entire country. The program could be financed with funds raised under the Meat Law. Acceding to this advice, the Justo administration promptly founded the Markets organization by presidential decree.[15]

The creation of the Markets brought a halt to financial sup-

[13] Junta Nacional de Carnes, *Informe de la labor realizada desde 1935 hasta 1937*, pp. 88–89, 175–77. A full text of the decree is in *Buenos Aires y La Pampa*, III, no. 25 (April, 1937), 155–59.

[14] *Buenos Aires y La Pampa*, III, no. 25 (April, 1937), 149–50; editorial approval is on 154–55.

[15] Junta Nacional de Carnes, *Informe de la labor realizada desde 1935 hasta 1937*, pp. 36–49.

port for the CAP, as the funds that were previously given to the Corporation—80 per cent of the total Meat Board revenues, as stipulated by the law of 1933—were now diverted to the Markets. In mid-1937 CAP payments were stopped. This meant, of course, that the Corporation would not be able to obtain its own packinghouse. Financially, the CAP and the Livestock and Meat Markets seemed to be mutually exclusive entities.

During this period the Meat Board also worked on the classification and grading of cattle, which was widely regarded as a means of gaining protection against discriminatory treatment from the packers. Yet nothing of practical value was accomplished. In June 1936 a system was imposed on transactions at Liniers, but soon had to be dropped because the packers—who opposed the establishment of any such standards—sidestepped the new regulations by making virtually all their purchases on the ranches. This only drove the Liniers prices down, so the abortive attempt was abandoned.[16] In the wake of this failure, the Meat Board appointed a committee to study the problem and draft new classification proposals.

COMPLAINTS OF THE BREEDERS

As the Meat Board pursued its general policy of "solidary action" with the packers, the breeders—as represented by CARBAP—formulated a series of specific and ardent complaints.[17] Their basic charge was that the Meat Board promoted the interests of the fatteners only. The roots of this issue ran back to the problem of representation. Despite the breeders' partial triumph on this question in the 1933 congressional debates, the Board was largely controlled by the fatteners. Of the

16 *Ibid.*, pp. 111–13. Interestingly enough, the packers reportedly considered the plan for classification and grading "the most dangerous" of all the provisions in the Meat Law. N.A., D.S., 835.6582/80, 83, memos by J. C. Pool, September 1 and October 3, 1933.

17 The most comprehensive statement of the breeders' position is in a CARBAP petition submitted to both houses of Congress in July 1939. See Diputados, 1939, II (July 13), 328–61; and CARBAP, *Recopilación*, pp. 759–83. Also see the article entitled "Cuarenta razones que justifican una enérgica intervención del Gobierno y del Parlamento" in *Edición Rural*, June 14, 1940.

20 governmental or rancher representatives who served on the Board from 1934 to 1945, at least ten owned land in the fattening zones. More specifically, the organization was dominated by delegates from the 1932–33 Board of Directors of the Argentine Rural Society, which had proposed the original Meat Law and taken a pro-fattener stand itself. Horacio Bruzone, previous president of the Society, was made president of the Meat Board, and no less than seven of the men who had served with him in the Society received presidential appointments to the Board at one time or another. Through their influence with the Executive, the fatteners had secured disproportionate control over the policies of the Meat Board.[18]

This imbalance was further aggravated by a 1939 order which decreed that rural societies of the interior which distributed dividends to their associates could not participate in the elections for representatives on the Meat Board. Furthermore, votes were to be counted according to the number of members in each society—rather than one vote for each—the only reservation being that no single association could have more than one-third of the total votes.[19] In an angry gesture of protest, CARBAP and other institutions claimed that these regulations would unjustly reduce the representation of many breeders and they boycotted the following elections to the Board.[20]

In view of this inequitable representation, the breeders declared that official policy favored the fatteners in numerous ways. They complained about classification and grading. On the face of it, the application of such a system should be desirable to all cattlemen, since it would prevent discriminatory purchasing practices by the packers. Classification was particularly important to the breeders, though, because it would prohibit the favoritism with which the packers treated many of the large-

18 See the CARBAP petition, Diputados, 1939, II (July 13), 329, and CARBAP, *Recopilación*, pp. 235–50. It should be noted that Horacio Pereda, the first president of the CAP, also served on the Rural Society's Board of Directors in 1932–33.

19 Both decrees were dated July 28, 1939, and can be found in the *Novísima recopilación de leyes usuales de la República Argentina,* ed. Orlando Gil Navarro, II (Buenos Aires, 1943), 1012–14.

20 *Edición Rural,* August 23, 1939.

scale fatteners.[21] Yet the Meat Board did nothing practical about it. In CARBAP's opinion, the delay had little to do with the technical complexity so often cited by members of the Meat Board. On the contrary, it merely reflected the Board's desire to perpetuate the system of packer-fattener favoritism.[22]

Breeders also charged that the Meat Board gave undue protection to chilled beef—and therefore to the fatteners. Their most obvious claim concerned the subsidy scheme of December 1936, which was applied only to chilled beef. In fact the subsidy's main practical effect was to increase the profits of the packers, who handled the funds, since the interplay of market forces had ultimately (if somewhat surprisingly) passed the burden of the British import tax onto the British consumer. In the meantime, the struggling producers along the upper Littoral were ignored by the Board. And despite the creation of the Livestock and Meat Markets, no serious effort had been made to expand the domestic market or find new outlets abroad for medium-quality beef.[23]

Arguments over the CAP were both more damaging and more complex. Basically, the breeders asserted that the Meat Board was trying to prevent the CAP from reaching its full potential in the cattle market. One reason was that extended Corporation activity would reduce the packers' profit margins, thus leaving them less resources with which to favor large-scale fatteners. Another was that the CAP, if given the opportunity, would stimulate the Liniers Market; this would offer the breeders an acceptable alternative to selling their stock to the fatteners, thereby driving up the prices that fatteners would have pay for their steers.[24]

In this connection, CARBAP spokesmen charged that the Livestock and Meat Markets was intended to sabotage the CAP. By this argument, the Markets did nothing to strengthen the domestic market; instead of reducing the cost of meat for the

[21] *Buenos Aires y La Pampa,* IV, no. 37 (April, 1938), 173.
[22] CARBAP, *Recopilación,* pp. 305–10.
[23] CARBAP petition, Diputados, 1939, II (July 13), 330.
[24] For a lucid discussion of this point see Pereda, *La ganadería argentina,* pp. 113–15.

consumers, it only added "one more intermediary" to the already crowded local market.[25] More significantly, breeders also maintained that this whole venture had been undertaken in order to divert Meat Law funds away from the CAP and thus make it impossible for the Corporation to get its own packinghouse. CARBAP leaders were quick to point out that deflection of funds from the CAP was illegal, since the Meat Law specifically stated that 80 per cent of its revenue should be turned over to the Corporation. To use the funds in any other way infringed upon the statutory autonomy of the CAP and betrayed a flagrant abuse of power by the Meat Board.[26]

Furthermore, breeders argued that the Meat Board's efforts to elevate cattle prices served only to detract from the resources and efficacy of the CAP. Haphazard subsidy schemes, even when granted to producers of the northern Littoral, wrecked the Liniers Market,[27] and provided no real substitute for the "effective action" of competition from the CAP.[28] Price regulation was not any better. In 1937, under the Integral Plan, the minimum price for chiller steers was steadily raised from 26 to 31 centavos per live kilo. When Bruzone announced his intention to push up the price to 32 centavos, Corporation managers declared that the boost would drive it into the red. But Bruzone hiked the price.[29] This move seemed to provide still further proof of the Meat Board's conspiracy to rob the CAP of its purpose, restrict its freedom of action, and ultimately force it out of business.

According to some breeder spokesmen, the Meat Board's anti-CAP policy opened such deep divisions within the Corporation's management that it was unable to meet its special obligations. Horacio Pereda resigned from his post because of the Board's decision to set up the Livestock and Meat Markets.

[25] CARBAP petition, Diputados, 1939, II (July 13), 330. *Edición Rural,* March 7, 1939; July 20, 1939; March 28, 1940.

[26] CARBAP, *Recopilación,* pp. 275–76; *Edición Rural,* February 10, 1939.

[27] *Buenos Aires y La Pampa,* III, no. 31 (October, 1937), 640–41.

[28] *Edición Rural,* February 27, 1939.

[29] Junta Nacional de Carnes, *Informe de la labor realizada desde 1935 hasta 1937,* pp. 20–21. The CAP's statement is mentioned in the CARBAP petition, Diputados, 1939, II (July 13), 342.

The cost-price squeeze that followed the 32-centavo price minimum apparently persuaded some directors of the need to reduce losses—that is, to run the CAP as though it were a profit-seeking company and not a service to the producers. These new commercial standards, in turn, led the CAP to make its purchases mainly on the ranches, not at Liniers, thereby abandoning the breeders to their economic fate.[30] (As a matter of fact, official CAP records reveal a 21 per cent drop in Liniers purchases between 1936–37 and 1937–38.)[31] In short, the Corporation was finally compelled to fall in line with the policy of the Meat Board.[32]

From the breeders' viewpoint, the only conceivable solution to this problem was to gain control of the CAP.[33] This would not be easy. Under the Meat Law, shares in the CAP were distributed in accordance with the amount of "contribution" exacted from each cattle seller; and since payment credits generally went to the fatteners and not to the breeders, the fatteners controlled a disproportionate share of stock in the Corporation. The map on page 207 which shows the regional distribution of CAP funds in 1939, clearly illustrates the situation: concentration was much heavier in the fattening zones, which contained about one-quarter of the ranches, than it was in the areas for breeding.

This imbalanced control of the CAP was further distorted by one of the Corporation statutes, which divided stockholders into three separate categories—based on the size of individual contributions, rather than the number of contributors.[34] Since each of these categories had equal representation on the Board

30 *Edición Rural,* May 17, 1939; CARBAP, *Recopilación,* pp. 266–70.

31 Corporación Argentina de Productores de Carne, *Memoria y balance,* VII, 33, Cuadro 2.

32 See the additional complaint in *Edición Rural,* April 14, 1939, over the CAP's failure to protest the Meat Board's distribution of a corned beef contract mainly among the foreign packinghouses.

33 *Edición Rural,* February 28, 1940.

34 With each share worth ten pesos, the categories were as follows: A, those with no more than 75 shares; B, 76–150 shares; C, over 150 shares. As "contributions" amounted to 1 per cent of cattle sales, this meant that ranchers in category C would have to have sold over 150,000 pesos worth of cattle—indeed, a large-scale category.

Regional Distribution
of Contributions
to the CAP, 1939

Breeding Zone

Fattening Zone

*Each dot represents a unit of
funds contributed to CAP.*

Source: Corporación Argentina de Productores de Carne, *Memoria y balance,*
IV (Buenos Aires, 1939), 15.

of Directors, this meant that large-scale cattlemen, who formed
a numerical minority, would have much greater per capita
representation than the smaller ones.[35] So CAP administrative
procedures not only favored the fatteners; they specifically

[35] This stipulation led to a number of electoral absurdities, as shown by
the voting statistics in *Buenos Aires y La Pampa,* VI, no. 62 (1940), 7. CARBAP
discussed the category system in September 1941: CARBAP, *Recopilación,* pp.
254–58.

favored the *large-scale* fatteners. In order to obtain control of the Corporation, the breeders would first have to obtain a change in the statutes.

In summary, the breeders' main arguments concerned four different points: (1) under-representation on the Meat Board; (2) subversion of the CAP by the Meat Board, especially through the diversion of funds to the Livestock and Meat Markets; (3) the Board's failure to establish an effective system of classification and grading; and (4) injustice in CAP voting procedures.

THE REPORT OF THE JOINT COMMITTEE

Into the midst of this mounting quarrel came the report of the Joint Committee of Enquiry into the Anglo-Argentine Meat Trade, set up in accordance with the Roca-Runciman Pact. Issued in September of 1938, it was by far the most impartial and soundly documented investigation that had ever been made into the subject. Beginning in 1935, the Committee had held some 60 meetings, conducted lengthy interviews, and taken testimony on both sides of the Atlantic. As De la Torre—and his opponents—had complained during the Senate investigation, information was difficult to get: almost all the packers, said the report, "definitely refused to give us facilities to collect evidence which we considered necessary." [36] Even so, the findings were highly important.

In its analysis of the Anglo-Argentine commerce, the Committee explained that most of the business was controlled by the meat-packing pool. Before 1933, the packers exercised "a *de facto* monopoly" over the trade. Despite the Roca-Runciman Pact and governmental supervision, competition in the purchase of cattle still "does not normally exist in practice . . . whatever may be the truth as to the way in which the Packing Companies have behaved in the past, the fact remains that they

[36] *Report of the Joint Committee,* p. 5; the report was also issued in an official Spanish edition, which has been cited above.

are in a position which, unless proper safeguards are provided, can be only too easily abused and which in any case is likely to lead to suspicion and misunderstanding." [37]

Because of their economic strength, the packers made profits that were excellent—but difficult to estimate. The companies juggled their accounts, somewhat as De la Torre had claimed, often shifting profits to an international branch. The Committee noted that published statements showed losses in the domestic trade, and broadly hinted—as De la Torre had also suggested—that the companies might be dumping goods on the local market in order to gain ultimate control. Through these and other means the packers maintained "a high level of distributable profit," even during the Depression, passing most of the economic shock on to Argentine stockmen.[38]

In this regard the Joint Committee suggested that the best way to thwart the power and profits of the packers would be to encourage the CAP. By competing in the trade, the CAP would be able to determine how and to what extent the packers sought to abuse or monopolize the market. In the Committee's opinion, "the activities of the Corporación have, up to the present, not been developed to their full potentiality." The report strongly recommended that the CAP's participation in the meat market be increased as much as possible.[39]

Speaking of profits, the Committee also dealt with the relative position of the breeders and the fatteners. "It is probably true," observed the investigators,

that the position of the fattener is less vulnerable than that of the breeder, for the risk of market fluctuations which he has to run begins nearer to the date of the realization of his product. It would only be natural to expect the fattener to adjust his principal working expense, namely the prices which he pays to the breeder for calves and fattening steers, according to the market conditions at the time of purchase, and thereafter he has to carry the risk of the market for only about a year. The breeder, on the other hand, would not appear to have the same control over his working costs, while he cannot, without going out of business altogether,

[37] *Report*, pp. 17, 34, 36–38.
[38] *Ibid.*, pp. 56, 63.
[39] *Ibid.*, p. 12.

make any important reduction in his operations, and his decision whether to make any reduction at all has to be taken as long as two and even two-and-a-half years before the first realization of the cattle produced.[40]

In other words, the workings of the market favored the fattener more than the breeder.

Turning to another issue, the Joint Committee stated that the Meat Law's provision for a system of classification and grading had so far had "little practical effect pending the prescription of the necessary official standards." Sansinena, Gualeguaychú, and the CAP had adopted private systems for any producers prepared to accept them, but that was all. If the task was complex, the need for decisive action was also very great: the Meat Board should try to set up standards "as soon as possible." [41]

Aside from the proposals for classification and grading and the strengthening of the CAP, the report ended with a general set of recommendations concerning two major problems: (1) controlling the profits of the packers and (2) adjusting supply and demand through improvements in market intelligence, cultivation of the domestic market, and numerous other measures. On all these counts, it should be noted, the Joint Committee called for the intensification of activity in the beef trade by the Argentine State.

This report was vastly significant—not only for its dispassionate dissection of the beef trade, but also because of its relationship to the growing conflict between Argentine ranchers. Breeders immediately claimed that the Joint Committee confirmed the validity of their grievances. The report showed that breeders suffered more economic hardship than fatteners—a fact which, according to CARBAP, would justify separate representation on the Meat Board; the activities of the packers were suspicious; classification and grading were badly needed; and the CAP, above all, must be greatly fortified.[42] In this way

40 *Ibid.*, p. 29.
41 *Ibid.*, pp. 14, 33.
42 See the message from CARBAP to the Minister of Agriculture in *Buenos Aires y La Pampa*, IV, no. 43 (October, 1938), 157–58; and also *Ibid.*, IV, no. 44 (November, 1938), 23–26. Almost a year later, *Edición Rural* printed the

the Joint Committee's report gave CARBAP and the breeders the courage of their convictions and, if anything, stepped up the energy of their campaign against the fatteners.

CONGRESSIONAL ACTIVITY

Like most previous fights within the beef industry, the struggle between livestock breeders and fatteners eventually reached the halls of Congress. In July 1938, just after a spirited CARBAP assembly, virtually identical requests for explanations of government policy were made in the Senate and Chamber of Deputies, both by Radical lawyers from Entre Ríos. Almost all the familiar questions were raised: what had the Meat Board done about classification and grading, how much money had been invested in the Livestock and Meat Markets, had funds been withheld from the CAP, what steps had the Meat Board taken to uphold the price of lower-grade cattle, whether the Board was seeking to open new markets abroad or expand the domestic one, how the export quotas had been distributed, whether the composition of the Meat Board could or should be changed.[43]

In answer to these demands, Minister of Agriculture Cárcano forged a strongly worded but somewhat elusive response.[44] It was too early, he argued, to say whether the Meat Law should undergo reform; in the meantime, the composition of the Board was strictly in accord with the law. The establishment of regulations for classification and grading (four years after the inauguration of the Board!) was an extremely complex matter that would demand further study. The Markets system complied with the Meat Law's provisions for improvement of the domestic market, and only time could tell if it would be suc-

general conclusions of the Joint Committee's report under the title "Un documento sensacional," June 30, 1939.

[43] Senadores, 1938, I (July 12), 370–71; Diputados, 1938, II (July 13), 729–30.

[44] The Executive's answers to both inquiries are published together in Junta Nacional de Carnes, *Respuestas*. The response to Atanasio Eguiguren is also given in Senadores, 1938, II (September 21), 319–59. The reply to Bernardino Horne's questions is not in the *Diario de Sesiones*, but is mentioned in Diputados, 1938, VI (September 28–29), 3.

cessful; it was by no means intended to conflict with the CAP. The government gave subsidies only to chilled beef because that was the kind that suffered from the British import duty, the tax on lower grades having been absorbed by the British consumer; besides, price movements for chilled set the trends for all the other grades.[45] Cárcano avoided the question of packinghouse profits. From the over-all tone of the Minister's reply, it is clear that the Justo administration wanted to bring conflicts within the country's cattle-producing sector to an end.

But breeder representatives were not satisfied. In September 1938 Juan Carlos Agulla proposed that the government lend 50 million pesos to the CAP "for the construction or acquisition of a central packinghouse." [46] The next year Bernardino Horne publicly criticized Cárcano's statement,[47] and that June a group of National Democrats from Entre Ríos presented a plan to reform the Meat Board and increase breeder representation. The point, as Justo Medina explained, was to end the Board's domination by "members of the governing board of the Argentine Rural Society." [48]

In August 1939, in the Senate, Atanasio Eguiguren introduced two related proposals that would (1) reorganize the composition of the Meat Board along regional lines, while four of the six rancher representatives would have to be breeders; (2) give the breeders share credits for half the contributions to the Corporation; (3) specify that 80 per cent of the funds received by the Meat Board would have to go to the CAP; (4) dissolve the Livestock and Meat Markets; (5) authorize the Corporation to construct its own packinghouse; and (6) reform

---

[45] Governmental spokesmen often stressed this last point. See the comparative price graph in Junta Nacional de Carnes, *Respuestas*, pp. 109–10.

[46] Diputados, 1938, IV (September 13), 773–78. The bill was supported by CARBAP resolutions in November 1938 and May 1939: CARBAP, *Recopilación*, pp. 276–77.

[47] Diputados, 1939, I (May 31), 233–34.

[48] *Ibid.*, 1939, I (June 7), 361–63. A retort by the Rural Society is given in *Ibid.* (June 14), 541. A few years later the bill was reintroduced: Diputados, 1941, II (July 23), 476–79. This time the complaints were answered by Horacio Bruzone, president of the Meat Board: Biblioteca del Congreso, División de Archivo, Museo, y Publicaciones, 1941, Caja 1985, Obras Varias 41.

CAP voting procedures so that two-thirds of its directors would be livestock breeders.[49]

About two weeks later, in the Chamber of Deputies, Nicolás Repetto presented a resolution to interpellate the Minister of Agriculture (at this time Padilla) about the application of the Meat Law and the actions of the Meat Board.[50] The spectacle was reminiscent of the consumer-producer alliance during World War I that helped bring eventual passage of a general anti-trust law: Repetto, Socialist from Buenos Aires and frequent spokesman for lower-class urban consumers, took up the cause of rural cattle breeders, many of whom belonged to the aristocracy. Nor was this an isolated personal whim, since the Socialist paper *La Vanguardia* ran a steady stream of editorials in behalf of the breeders.[51] Though the debate yielded no new information,[52] Repetto's emphasis on the issue suggests that rural conflicts could still influence the political loyalties and actions of an urban audience.

None of this congressional activity yielded any positive or concrete results. The various proposals for helping the CAP, reforming the Meat Law, or changing the Meat Board were all shunted off to uninterested committees; not one of the initiatives was ever brought to the floor for debate. The efforts no doubt tended to crystallize and publicize the issues, but also revealed the futility of parliamentary action. If the breeders wanted truly effective political representation, they would have to look outside the Congress.

Despite the inefficacy of these proposals and statements, their political origin helps shed light upon the basic character of the conflict. First, both sides were represented mainly by uncharismatic and upper-class adherents of the Concordancia (particularly National Democrats); fatteners drew support from

[49] Senadores, 1939, I (August 22), 548–52. CARBAP support for the plan is given in *Edición Rural,* September 7, 1939.

[50] Diputados, 1939, IV (September 8), 32–34.

[51] Most of these editorials were quoted by *Edición Rural* throughout the year 1939.

[52] Diputados, 1939, IV (September 26–27), 813–83.

the provinces of Córdoba and Buenos Aires while several breeder spokesmen came from Entre Ríos, but these regional overtones did not define the issue. Even in the political arena, this was an economic struggle between cattle breeders and fatteners. Second, both sides recruited representatives primarily from non-livestock professions: doctors, lawyers, one sugar-cane grower. Though fighting among themselves, cattlemen spoke out less and less in their own behalf. What this illustrates, again, is professionalization; to an increasing degree, politics was becoming the province of politicians.

INTERVENTION OF THE
EXECUTIVE POWER

The resolution of the breeder-fattener conflicts was brought about not by the Congress but by the Executive branch of the government. This was due partly to the nature of the struggle: since the battles were being fought within and over institutions set up by the State, they could be decided simply by decree. It also derived from widespread awareness of the weakness of Congress and the decay of the country's representative political system. In addition, this intervention of the Executive revealed a possible shift in the political balance. The breeders, whose political power had always been secondary to that of the fatteners, began to find great influence in the Ministry of Agriculture. With this new resource, they might be able to match or even defeat the economically superior fatteners and their National Meat Board.

In some ways the process began when President Justo replied to pressure from the breeders by proposing a bill that would authorize a loan of 30 million pesos to the CAP for the specific purpose of buying or building a meatpacking plant. Referring to the present system of subcontracts with the private companies, Justo's message flatly stated that the Corporation should not have to "depend on them" for the preparation and sale of its products.[53] Though the President's bill died in the

53 Diputados, 1938, I (May 13), 65–66.

Chamber of Deputies, it still showed some recognition of the breeders' claims.[54]

It was in 1940 that Executive support for the breeders became clearly apparent. In March of that year, the new Minister of Agriculture, Cosme Massini Ezcurra, named a commission to advise the government on the negotiation of international meat contracts. The appointment was significant for two reasons: first, because such advice had previously been taken from the National Meat Board; second, because the breeders got the majority representation.[55] At least on one important matter, the breeders were given a chance to replace the influence of the fattener-oriented Meat Board.[56]

This trend picked up rapidly, as the breeders soon registered a major triumph: dissolution of the Livestock and Meat Markets. In April 1940 the Markets administration buckled under mounting waves of criticism, mainly from the breeders, by resigning en masse. CARBAP continued to press for termination of the entire scheme, although the Argentine Rural Society argued in favor of its reorganization and improvement.[57] Within weeks, the Markets system was undone by presidential decree.[58] To be sure, this was not a clear-cut victory, since the Markets organization partly collapsed of its own accord. But Ezcurra made no attempt to revive or rejuvenate the Markets, as the Rural Society wanted; he just abandoned it. In time, as the breeders had requested for so long,[59] the funds that had been allotted to the Markets were turned back over to the CAP.

Subsequently Daniel Amadeo y Videla, an aristocratic National Democrat from the province of Buenos Aires, took over the portfolio of agriculture. Ministerial representation of the breeders became more and more explicit under his rule. In

[54] Support for the bill came from a CARBAP meeting in May 1938: CARBAP, *Recopilación,* p. 276.

[55] For the text of the decree see the *Boletín Oficial,* April 8, 1940.

[56] See the notes of self-congratulation in *Edición Rural,* March 20 and April 12, 1940.

[57] CARBAP, *Recopilación,* pp. 328–33; *Edición Rural,* April 12, 1940; *Anales,* LXXIX, no. 6 (June, 1940), 483–85.

[58] The text is in *Edición Rural,* May 3, 1940.

[59] See CARBAP, *Recopilación,* pp. 333–35.

January 1941, Amadeo y Videla won the breeders' confidence by asking the Meat Board for information on the problem of classification and grading, then setting up regulations for the sale of consumer cattle. The scheme did not work well, mainly for the same reason that the Meat Board's abortive effort fell through in 1936: the packers dodged the regulation by purchasing stock on the ranches, leaving prices to fall at Liniers.[60] But Amadeo y Videla refused to give up; by the end of the year, in accord with the breeders' longstanding desires, he established permanent and workable norms for the classification and grading of export-type cattle.[61]

Yet the most important action of the Executive concerned the administrative procedures and control of the CAP. The stakes were high. In September 1940 the annual meeting of Corporation stockholders, in which every man had one vote, approved an ambitious plan for the purchase of an extensive packinghouse network stretching from Entre Ríos to Patagonia. That December the Ortiz government sanctioned the measure, giving official permission for the CAP to increase its capital by 30 million pesos in order to complete the purchase.[62] These developments provided the basis for a bitter struggle; breeders favored the purchase plan, which they had pushed through the assembly with their numerical strength, while the fatteners tended to oppose it.

Apparently under pressure from some fatteners, CAP managers called a special assembly of stockholders in July 1941 to reconsider the packinghouse plan. Two days before the meeting, the four leading breeder organizations (CARBAP, Littoral, Middle and Western Littoral, Patagonia) convened in order to coordinate their efforts in favor of the purchase; significantly enough, Amadeo y Videla was present and pledged his support to the scheme. The special assembly then reapproved the plan. "TRIUMPH!" crowed the partisan *Edición Rural,* which de-

[60] *Edición Rural,* January 13 and 27, 1941.

[61] Junta Nacional de Carnes, *Síntesis de la labor desarrollada, 1933–1945* (Buenos Aires, 1945), pp. 59–82.

[62] The text of the decree is in *Buenos Aires y La Pampa,* VI, no. 63 (1940), 20; also see *Edición Rural,* January 10, 1941.

fined the outcome as a victory of the genuine "producers" against "a mixture of fatteners, lawyers, bankers, traders, and auctioneers, whose conduct played into the hands of the interests of the meatpacking monopoly of international capital." [63] Alone, the men of the Argentine pampa defeated a vast and vicious conspiracy.

Reapproval of the plans for CAP packinghouses only broadened the rift between the breeders and the fatteners. At the special assembly, several fatteners brought a censure motion against the directors of the CAP (and found support among four members of the Meat Board, including its vice-president).[64] Within a week after the meeting, dissident stockholders in the Corporation brought suit against the directors, in hopes of having the decision annulled on the grounds that the assembly was illegal. There was even a split within the ranks of the Rural Society, as a group of prominent breeders came out in favor of the CAP purchases, publicly condemned the Board of Directors' opposition to the scheme, and started a campaign to capture control of the Society.[65] The breeder-fattener conflict had never been more open or intense: as both groups fought for their interests, charges of fraud, treachery, and deceit were hurled back and forth. A general assembly of the CAP, scheduled for September 1941, promised to widen the breach even more.

Suddenly the Executive cancelled the assembly and intervened in the Corporation. The breeders supported the move in hopes that it might lead to changes in voting procedures.[66] With a good deal of justice, the Argentine Rural Society pointed out that the intervention was illegal since it violated the autonomy of the CAP.[67] CARBAP acknowledged the juridical problem,

[63] *Edición Rural*, July 18, 1941. Here the term "producers" is used to mean "breeders."

[64] *Ibid.*

[65] For the Society's stand against the purchase plan see *Anales*, LXXIV, no. 10 (October, 1940), 779–813. The internal opposition within the Society is discussed in *Edición Rural*, July 28 and September 19, 1941.

[66] *Buenos Aires y La Pampa*, VI, no. 65 (September, 1941), 12–13, 49–59.

[67] *La Res*, IX, no. 188 (November 5, 1941), 12, 158–60. *La Prensa* also took this stand on November 4, 1941.

but preferred to justify the means in terms of the ends; besides, argued the breeders, if the Corporation had been established by decree it could be changed by decree.[68] The rhetorical paradox is worth noting: CARBAP, which had always defended the autonomy of the CAP against the intrusion of the Meat Board, now freely acquiesced in Amadeo y Videla's intervention; the Rural Society, which in recent years had supported the Meat Board's claim that the CAP was a subordinate entity, stoutly upheld the Corporation's independence.

The climax soon followed. In October 1941 the Executive Power, now under Ramón Castillo, bypassed the Meat Board and decreed that no director of the Corporation could have any connection at all with any organization under the vigilance of laws controlling the meat trade (packinghouses, livestock auction houses, etc.). Even more significant was the abolishment of the hated categories for CAP voting procedures, in a decree that directors should be elected by region and not by the number of shares in the Corporation.[69] At last, the breeders had a chance to gain control of the CAP.

As preparations were made for the next CAP election, the issue was clearly defined as a struggle between the breeders and the fatteners, between the Corporation and the Meat Board.[70] Rivalries were bitter and the campaign was intense. In the end, through their numerical superiority, the breeders won a smashing victory. As *Edición Rural* exulted in the outcome,[71] the new CAP administration consisted entirely of breeders.[72] They finally gained control of the CAP, and the CAP soon had its own meatpacking plants.

IDEOLOGY AND THE SCOPE OF THE STRUGGLE

Throughout this entire struggle for control, the ideological content of the breeder-fattener debates was kept on a generally

[68] *Edición Rural,* September 29, 1941.
[69] *Ibid.,* October 25 and December 19, 1941.
[70] *Ibid.,* March 13, 1942.
[71] *Ibid.,* May 13, 1942.
[72] *Ibid.,* July 14, 1943. This issue lists the occupations of all the CAP directors.

low key. For the most part, nationalistic rhetoric was lacking. This was true despite the breeders' anti-imperialist inclinations, witnessed on multiple occasions above, and even during CARBAP's attack on the Meat Board for its policy of "solidary action" with the packers. In striking contrast to the artful and vociferous anti-imperialism of Lisandro de la Torre, most of the discussion concerned issues and interests rather than matters of doctrine.

This paradox demands a careful explanation. There is no indication that the breeders had lost their nationalistic impulses. From time to time such tendencies showed through, as in *Edición Rural*'s identification of an international conspiracy in the conflict over the CAP. In fact the high priest of cattle breeder ideology was a longtime president of CARBAP, Nemesio de Olariaga, whose most cogent statement of the creed came with the publication of a book called *El ruralismo argentino* in 1943.[73]

This work provided a classic example of what I have described as traditional anti-imperialism. It was anti-modern, anti-urban, anti-foreign, anti-democratic, and highly moralistic. Its content could have been easily used to justify State action in behalf of livestock breeders—and was, but only to a minimal extent in the late 1930s. For Olariaga's avowed purpose in writing the book was not to mobilize support or approval for the breeders' campaign to gain control of the CAP, but to explain Olariaga's own identification with the revolution of 1943, described in the following chapter.[74] So the essential fact remains: despite the intensely nationalistic feeling of the CARBAP leaders, they did not employ anti-imperialism as a major weapon during this battle against the fatteners and the Rural Society over the Meat Board and the CAP.

The basic explanation for the conflict's lack of ideological content appears to lie in the struggle itself. As suggested above, these breeder-fattener battles were largely semipublic. They took place mainly within and over the Meat Board and the CAP, and did not concern non-cattleowning groups in any

73 Cited above.
74 *El ruralismo argentino,* pp. 41, 345.

significant way. Despite a few ineffectual proposals, interpellations, and inquiries, Congress did not arbitrate the fights;
settlements came through the Executive power. There was no
real audience for the debates. It was therefore unnecessary for
the stockmen, breeders or fatteners, to identify their interests
with Argentine national sovereignty. Rather than talk about
the opponents' alleged connection to foreign capital, as
Lisandro de la Torre had done, they merely talked about each
other. Rhetoric would have mostly been a waste of energy and
time.

In view of this situation, it should come as no surprise that
outside sectors failed to participate directly in breeder-fattener
politics. As on other occasions, the C.G.T. maintained absolute
silence. The wheat farmers and the industrialists did not take
any sides either. But they did acknowledge the conflict, possibly
because of the popular interest in beef politics awakened by
the Senate debate of 1935.

In this connection, the central preoccupation of the wheat
growers' Agrarian Federation did not so much concern the
struggles between the different stockmen as the rivalry between
agricultural and pastoral sectors. Departing from its fraternal
opinion of the early 1930s, *La Tierra* took a deeply hostile view
of ranchers in general. First, wheat farmers resented the lavish
attention paid to livestock matters by the Concordancia administrations—as one editorial griped, "We are regarded as
inferior to cattle." Second, attacks on the leisurely existence of
aristocratic cattle barons reflected a renewal of the longstanding
quarrel between cattlemen as landowners and wheat farmers
as tenants. Third, the Federation denounced the CARBAP
and other local rural societies for trying to enlist farmers in
their ranks, "sowing confusion everywhere and debilitating
the true agrarian organizational movement of the country." [75]
This is a significant complaint. Offhand, one might have expected an alliance between these two groups, based on their
mutual opposition to the Rural Society and what they called

[75] *La Tierra,* July 18, 1941; also February 10, April 18, April 21, and October
6, 1939.

the ranching "oligarchy." As another indication of organizational modernization in the rural sector, however, the institutions fought because their functions were specific, distinct—and perhaps narrowly perceived. Given its opposition to all cattlemen, therefore, the Federation did not join the politics of beef.

The Industrial Union also abstained from positive action in the breeder-fattener struggles, but revealed a growing rivalry with the cattle-producing sector. Like the wheat farmers, manufacturers repeatedly complained about the excessive governmental attention to matters of livestock. In apparently rising opposition to the traditional export-import economic structure, too, the Union made frequent demands for tariff protection—sometimes against the wishes of the ranchers. As a matter of fact, the Union objected to Justo's proposal for creating a CAP packinghouse—not out of any solidarity with the fatteners or private packers, but because one of the bill's clauses would have permitted the free importation of machinery and materials necessary for the plant's construction. At the same time, disclaimers about antagonism between the industrial and pastoral sectors revealed a reluctance to engage in an all-out war with the cattlemen.[76] The Union's attitude was ambiguous: it pursued interests of its own, in occasional opposition to the stockmen, but shied away from outright conflict.

To summarize, livestock breeders managed to gain some significant victories over the fatteners in the semipublic battles of the late 1930s. This outcome indicates that, for the first time in all the conflicts connected with beef, political action could bring meaningful redress for economic grievances—but with two important limitations. One, the fights between breeders and fatteners took place essentially *within* the rural upper class. Two, effective influence resided in the Executive branch of government, not the discredited Congress. So these develop-

[76] *Boletín*, L, no. 818 (February, 1937), 8; LII, no. 852 (December, 1939), 55–57; LV, no. 882 (June, 1942), 31–33. Opposition to the CAP packinghouse plan is in the *Boletín*, LI, no. 838 (October, 1938), 6–7; and Biblioteca del Congreso, División de Archivo, Museo, y Publicaciones, 1938, Caja 1683, Expediente 463.

ments do not necessarily reveal any increase in the absorptive capacity of Argentina's political system; if they pointed to modernization, they occurred within exclusive circles. How the country's leadership responded to demands from other groups is the subject of the following chapter.

IX

Realignment of the Conflict

THE Rural Society's livestock exposition of 1939 was an elegant occasion.[1] Dressed in morning coats and top hats, their ladies puffed and powdered in the latest Paris fashion, Argentina's leading landowners came out to watch the parade of champions in the show ring at Palermo. A military escort ushered President Roberto M. Ortiz to his place of honor, and then Adolfo M. Bioy, president of the Society, began the round of speeches. His discourse struck a strangely discordant note: "The cattle ranch," contended Bioy, "was never the residential fief of an idle lord, indulging himself on the labor of his serfs; the ranch was always the laboratory, the storage place for tools of work; it was not and is not defended by moats or ramparts, and if it has a door it has no lock. It must be seen from the countryside, and the vast countryside . . . must be seen from it." [2] An apology like this, under conditions like these, was completely without precedent. It provides eloquent testimony to the shifting social, economic, and political forces of the time.

What Bioy's comment essentially recognized was the rising restlessness of the nation's urban masses. As shown in Chapter I, social and economic changes were producing a large and active working class. By 1947, Greater Buenos Aires accounted for 28 per cent of the national population; about 60 per cent of the city's inhabitants belonged to the lower class.[3] Some of these

[1] Some of the material in this chapter appears in my article on "Social Mobilization, Political Participation, and the Rise of Juan Perón," forthcoming in the *Political Science Quarterly*.

[2] *Anales*, LXXIII, no. 9 (September, 1939), 5.

[3] Germani, *Estructura social*, pp. 67, 69, 210.

people had been "pushed" from the countryside by the difficulties of finding jobs or land; others were attracted by the "pull"
of urban comforts and employment. Indirectly protected by the
reduction of world trade, Argentina's industrial output was
growing faster than the gross national product, and also showed
structural changes: quickly gathering momentum, manufacturing and some "heavy" activities were gaining predominance
over the preparation of textiles and foodstuffs.[4] At any rate, by
socio-economic standards, members of the working class were
highly mobilized.[5] They were urban, they were literate, they
were often migrants, they had jobs.

Eventually, they began making demands on the nation's political system. Under the Saenz Peña law, many of them voted
in elections. Table 9.1 indicates the growth of a "mass" political
audience in Buenos Aires; it also shows that voter participation
in the capital city, with its large lower class, consistently outstripped the national average.[6] Before 1930, however, lower-
class voters seem to have been responding to political initiatives of the upper and middle classes in a generally passive way.
After that date, their posture appears to have become more
aggressive—as suggested by Buenos Aires' repeated opposition
to the pro-aristocratic Concordancia.[7]

Even as lower-class groups exerted pressure for change, the
political system was disrupted by another revolution. On June
4, 1943 a group of military officers known as the "G.O.U." suddenly took over the government and set up a dictatorship.[8]
Conservative Catholic nationalists under General Pedro Ramí-

[4] Economic Commission for Latin America (United Nations), "El desarrollo
económico de la Argentina," E/CN.12/429/Add. 4, Pág. 4; IV° censo general de
la Nación, III (Buenos Aires, 1947), 15; and Dorfman, Evolución, p. 115.

[5] For a discussion of this concept see Deutsch, "Social Mobilization."

[6] The progressive decline in the proportion of unnaturalized immigrants
greatly expanded the electorate. In the presidential elections of 1916, barely
50 per cent of the adult male population was registered to vote; in 1946, about
73 per cent was registered. Ministerio del Interior, Las fuerzas armadas, I, 368,
and II, 431–548; and IV° censo general de la Nación, I, 5.

[7] See data in Ministerio del Interior, Las fuerzas armadas, I, 464, 476,
589–90.

[8] The letters are generally said to stand for "Grupo de Oficiales Unidos," but
other variants include "Grupo Obra de Unificación" and "Gobierno, Orden,
Unión." Whitaker, Argentina, p. 103n.

Table 9.1. *Participation in Selected Elections, 1912–1946* [9]

Year	Nation		City of Buenos Aires	
	Registered (Thousands)	% Voted	Registered (Thousands)	% Voted
1912	934	68.6	126	84.1
1920	1,445	53.1	222	73.0
1928	1,808	80.9	304	91.6
1934	2,395	65.1	415	80.2
1938	2,745	67.9	492	77.9
1940	partial elections	70.1	509	80.9
1946	3,480	82.2	694	82.9

Source: Ministerio del Interior, *Las fuerzas armadas,* I, 331, 340, 383–87, 427–28, 481, 592–95, 600, 602; II, 431–548.

rez dominated the regime at first, and showed no particular inclination to aid the urban masses. In March 1944 a colonels' clique, led by the able and ambitious Juan Domingo Perón, pushed aside the right-wing rulers. As Edelmiro Farrell stepped into the presidency, Perón took over both the vice-presidency and the Ministry of War—in addition to retaining his position in the Secretariat of Labor and Social Security, which he had run since October 1943. With this multiple leverage, he forged a formidable alliance between the military and the lower-class *descamisados* (literally, "shirtless ones") of the city. After falling out with Farrell, he launched his "impossible candidacy" for the presidency [10] and won the 1946 elections with a thumping 56 per cent majority.

In retrospect, it is quite clear that Perón exploited the working class for the sake of his own ambitions. But why did the urban masses support him in the first place? Why did they regard his dictatorship as a legitimate government? One way to shed light on these questions, in addition to the other concerns of this book, is to analyze the political activity of two urban

[9] Most of these contests concerned only congressional representation; presidential elections took place in 1928 and 1946. Data for the 1940 elections in the province of San Luis have been added to the national totals for 1934 and 1938, as that province did not hold elections in those years.

[10] See Robert J. Alexander, *The Perón Era* (New York, 1951), pp. 42–53.

lower-class groups connected with the beef industry: the consumers of municipal Buenos Aires and the packinghouse workers.

THE CONSUMERS AND THE
CITY COUNCIL

As a group, the consumers did not display any notable political power before the 1930s. Just after World War I they helped the ranchers gain passage of a general anti-trust bill, but as junior partners in a tactical alliance; in the mid-1920s the Buenos Aires City Council founded a new municipal packinghouse, but only with the explicit approval of the Argentine Rural Society.[11] Whenever the consumers clashed with cattlemen, they lost. Nor did they show much economic influence. Though the domestic market came to account for over 70 per cent of total beef production,[12] consumers had no cooperative arrangements or other organized means of asserting their potential power. This weakness became painfully apparent in the post-Depression period. Along with the cost of living, prices for beef climbed from an average of 57 centavos per kilo in 1935 to 85 centavos in 1945. The situation was particularly acute from 1942 to 1944, when meat prices rose sharply in relation to the cost-of-living index—and when Perón began his climb to power. In a country that was famous for its cattle, beef was becoming difficult to buy. (See Table 9.2.)

The highly carnivorous Argentines promptly sought to remedy these economic ills through political action, first on the municipal level. It should be noted that ordinances of the City Council were subject to the veto of the Mayor, who was appointed by the President. Possibilities for conflict were particularly apparent in the 1930s, when national politics was dominated by the conservative Concordancia and the most vocal (if not always the largest) group in the Buenos Aires City Council belonged to the Socialist Party.

[11] Concejo Deliberante, 1926, III (December 29), 2523–34.
[12] Junta Nacional de Carnes, *Estadísticas básicas,* p. 8.

Table 9.2. *Beef Prices and the Standard of Living, 1935–1945*
(Index: 1936–39 = 100.00)

	Cost-of-Living Index	*Average Retail* Price of Beef (Pesos/Kilo)	*Index of* Beef Prices
1935	90.4	0.57	91.2
1936	98.1	0.65	104.0
1937	100.7	0.62	99.2
1938	100.0	0.61	97.6
1939	101.6	0.62	99.2
1940	103.9	0.65	104.0
1941	106.6	0.67	107.2
1942	112.6	0.73	116.8
1943	113.9	0.76	121.6
1944	113.6	0.81	129.6
1945	136.0	0.85	136.0

Source: Junta Nacional de Carnes, *Estadísticas básicas,* p. 14.

The pattern of struggle was first revealed in 1932, when an aristocratic Mayor, Rómulo S. Naón, proposed nationalization of the city-owned slaughterhouse. Socialists in the Council bitterly opposed the scheme, loudly proclaiming that it would benefit upper-class cattlemen at the expense of the consumers and (to a lesser extent) the workers in the slaughterhouse. As José M. Penelón declared, urban Buenos Aires would once more become "the specially sacrificed victim of . . . the stockmen and the speculators in land." [13] Despite this opposition, as described in Chapter VI, Naón's recommendation was adopted by the national Congress as part of the 1933 Meat Law.[14]

In March of the following year, a new Mayor—Mariano de Vedia y Mitre, another scion of the landed aristocracy—decreed a change in the working schedule at the municipal slaughterhouse which meant that its beef would reach the markets one

[13] Concejo Deliberante, 1932, III (October 6), 3210.

[14] The Socialists protested again after the passage of the Meat Law, but without success. Concejo Deliberante, 1933, IV (December 28), 4688. Though the plan for nationalization was later abandoned, it was not so much the result of consumer pressure as a policy decision by Horacio Bruzone, president of the Meat Board. Junta Nacional de Carnes, *Informe de la labor realizada desde 1934 hasta 1935,* p. 64.

day after slaughter. Speaking for the consumers again, Socialists complained that the measure would give private and mainly foreign-owned packinghouses a commercial advantage—and lead to a rise in retail prices. After a Socialist move to override the decree was defeated by only one vote (15–14), the Council unanimously approved another proposal to create a committee to investigate the municipal beef business. On the somewhat specious grounds of imprecise language, however, De Vedia y Mitre vetoed the resolution.[15]

Conflicts between the Council and the Mayor soon became a political routine. Late in 1933, Socialists sponsored a measure to expand the city slaughterhouse's control over the local market and presumably keep prices down; the bill was passed by a two-thirds vote, then vetoed by the Mayor. In 1934, the Council approved a Socialist plan to give the municipal slaughterhouse an outright monopoly over the urban market by 13 votes against 7; the Mayor promptly vetoed it. In 1935, a nonpartisan proposal to reorganize and strengthen the municipal slaughterhouse was quickly passed, and just as quickly vetoed. In 1937, the Mayor vetoed still another ordinance requiring that all beef from the private packinghouses be given hygienic inspections by agents of the city slaughterhouse.[16]

On the municipal level, political efforts in favor of urban consumers met with repeated frustration. The ruling group

[15] Concejo Deliberante, 1933, I (May 11), 616; (May 12), 655–56; II (June 2), 842–44. Fernando Ghío later claimed a Socialist victory in the battle over day-old meat: Ibid., 1934, I (July 10), 959. De Vedia y Mitre apparently revoked the original decree through his own volition, though, rather than as a result of consumer complaints.

[16] Concejo Deliberante, 1933, III (September 15), 1904–5; (October 10), 2323; (October 27), 2841–43; IV (November 14), 3330; 1934, I (July 10), 958–70; II (July 27), 1247–48, 1289, 1291; (July 31), 1446; (August 10), 1682–88; 1935, II (August 16), 1592–1609; III (September 17), 1727; 1937, III (October 15), 2270–72; (November 30), 3079–87, 3099; IV (December 17), 3541–42; (December 23), 3829–33. But the Mayor did not oppose the Council on issues which posed no potential threat to the stockmen or the leading packing plants. A bill against the clandestine entry of meat into Buenos Aires was easily passed through a nonpartisan commission without any perceptible opposition from the Mayor. Ibid., 1934, III (November 16), 2878–79; IV (December 7), 3417. Another bill whose main effect would be to tighten hygienic regulations was passed by the Council and apparently approved by the Mayor. Ibid., 1934, IV (December 11), 3477–84.

made not a single concession. As De Vedia y Mitre explained one of his decisions, "any measure which ties up the commercial development [of the Buenos Aires meat market] can impinge upon one of the most important sources of the country's wealth, the production of livestock." [17] Liberally interpreted, this meant that De Vedia y Mitre, even as a municipal official, would take no action in behalf of consumers that was prejudicial to the cattlemen. If the consumers and their leaders were to gain access to an effective decision-making apparatus, they would have to look outside the City Council.[18]

CONSUMERS AND THE CONGRESS

As if in recognition of this situation, consumer spokesmen turned to the national Congress. In June 1937, a Socialist Deputy requested information on the rising cost of living from the Concordancia administration. The next year Nicolás Repetto (who later took the side of the breeders against the fatteners) claimed that beef prices were being driven up by the CAP and the National Meat Board. Ranchers controlled both institutions, he observed, and their explicit purpose was to increase the cost of cattle. This could only elevate the cost of beef. The State, he implied, was protecting the producers at the expense of the consumers.[19]

Though Repetto's attack on the Meat Law institutions became the focal point of subsequent debates, consumer spokesmen displayed a cautious attitude toward ranchers—probably because of the creation of the Livestock and Meat Markets with the alleged purpose of bringing salubrious beef to Argentines at economical prices. But after the dissolution of the Markets, consumer leaders hardened their position. In 1940, Benjamín Palacio evidently tried to strengthen the temporary alliance between consumers and breeders, illustrated by Repetto's state-

[17] *Ibid.*, 1937, IV (December 17), 3542.

[18] In the name of consumers, another upper-class Mayor later proposed and gained approval of a plan to put more beef from the private packinghouses on the municipal market—a plan which would clearly help the producers as well. *Ibid.*, 1942, I (May 12), 51–52; (June 2), 154–55.

[19] Diputados, 1937, I (June 10), 598; 1938, II (July 13), 741–44.

ments in 1939; to demonstrate the compatibility of interests, Palacio argued that expansion of the domestic trade would increase the market for breeders and reduce retail prices for consumers. But the Socialists rejected his overtures. Américo Ghioldi brought up the basic point: the Meat Law could help either producers or consumers, but not both. The Livestock and Meat Markets, he charged, were nothing but a hoax. Consumers needed purchasing power, not distributing facilities.[20] In short, the interests of the two groups were inherently and irrevocably opposed.

Despite the passage of a general law for the control of retail prices,[21] consumer resentment against the Meat Law and especially the CAP mounted rapidly during the early 1940s. In 1941, when the Minister of Agriculture was forced to explain the rise of meat prices to the Chamber of Deputies, Socialists and even some Radicals charged that consumers were neglected by the government. Silvio Ruggieri bluntly denied Amadeo y Videla's assertion that an excessive number of butcher shops had pushed up the prices for beef, claiming instead that "the great producers' corporations and the wholesale distributors are the ones who determine the rise in prices. . . ." As a result, insisted this Socialist, State action was needed to help the consumer.[22]

Congress was deeply concerned about the price of beef in 1942. Within a fortnight, a Radical proposed a special investigation of the meat market; a delegate from Córdoba suggested a subsidy fund; Socialists presented a plan for stricter price controls; and spokesmen from stockraising areas advocated a greater role for the CAP in the local meat market.[23] In addition, three young intellectuals from Buenos Aires sent a learned and lengthy memorandum to Congress, pinning the blame for the price rise squarely upon the CAP.[24] But as stockmen confronted consumers, no positive action was taken.

[20] *Ibid.*, 1940, I (June 12), 493–504.
[21] *Ibid.*, 1939, V ("Leyes sancionadas"), 290–91.
[22] *Ibid.*, 1941, III (August 27–28), 485–99, 515–55.
[23] *Ibid.*, 1942, I (May 29), 145–47, 171–72; (June 3), 579–81; (June 12), 860–61.
[24] José Mármol, Horacio Giberti, and Ricardo Olivari, *Por qué está cara la carne* (Buenos Aires, 1942).

This congressional deadlock was broken by Executive decree in 1943, when President Ramón Castillo gave responsibility for retail beef prices to the CAP—of all institutions. As his message blandly stated, the Corporation should protect both ranchers and consumers, "whose interests, far from being antagonistic, are harmonized on the level of national welfare." [25] An organization which had been completely dedicated to raising livestock prices now assumed the supposed task of lowering the market price of beef. A measure that was nominally taken in behalf of the consumers placed the domestic trade under the control of the producers.

Under existing political conditions, the consumers and their spokesmen were unable to make any headway. Efforts to work through established governmental institutions were utterly futile. The City Council was blocked by the Mayor. Parliamentary demands made no impression on a Congress which, under the Concordancia, was losing its role as an open arena for competition. And the Executive favored the producers. Highly mobilized and actively seeking political power, Buenos Aires' urban consumers needed a meaningful way of promoting their interests, perhaps through a whole new political system.

THE CONSUMERS AND THE REVOLUTION

It was after the 1943 coup that the consumers began to get some governmental attention, though this was not clear during the first stage of conservative military rule. Along with all the provincial governments and other major institutions, the CAP was intervened at the time of the revolution and taken over by Colonel Luis Elías Schulze. The meaning of this move was hard to ascertain. The Argentine Rural Society maintained a diplomatic public silence, while breeders expressed the hope that this action would strengthen the CAP in its struggles against "the two enemies of rancher prosperity: the privileged group of cattlemen, direct agents of the packinghouses, and

[25] The text of the decree appears in Junta Nacional de Carnes, *Síntesis*, pp. 95–97. Also see the explanation in *Edición Rural*, March 26, 1943.

the monopoly which uses them as tools. . . ." [26] In one way or another, it looked as though cattlemen were keeping control.

After the conservative leaders were ousted by Perón's clique of colonels in 1944, however, the State began to demonstrate positive concern for the lot of urban consumers. Late that year, the Farrell administration announced its intention to place the CAP at the service of the consumers and not the producers. Cattlemen stoutly resisted this idea, as CARBAP and other breeder organizations joined the Rural Society in opposition to the plan.[27] But eventually, the ranchers had to settle for a draw. In early 1946, the government declared that the CAP would henceforth be considered a "semi-official" entity and not the exclusive property of cattlemen, thus placing strict limits on any efforts to drive up livestock and beef prices.[28]

Rising pressure from the consumers—or rather, their defenders in the Farrell administration—even influenced the policy of the National Meat Board, still under the leadership of Horacio Bruzone. In June 1944, a permanent classification and grading scheme was applied to the domestic trade, assuring purchasers of the quality and proper price of beef. That same month, limits were placed on the canning of meat for export so that more would be available for local consumption, and at lower prices. And in July, against open protests from *Edición Rural*,[29] the Meat Board suggested a new schedule of price ceilings that was promptly applied by the national government.[30] Though none of these measures threatened the interests of the stockmen to any great degree, they showed some concern for the consumers. They also appear to have had some results. According to Table 9.2, meat prices rose much faster than the cost-of-living index from 1942 to 1944; but, quite suddenly, they fell back in line with the index during 1945.

Thus Argentina's urban consumers finally gained effective representation in the political sphere under the Farrell admin-

[26] *Edición Rural,* March 8, 1944.
[27] *Anales,* LXXVIII, no. 11 (November, 1944), 709–14.
[28] *Edición Rural,* February 20, 1946.
[29] April 9, 1944.
[30] Junta Nacional de Carnes, *Síntesis,* pp. 35–40.

istration, whose dominant figure was Juan Domingo Perón. This long-awaited political power was neither direct nor constitutional: it was found in decisions from above, imposed on the country by dictatorship. But in contrast to previous times, when consumer interests were politely expressed by parliamentary delegations, pro-consumer action was successful.

PACKINGHOUSE WORKERS AND PARLIAMENT

Like the consumers, packinghouse workers displayed little political activity before the 1930s. The strike in 1917 was broken by the combined efforts of management and the Radical government of Hipólito Yrigoyen. Despite continued grievances, the laborers remained passive until 1932, when they staged another major strike; this one, too, was broken by the management.[31] Though they were nearly 40,000 strong, packinghouse workers possessed neither economic nor political strength in the early years of the Depression.

As explained in Chapter II, one reason for this weakness was organizational. There were unions—but for each separate packinghouse, not for the industry as a whole. Of course, this dispersion limited the bargaining strength of labor leaders. In 1932, just before the strike of that year, an effort to solve this problem was made by José Peter, a well-known Communist, who set up a Federation of Workers of the Meat Industry with the purpose of uniting all the separate worker organizations. Peter's success was notable but incomplete.[32] Even after the Federation joined the C.G.T. in 1936, the packinghouse workers remained in relative disarray.

Despite this state of affairs, Peter stimulated the workers' desire for political action by giving articulate expression to

[31] Rodolfo Puiggros, *Libre empresa o nacionalización en la industria de la carne* (Buenos Aires, 1957), pp. 152–61. An unsuccessful strike in 1930 is also reported in N.A., D.S., 835.504/55, White to Secretary of State, February 16, 1930.

[32] Manuel Reche, president of the Meat Workers' Federation, said many workers resented Peter's Communist and internationalist leanings. Interview, November 9, 1965.

their grievances. As he forcefully argued, packinghouse managers paid pitiful wages, ignored such labor laws as there were, laid off workers without reason, put labor organizers on a "black list" and sometimes had them beaten. Complaints about working conditions referred to the unhealthy atmosphere in freezing rooms, the risk of contamination on the killing floors, and the danger of accident in the cutting and chopping areas.[33] His most passionate statements concerned the "standard" system, under which workers were paid to perform a minimum amount of labor—or be fired—and then rewarded for extra efforts on a declining scale. Steady increases in the minimum schedule and the declining scale of payments for extra accomplishment made the "standard" a symbol of proletarian oppression. As Peter once declared:

The standard system is a brutal and intense rhythm which converts the worker into much less than a machine; because a machine is given rest, it is oiled, it is cared for and repaired, while only illness and unemployment are left to the worker after the standard . . . has extracted his last drop of energy and ruined his health. The standard system has managed to make the worker lose even the faculty for thought. Not to be able to read, except with a great deal of effort. To lose interest in life. Not even to want to go to the movies, or take a walk. To await the horrible hour of work in agony. To beg for the hour of payment. To lose the possibility of sleep, because the barbaric rhythm of the standard takes over the nerves. . . . The laborer is turned into a shadow of his former self. Tuberculosis, rheumatism, insomnia, mental ruin, a permanent picture of misery and helplessness, a tenement house, hungry children, a consumptive wife. This is what the standard signifies, comrades! [34]

As Peter intensified his Federation's campaign for better wages and working conditions, he won the full support of the C.G.T. In 1939, for instance, the C.G.T. publicly backed up Peter's dealings with the packinghouse management.[35] This greatly strengthened his hand, of course, but was significant for another reason: it was the only way the C.G.T. took part in beef politics. Completely oblivious to all the other struggles

[33] See *C.G.T.*, for example October 27, 1939; April 19, June 21, September 6, October 11, and November 29, 1940.
[34] *Ibid.*, July 28, 1939.
[35] *Ibid.*, August 25, 1939.

connected with meat, the labor organization would only come to the aid of its working members.

Possibly because of this affiliation with the C.G.T., Peter's efforts began to show some slight political results in 1936.[36] At the behest of two Socialists in the Chamber of Deputies, a committee was named to investigate working conditions in the packinghouses and to recommend any necessary legislation. Only one of the six committee positions was given to the Socialist Party, however, and the chairman was a cattle-raising aristocrat. As a result, nothing was accomplished. In 1938 another committee was appointed for the same purpose; again, leadership was given to upper-class landowners and no concrete action was taken.[37]

Pro-labor activity in Congress intensified in 1939, when the Socialists introduced a bill to set up a commission (including representatives of Peter's Federation) to supervise working conditions, establish a minimum wage, resolve labor-management conflicts, and draw up a general labor law for the meat industry. Later that year, some members of the Radical Party suggested inclusion of the packinghouses under a general labor law of the early 1920s, and in 1940 some other Radicals presented a plan to set up retirement and compensation funds for the workers.[38]

Though the packinghouse workers drew encouragement from many groups,[39] they also sought support from CARBAP. Feder-

[36] Significantly enough, the C.G.T. abandoned a previous policy of apolitical unionism in late 1935 and started promoting political action—usually through the Socialist Party. Baily, *Labor*, esp. pp. 51–61.

[37] Diputados, 1936, V (December 21–22), 573–75. The committees' paltry meeting and attendance records are given in *Ibid.*, 1937, I (August 5), 1167; 1938, I (June 1), 281, II (June 22), 183, and VI (September 30), 322. Packinghouse workers did not work through the Municipal Council, incidentally, because they lived outside the city limits.

[38] *Ibid.*, 1939, III (August 16), 49–53; 1939, V (September 29–30), 124–25; 1940, III (August 14), 46–63.

[39] Petitions in favor of labor legislation came from Peter's Federation, the Congress of Institutions of Ensenada, the Committee of Packinghouse Employees and Workers for a Pension Law, the Foodstuff Workers' Federation, and the Mutual Association of Employees of the (Frigorífico) La Negra. Biblioteca del Congreso, División de Archivo, Museo, y Publicaciones, 1940: Caja 1871, Expediente 1494; Caja 1847, Expediente 190; Caja 1685, Expediente 1100; Caja 1872, Expediente 1537. Some of the petitions are mentioned in Diputados, 1940, I (June 5), 280; III (September 5), 848; IV (September 27), 892 and (September 30), 962.

ation delegates attended the breeder congresses of 1939 and 1940, and José Peter told the ranchers that "Your problems are at the same time our problems; and by the same token, our problems as meat workers are vitally linked to your interests and aspirations." The two groups should join in opposition to "an oligarchic and privileged minority," and if the breeders wanted their own packinghouse the laborers would be glad to see them have it; as Peter put it, working conditions could only improve with a change in management.[40] In this way urban workers tried to awaken rural sympathy for their cause and perhaps, in accord with Marxist doctrine, launch a broad class struggle against the aristocracy. But the breeders, who might have been grateful for Peter's support, did not join the workers' side.

Despite their intensity, none of these political efforts in behalf of the laborers bore any perceptible or practical results. Two of the congressional bills were reintroduced later on,[41] but neither of them was brought to the floor for debate and no laws on the matter were passed. Under Peter's leadership and the existing political system, the packinghouse workers could not accomplish their goals.

LABOR AND PERÓN

It was not until the revolution of 1943 that prospects improved for the packinghouse workers. Specifically, the change began in October of that year, when the Department of Labor was turned over to Perón. Renamed the Secretariat of Labor and Social Security, the new department sought to stimulate labor organization and promote the interests of the workers. Openly courting the laborers, using both the carrot and the stick, Perón made this office a political base which eventually helped carry him into the presidency.

Perón's technique was nowhere better exemplified than in his treatment of the packinghouse workers. After taking over

[40] *C.G.T.*, July 26, 1940; also see June 2, 1939. *Edición Rural*, May 24, 1939.
[41] Diputados, 1941, I (June 5), 267; 1942, I (June 10), 678.

the labor department, he helped establish a whole new organization to replace Peter's ineffective Federation.[42] With his approval, Peter's internationally oriented Communists were pushed aside by a young, nationalistic team of native Argentines headed by Cipriano Reyes—a typical expression of the rising influence of indigenous elements among the urban laborers. Called the Federation of Labor Unions of the Meat Industry and formally christened in June 1944, the new syndicate included workers at every level of employment and encompassed all the packinghouses together. The problem of organization was finally solved.

As a matter of fact, the workers started to act even before the new union was set up. After some workers were laid off their jobs in early 1944, a strike was held at the Armour plant. In March, Perón himself proposed a settlement that would have included a five centavo per hour wage increase, half pay for vacations, a guarantee of 60 hours of work every fortnight, the return of suspended workers to their jobs, and the stoppage of brutality by the foremen. The Armour management refused to accept these terms, and the strike dragged on for a number of months. On June 1, Perón took decisive action and a government decree brought the strike to a compulsory end. Wages were boosted by ten centavos an hour—about a 30 per cent increase—and overtime work would be paid an extra 25 per cent. In return, the workers were required merely to promise not to strike for at least another year.[43]

Government intervention soon became the rule in clashes between management and the workers. Late in 1944, Perón imposed a settlement on the Smithfield & Argentine firm. In April of 1945, he arranged a minimum-wage agreement for workers employed by the CAP.[44]

Labor-management relations took a decisive turn for the worse in early 1945, when the packinghouses took joint action

[42] Some of Perón's tactics are described in Alfredo López, *La clase obrera y la revolución del 4 de junio* (Buenos Aires, 1945).

[43] Secretaría de Trabajo y Previsión, *Revista de Trabajo y Previsión*, 1944, no. 2, 604–7.

[44] *Ibid.*, 1944, no. 4, 1615; 1945, nos. 7–8, 1196–97.

by suspending thousands of workers, partly for "disciplinary reasons" and partly because of a reduction in the volume of trade.[45] On March 31 a general strike was called in all the packing plants. A deadlock ensued, with both sides determined not to back down. On April 24, it happened again: the government intervened and ordered the management to take the workers back. If it proved impossible for the packers to absorb them all for economic reasons, the State would pay the salaries of up to 12,600 workers for as long as three months as a matter of social justice. And pay it did; in the end, this program cost the Argentine government nearly 10 million pesos.[46] Few measures ever captured the *Peronista* concern for the packinghouse laborers quite so neatly.

Later that year the workers had a chance to show their gratitude, when Perón was imprisoned by the shaky Farrell government. After a few days of frantic negotiations, some with the extraordinary Eva Duarte, Cipriano Reyes commanded his followers to go to the Plaza de Mayo and demand the release of Perón.[47] In they came, marching all night from the Avellaneda slums, swarming in front of the government palace and calling for their hero. Late that evening the government gave in to this pressure, brought Perón back to the city and let him address the jubilant throng. This was one of the most dramatic moments in Argentina's political history: the famous *17 de octubre,* the first major mass action that the country had ever known. More than any other single event, this was the occasion that marked the rise to power of both the urban lower class and its dynamic leader.

In addition, the demonstration of October 17 points up the newly emerging importance of personal charisma in the politics of beef. As all observers had testified, one of Perón's greatest

45 See the managers' subsequent statement in *Edición Rural,* March 20, 1946.

46 *Revista de Trabajo y Previsión,* 1945, nos. 5–6, 162–63, 165–67; 1945, nos. 7–8, 738–39; 1946, no. 9, 130–32. These payments were probably made from the vast stores of foreign exchange that had accumulated in Argentina during World War II.

47 See Cipriano Reyes, *Qué es el laborismo* (Buenos Aires, 1946), esp. pp. 45–52. This event marked the beginning of Evita's active intervention in labor politics; but it was not until Perón's inauguration as President, the following year, that she assumed major responsibilities in this area.

weapons was his own attractiveness and charm. His handsome smile inspired confidence; his notorious affair with Eva Duarte (followed by marriage) played upon sexual aspects in the cult of *machismo;* his military bearing further emphasized virility; his own humble origins gave him a sense of identity with the masses; and most important, his political actions and masterful rhetoric convinced the crowds that he shared their highest goals and aspirations. Many followers considered him a saviour, and gave him their total devotion.[48] There have been other charismatic leaders in Argentina, but none so magnetic as Perón.

After the October demonstration, Perón was quick to repay the workers' loyalty.[49] Late in 1945, packinghouse managers refused to cooperate with a newly created labor relations board that was supposed to establish minimum wages, in effect eliminating the "standard" system. Reyes responded by calling a general strike. A frequently violent stalemate ensued for three months, and then the climax began. The government declared the strike to be legitimate, decreed that working hours should be reduced in freezing rooms, and publicly condemned the management's intransigence. In March 1946—significantly enough, in President Farrell's office—the packing companies surrendered. They promised to comply with a minimum wage decree. They pledged their cooperation with the labor commission. They said they would reincorporate all the workers suspended since the beginning of 1945. They agreed to provide for some job stability. They consented to a full day's pay for six hours of work in the freezing rooms. They left the decision as to whether the workers should be paid for the three months' strike time in the hands of a pro-labor government. The union, on the other hand, made no concessions at all: its only obligation was to enter all future negotiations with "good will." [50]

[48] For a self-conscious and propagandistic statement about Perón's "missionary" qualities see Eva Perón, *La razón de mi vida,* 12th ed. (Buenos Aires, 1952).

[49] Although Perón was running for the presidential elections of February 1946 at the time, the Secretariat of Labor and Social Security was clearly under his influence.

[50] *Revista de Trabajo y Previsión,* 1945, nos. 7–8, 911–27; 1946, no. 9, 30–32, 144–47, 300–2. A protest by the slaughterhouse managers against governmental favoritism to labor during the middle of the strike was printed in *Edición Rural,* March 20, 1946.

Rarely had a triumph ever been so clearly cut. Furthermore, this agreement served as the basis of labor-management relations in the meatpacking industry for many years to come, as the workers continued to benefit from governmental protection. Between 1946 and 1949, one writer estimates, their nominal wage actually doubled.[51]

By 1946, it had evidently become clear to the urban masses that the way to gain power was through the elevation of Perón. In the elections of that year, the central issue was quite clearly drawn: whether Argentina should continue with her openly authoritarian political system, or return to time-worn constitutional procedures. The contest pitted Perón's new Labor Party, which Cipriano Reyes helped form, against a broad coalition containing virtually every other party in the country—including the Socialists, deeply committed to parliamentary practice and resentful of Perón's courtship with the urban lower class.[52] Perón obtained a good deal of electoral support from rural peons and some portions of the lower middle class, but scored most heavily among the urban masses. Even with its sizable middle class, the city of Buenos Aires gave Perón a 54 per cent majority. And in Avellaneda, the major packinghouse district, the results were overwhelming: 87 per cent of those eligible cast ballots, 68 per cent of which were for Perón.[53] Ironically, it was through this most scrupulous and "democratic" election in Argentine history that Perón was given the authority to install his undemocratic regime.[54]

In general, these developments indicate some fundamental

[51] Horacio J. Noboa, *Política nacional de carnes* (Buenos Aires, 1956), p. 17. This meant that the laborers kept substantially ahead of the rise in the cost of living. Junta Nacional de Carnes, *Estadísticas básicas*, p. 14. On the whole, labor made solid gains in the early Perón era; the share of national income comprised of wages and salaries jumped from 42.3 per cent in 1945 to 54.0 per cent in 1950. Torcuato S. di Tella, *El sistema político argentino y la clase obrera* (Buenos Aires, 1964), p. 104.

[52] The Socialist position is explained in López, *La clase obrera.*

[53] Ministerio del Interior, *Las fuerzas armadas*, II, 433, 443. The active intensity of lower-class appreciation of Perón is also noted by Torcuato S. di Tella, who holds that *Peronismo* combined "Bonapartist" leadership with "worker spontaneity." *El sistema político*, pp. 54–64.

[54] Adding to the irony, Perón subsequently broke with Reyes and destroyed the Labor Party in an effort to gain complete control over the working-class movement. Baily, *Labor*, pp. 105–8.

changes in the politics of beef. First, in contrast to all the previous fights within the rural sector, these were urban-rural struggles. In a demonstration of rural unity against the urban threat, cattle ranchers and wheat farmers joined in condemnation of the packinghouse strikes.[55] Second, these were essentially class conflicts. The urban lower class was challenging the rural upper class. Some portions of the middle sectors sided with Perón, but most went with the aristocracy; at any rate, the middle classes did not lead the movement. Third, while economic strength predominated before, these fights were resolved by political power. It is true that the breeders gained some redress for economic grievances in the late 1930s; but the victories achieved by the workers and consumers, through an authoritarian system, clearly suggest that political strength reached a level of unprecedented effectiveness.

As Perón rose to power, that is, the hitherto characteristic pattern of intraclass rural conflict came to an end. The breeders, fatteners, packers, and even wheat farmers continued to pursue their own interests, of course, but their particular considerations claimed secondary importance in comparison to the broader conflict with the urban masses. The phase of functional fights, in which upper-class rural groups could afford to pursue their economic interests with impunity, was over; now, they were confronted by groups that were urban, lower-class, devoted to a charismatic leader and aided by the government. Like the politics of almost everything else, the politics of beef entered a new era when Perón came onto the scene.

THE ESCALATION OF ANTI-IMPERIALISM

The realignment of the participant groups brought a change in ideologies too. Having issued a challenge to the landed aristocracy in 1944 [56] and taken over the presidency in 1946, Perón sought to build up the country's industry. For several years his

---

[55] *Edición Rural*, May 23, 1945; March 21, 1946. *La Tierra*, March 12, 1946; also see January 15, 1946.

[56] Juan Perón, *Perón expone su doctrina* (Buenos Aires, 1947), esp. pp. 47–48; *Anales*, LXXVIII, no. 11 (November, 1944), 715.

Argentine Institute for the Promotion of Trade (better known from its Spanish initials as IAPI) managed to buy agricultural and pastoral products at low prices, sell them on a bustling world market, and invest the difference in industrial growth. More specifically, the governmental goal was to encourage both the manufacture of consumer goods and the development of heavy industry—steel, coal, oil, and electric power.[57] For this purpose—and also to offset the influence of the Argentine Industrial Union, still reluctant to defy the rural producers— Perón helped set up an organization called the General Economic Confederation which was dedicated to the cause of intensive industrialization.

This economic policy evidently sought to attract the support of three major constituencies in Argentine politics. One consisted of urban workers, who stood to gain additional jobs. Another was the military, which considered industrial growth as a logistical necessity for the effort to dominate the lower portion (*"el Cono Sur"*) of South America.[58] A third was composed of middle-class industrialists, who tended to regard Perón's populism with suspicion and even hostility. To this extent, Perón was using industrialization as a means to sustain the crucial bases of his power, labor and the armed forces, and to win the industrialists over to his side.

The policy was justified by modern anti-imperialism. As Perón introduced his famous Five Year Plan to the Congress of 1946, he claimed that Argentina's economic independence was still waiting to be won. "In 1810," he said, "we were politically free. We now desire to be economically independent. Vassalage for vassalage, I don't know which would be worse." In his view economic sovereignty could be reached only through industrial development, since that would free the country from its dependence on foreign markets and provide genuine self-

[57] Instituto de Investigaciones Económicas y Financieras de la Confederación General Económica, "Elementos para la historia de una moderna acción empresaria," mimeographed (Buenos Aires, 1965), esp. pp. 52–53.

[58] For good examples of the military emphasis on industrialization, especially the production of iron and steel, see the speeches by Colonel Mario N. Savio and Colonel Carlos J. Martínez in the *Boletín*, LV, no. 885 (September, 1942), 37–47 and LVI, no. 898 (October, 1943), 3–14.

sufficiency. Without a strong manufacturing base, maintained Perón, few nations had managed to escape the problems of "a semicolonial economy." Furthermore, a viable industrial sector would aid the popular masses by furnishing employment opportunities and eventually offering goods at reduced retail prices. As part of Perón's over-all program, industrialization would thus help to "set up the economy in such a way as to be the patrimony of all instead of the privilege of a few." In this manner industrial growth would contribute to the establishment of social justice as well as to the economic independence of the Argentine nation.[59]

Whatever its effectiveness, Perón's anti-imperialist doctrine had the latent political function of attempting to mobilize urban elements in a common cause against the traditional aristocracy. Rural economic activities, which mainly produced goods for export, were identified with national inferiority and backwardness; urban efforts, manufacturing and labor, were linked to the prospect of independence, greatness, and strength. Furthermore, the emphasis on the novelty of an industrial Argentina served to awaken the interest of originally apathetic groups who had previously failed to articulate their demands on society; under the rule of Perón—however authoritarian it might be—there would be something for everyone in the future Argentina. In these ways, the official ideology sought to gain the allegiance of as many sectors as possible in the struggle with the status quo. It tended to widen the conflict as much as possible—whereas, on previous occasions, traditional anti-imperialism seemed to restrict and confine the intergroup fights within the beef industry.

Perón's ideological appeal did not fit classical molds. If he was anything he was eclectic. Specifically, he managed to combine the socio-economic content of modern anti-imperialism with strongly traditional claims to political authority. As a charismatic figure, he maintained a kind of *patrón-peón* relationship with his followers. His establishment of the "Justicial-

[59] Presidencia de la Nación, *Plan de gobierno 1947–1951* (Buenos Aires, 1946), I, 13, 62, 64.

REALIGNMENT OF THE CONFLICT

ist" State drew inspiration from the corporativist ideal of hierarchical order. His rhetoric emphasized spiritual values as much as material gains. Thus he mobilized previously unintegrated masses in a fashion that promised both change and tradition. In these paradoxical ways, Perón represented leadership of the "populist conservative" or "falangist" type.[60]

Yet his urban-based movement presented a definite challenge, and rural groups sprang to the defense. In varying moods, the Argentine Rural Society hotly denied the allegation that livestock production represented any kind of economic or social backwardness, and coolly argued that there was no necessary inconsistency between pastoral and industrial interests; in fact, industrialization might be necessary someday, but it would now be premature.[61] CARBAP, whose leaders fervently supported the 1943 coup, cautiously approved the efforts toward industrialization for a while. But in 1945, *Edición Rural* decried the dangers of "artificial industrialization"; in 1948 CARBAP leadership furiously assailed governmental overemphasis on manufacturing and maltreatment of livestock production, foremost among the forces "that sustain the structure and economic independence of the country." [62] Thus the ranchers united in opposition to the economic program of Perón. Significantly, the wheat farmers' Agrarian Federation also joined this anti-Peronist alliance against industrial development.[63]

As this confrontation emerged, an extraordinarily significant ideological battle developed, in which one kind of anti-imperialism was used to combat another kind of anti-imperialism. While Perón and his followers demanded industrialization in order to liberate the country from its imperialist yoke, the cattlemen demanded special privileges for livestock production

[60] K. H. Silvert, "Leadership Formation and Modernization in Latin America," *Journal of International Affairs*, XX, no. 2 (1966), 318–31, esp. 328. Also see Baily, *Labor*, pp. 71–135.

[61] *Anales*, LXXIX, no. especial (1945), 62; LXXX, no. 1 (January, 1946), 3–4; and LXXVIII, no. 11 (November, 1944), 712.

[62] *Edición Rural*, February 14, 1945; also see February 16, February 20, March 7, and March 27, 1945. And *Buenos Aires y La Pampa*, no. 98 (September–October, 1948), 9.

[63] *La Tierra*, October 11, 1946; November 30, 1946; and July 6, 1948.

—naturally, in order to liberate the country from its imperialist yoke. *Edición Rural,* the pro-breeder newspaper, put it in a nutshell: "Perhaps colonialism is not [the fact] that we export meat, but that Argentine stockmen have not managed to acquire their own packinghouse." [64] Aid to ranchers, not the industrialists, would establish Argentina's sovereignty.

The usage of nationalist rhetoric by both sides in this struggle aptly shows how anti-imperialism could grow as a function of internal politics. By this time, the assertion of economic independence was something of a political ritual: it was the *sine qua non* for the articulation of group interests. So when Perón accused the stockmen of being imperialist lackeys, they had no choice but to reply that they stood for the nation's true economic sovereignty, which would only be endangered by artificial industrialization. Thus the intensity of anti-imperialist rhetoric was greatly amplified by the urban-rural class conflict within Argentina, and (in many instances) had little or no direct connection with the actions of foreign investment. This internal dimension of anti-imperialism, in turn, might help explain some of its general usage in the Argentina of today.

As rural and urban groups engaged in ideological combat, they tended to harden their positions. The struggle concerned not only interests but also creeds. At bottom, this whole conflict involved opposing sets of values: populism vs. elitism. The urban masses were fighting for socio-economic power and mobility as well as personal dignity. They had moderate goals— cheaper meat, higher wages—but wanted them badly. When they could not achieve these ends through "democratic" political procedures, they were more than willing to work through Perón's authoritarian Justicialist regime. Meanwhile, the rural producers stoutly maintained their belief in stability, order, and rule by an enlightened elite. When they espoused the virtues of democracy, they meant limited democracy "in the Greek sense." All of their previous ideological acrobatics, the sudden switching from laissez-faire to anti-imperialism, took place within this

[64] April 12, 1945. Though the CAP had purchased some other packinghouses, as seen in the previous chapter, it had not yet built a plant of its own.

framework of elitist values.[65] But understandably, they chose not to dwell upon the liberal virtues of political or economic competition during a challenge from the urban lower class (especially after the 1946 elections). Traditional anti-imperialism had tactical advantages and, with its hierarchical emphasis on the superiority of rural life, emphasized the kind of values at stake. Thus the battle between the Peronists and their opponents turned into a kind of mutual crusade. Different classes fought for different values.[66]

Generally speaking, this pervasive realignment in the politics of beef provides some significant clues about Argentina's overall pattern of modernization. During the Depression, rapid changes in the social and economic spheres were combining to exert lower-class pressure on the political system. But the political system, despite its constitutional trappings and undoubted development, was controlled by the upper class and some middle-class groups. Even for them, it began to afford an effective counterweight to economic strength only in the breeder-fattener battles of the late 1930s—through influence with the Executive branch. By that time, representative institutions like the Congress were discredited and useless. In other words, Argentina's modernization was marked by a fundamental asymmetry: social and economic advances were matched by delay and retardation in the political arena. Thus highly mobilized urban masses sought to take part in politics, but could not gain access to power. The inevitable result was frustration. Perón was able to capitalize on this situation. His actions won the support of lower-class groups and, in their view, gave him the license to build a different political system.

[65] In their struggles with fatteners, breeders often imbued traditional anti-imperialism with populistic (if authoritarian) overtones; but in view of the Peronist threat, almost all ranchers now stressed the ideology's hierarchical and elitist content.

[66] It appears that various pressures in the early 1950s forced Perón to try stimulating agricultural-pastoral production, both to shore up the national economy and possibly to placate the landlords. But this change in economic policy (which did not achieve its ends) coincided with a demonstrable hardening of his political attitude. Partly as a result, the ideological confrontation between urban workers and upper- and middle-class groups—usually supported by the military—has continued to be one of the fundamental features of Argentine politics since Perón was overthrown in 1955.

Conclusion

TAKEN in retrospect, the conflicts concerning the Argentine beef industry can provide the basis for a broad analysis of the country's political modernization. The results are more suggestive than definitive, and empirical studies of other key issues— the wheat industry, the sugar industry, the petroleum industry, labor organization, among others—are badly needed to supplement, test, and refine the conclusions set forth here. Generalizations concerning the beef industry are subject to several inherent limitations. Despite its implications for some urban groups, cattle production was a decidedly "rural" activity. It was closely linked to the export-import economic structure, rather than to rising industrialization. The ranchers had extremely easy access to the decision-making centers of government. Foreign capital in the packinghouse business exercised strong (and possibly distorting) influence on group behavior. Yet a beginning has to be made in analyzing Argentina's development in the early twentieth century, and the sheer economic and political importance of the beef industry makes it as good a starting point as any other.

MODERNIZATION AND CONFLICT

The period from 1900 to 1946 in Argentina was characterized by intensive economic, social, and political modernization. Swelled by immigration from Europe, the national population rapidly grew. Extensive communications and transport systems, notably railroads, reached into the country's interior. The trend toward urbanization sharply increased. The upper circles of society became more and more open, especially for ambitious members of the middle sectors. The growth of the export-import economy led to the specialization of labor (as in the case of cattle breeders and fatteners), and per capita income went steadily up. Though its progress was uneven, political participation also expanded—as shown first in the rising importance of Congress and later in Perón's representation of lower- and lower-middle class groups.

Most of these developments took place under the rule of the rural aristocrats and their allies, and a good deal of political modernization occurred within the rural sectors. As cattlemen came to perceive emerging conflicts, they took their complaints to the State. They created voluntary associations for the expression of their interests, particularly the Rural Society and CARBAP. Their increasing reliance on some urban lawyers for spokesmen contributed to the "professionalization" of politics and also tended to broaden popular participation in the politics of beef, as did their frequent use of nationalistic ideology. In short, Argentina's political modernization during these years was not restricted to the city, nor was it based essentially on class-conscious urban-rural strife. It was a primarily rural phenomenon—led by members of the aristocracy.

As a further indication of this tendency, most of the struggles over beef broke out between the industry's rural or rurally oriented groups. Prior to the 1940s, the principal contestants were all linked to the export-import economic structure: the livestock breeders, the fatteners, and the packers. This was not always the case, since the laborers struck in 1917 and consumer spokesmen took some independent action during World War I. But it was not until the late 1930s that Argentina's urban groups mounted any serious challenge to rural domination.

The delay and suddenness of the urban attack shows not a gradual transition of alignments and power but a sharp break from previous practice. Though explanations for the abruptness of this change are hard to define, one senses a lack of coordination (or the existence of lags) between the locus and types of modernization. While economic and social development took place in both the cities and the countryside during this period, the rural and rurally oriented groups were the first to modernize their political procedures—that is, to consolidate their interests through group organization and make explicit demands upon the State. The effectiveness of this rural political action, in turn, might well have retarded the appearance of a truly urban challenge to the landowning aristocracy. The imbalance could not last indefinitely, however, and around 1940 lower-class urban groups finally made political demands corresponding to their growing social and economic importance.

In passing, these observations suggest some general points about politics and its analysis. First, as indicated, political modernization does not automatically follow socio-economic change. In fact the Argentine case implies nearly the opposite: under certain conditions socio-economic advance (consolidation of aristocratic strength, or rapid mass mobilization) might even deter some kinds of political progress. Second, political modernization can be selective. Most development indices—interest articulation, leadership broadening, institutional adaptability and specialization—appeared during the period of upper- and middle-class predominance. But when the lower class tried to take part, the political system collapsed. In the end Argentine workers achieved mass participation, but only under an authoritarian leader subscribing to semitraditional falangist values. Third, and most broadly, it is necessary to include the possibility of retrogression or decay in models of political change.[1] Argentina presents a striking sequence of modernization and breakdown; and the collapse, it seems, was closely related to prior patterns of economic, social, and political modernization.

THE PURSUIT OF INTERESTS

Almost all of the battles fought among the upper-class rural groups before the 1940s concerned economic issues. Of course it is not surprising that struggles originating within the beef in-

[1] For one effort to deal with this problem see Samuel P. Huntington, "Political Development and Political Decay," *World Politics*, XVII, no. 3 (April, 1965), [386]–430.

dustry dealt with economic matters. But even after the conflicts were transferred to the political sphere, they retained their economic character and definition. On several occasions, during the controversy over the Roca-Runciman Pact and the Great Debate, partisan considerations intruded into the argument. But in general, from the entry of American capital into the meatpacking business up to the struggles for control of the CAP, the groups steadfastly pursued their prosperity. As shown by the systematic analyses of biographical data on the political participants, party, region, class, ideology, or charisma did not alter the alignment or behavior of the contestants. Throughout these fights, the governing factor was economic interest.[2]

As these conflicts appeared, the rival groups resorted to differing weapons. The packers relied mainly on their tightly knit organization—the shipping pool—and the economic power that it brought them. This gave them a good deal of influence over trends in the market, and sometimes, as in the minimum-price battle of 1923, they could use this strength to alter policy decisions of the Argentine government. But for the most part their political power was weak, since, as private foreign investors, they had no direct representation in the workings of the State. They could frequently gain indirect representation through a community of economic interest, usually with the fatteners, but it was always indirect and uncertain. Though the fatteners supported the packers in 1923 and in the Great Debate, for instance, they staunchly opposed the packinghouse pool during the Meat Law debates of 1933.

According to available information, the British and United States governments do not appear to have taken much positive action in behalf of the packers. Throughout this period, both Washington and London paid more heed to the demands of domestic constituencies than to the needs of investors abroad. Though the British spoke up for their packers in 1913 and secured the 85-15 clause in the Roca-Runciman Pact, they also

2 This conclusion fully agrees with the central thesis of Miron Burgin, *The Economic Aspects of Argentine Federalism, 1820–1852* (Cambridge, Mass., 1946); and see Juan Álvarez, *Estudio sobre las guerras civiles argentinas* (Buenos Aires, 1914).

criticized packinghouse profits and agreed to place restrictive quotas on the Anglo-Argentine trade at the Ottawa Conference. For all these decisions, the guiding principle does not seem to have been solicitude for the packers, but deeply rooted concern for the welfare of two groups back in Britain: cattle farmers and consumers. Similarly, the United States' imposition of an embargo on Argentine meat responded to pressure from cattle ranchers in the West and the Middle West, and ran directly counter to the interests of the Americans in Argentina. In general, the packers could not rely on the diplomatic support of their own governments; whenever a choice had to be made between the companies and larger constituencies at home, the packers were quick to lose out.

When cattle ranchers opposed the economic strength of the packinghouse pool, they usually sought to exert their political strength. Argentine stockmen had several means of expressing their interests. First, there were institutional associations like the Argentine Rural Society, an elite and immensely influential organization. Yet the Society was not omnipotent, losing the 1923 battle over the minimum price and suffering some outright defeats from CARBAP and other associations toward the end of the 1930s. Second, ranchers had direct representation in the government. There the Rural Society enjoyed extraordinary power, as many of its members became Deputies, Senators, and Ministers. Third, the stockmen recruited increasing numbers of non-cattle-owning politicians as their delegates in government. As an illustration of this trend, the debate of 1913 was dominated by aristocratic cattlemen, mainly from the Rural Society; in 1923, some of the most influential pro-rancher spokesmen were urban lawyers, and from the Radical Party; by 1932 the Ministry of Agriculture was turned over to Antonio de Tomaso, ex-Socialist son of a bricklayer.

The gradual professionalization in the politics of beef is particularly significant insofar as it came to involve the defense of cattle-owning interests by members of the urban middle sectors. This has been noted at various points in the narrative, especially in the analysis of Radical Party behavior at the end of Chapter V. The first part of the twentieth century in Argentina was not characterized by urban-vs.-rural class combat. This point bears two critical implications about the nature of conflict during this phase of modernization. In the first place, it shows that the city was not inherently opposed to the countryside, and that fights originating within the rural sectors could be transferred to urban areas as well. This could be explained by the rapid development of the nation's export-import economy, which tied many of the country's supposedly "urban" activities (commerce, or industries that processed agricultural and pastoral goods) to the rurally oriented economic system. Up to the end of the 1930s, the city was not an inveterate rival of the rural areas, and its residents could frequently be persuaded to join hands with the landowners.

In the second place, the behavior of the middle classes—especially the upper-middle groups—indicates that they were by no means inclined to challenge the rural aristocracy. Their economic interests frequently coincided with those of the ranchers, a fact which nurtured social aspirations as well. Though it is hardly exhaustive, the evidence compiled throughout this book clearly suggests that Argentina's upper-middle sectors sought to join the aristocracy rather than destroy it. The behavior of less prosperous members of the country's lower-middle class was more erratic: sometimes they aided the oligarchy, sometimes they helped the lower class.

Through these differing delegations in politics, Argentine ranchers promoted their interests at the national level of government. The legislature of the province of Buenos Aires and the City Council of Buenos Aires, whose records have been examined for this study, showed a negligible amount of concern with the conflicts over beef compared to the activity of the central government. This might have been due partly to the geographical dispersion of livestock production over several leading provinces, but it also implies full recognition of the superior authority of the State. When the ranchers wanted action, they went straight to the top.

Figure 10.1. *Congressional Activity Concerning the Argentine Beef Industry, 1900–1942*

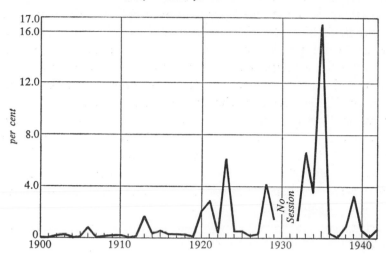

Once the stockmen shifted their struggles from the economic to the political sphere, various decision-making procedures were employed to settle the conflicts. Before the Saenz Peña law had taken full effect, as in the policy debates of 1913, most fights were liable to be resolved by "acuerdo."[3] Then the Congress became a widely recognized battlefield for the waging of intergroup warfare, and it was here that most of the action described in this study took place. Toward the end of the 1930s the political system was discredited by the exclusive and fraudulent rule of the Concordancia, however, and cattlemen turned for aid to the Executive, most notably the Minister of Agriculture. If one governmental institution did not work, the ranchers turned to another.

The transferral of economic problems to the political arena is depicted in Figure 10.1, which shows the annual percentages of pages in the *Diario de Sesiones* of both the Senate and Chamber of Deputies that were devoted to the politics of beef

[3] Generalization on this point is limited not only by the scope of this study, which scans only a decade or so of "acuerdo" type government, but also by the difficulty of detecting conflicts resolved by this method.

between 1900 and 1942.[4] The picture provides a neat summary. Up to 1912, as shown by the lack of activity, the Congress was of little use to the ranchers; if they needed a decision, they could probably get it by "acuerdo." After that point, a series of ascending peaks (especially for 1913, 1923, 1933) reflects the repeated attempts of cattlemen to offset economic crisis by the use of congressional action. From the beginning of the century until 1935, in fact, the graph describes a wide parabolic curve ending with the Great Debate, as stockmen and their representatives brought their complaints to the parliament (the ultimate height of the curve serving to illustrate the importance of beef politics in Argentina during this era).[5] Then the Congress was discredited, as seen in Chapter VII, and the curve suddenly drops; now conflicts were settled by the Ministry of Agriculture. At the same time, the rising signs of activity in the late thirties and early forties reveal the complaints of the consumers and packinghouse workers; the stoppage of the curve at 1942 represents the suspension of Congress by the revolution of June 1943, after which the surging urban groups could press their claims through new leaders and a new political system.

While ranchers frequently looked for help from the government, especially the Congress, they do not appear to have sought the active support of associations representing other economic groups—wheat men, industrialists, or laborers. One

[4] The curve is based on percentages in order to provide some idea of the relative political importance of the meat industry debates, as explained in the following footnote, although a figure depicting the absolute number of pages devoted to these issues would have shown the same general curve. Debates represented in the graph have been selected on the grounds of their relationship to the conflicts that took place between the interest groups. Routine, local, and purely technical matters have been omitted, though their inclusion would by no means have altered the curve in any significant way. All data have been adjusted to the calendar (not the congressional) year. The break in 1930–31 is due to suspension of the Congress after the revolution of 1930.

[5] Given the fact that so much of the *Diario de Sesiones* is concerned with routine and procedural matters, and that about one-fourth of all congressional activity dealt with the budget, I regard 5 to 15 per cent of all parliamentary action as an indication of extraordinary political importance for any single set of issues. It would be highly instructive to have a graph comparing the relative importance of other key problems—like petroleum and wheat—in this way, but that task lies outside the bounds of this study.

reason for this lack of outside participation is that stockmen failed to make any positive bids for aid from other sources, probably because they did not want to take the risk of spreading the conflicts beyond their own control. Yet the passive behavior of these other sectors is intrinsically important because it also betrays a "compartmental" quality in Argentine politics during most of this period. Individual groups tended to act in pursuit of immediate interests, not on the basis of permanent or widespread alliances; this was true even for the wheat farmers, who often complained about the ranchers' power but took no manifest action against it.

The nonparticipation of outside groups deserves some careful attention. It is naturally significant that the stockmen used various rhetorical devices to discourage action among these other sectors. It is also true that organized labor was too weak throughout most of this period to make any meaningful moves. On the other hand, the industrialists and the wheat men were relatively influential groups—but it is evident that they did not regard the politics of beef as pertinent to their own interests. As a hypothesis, one might attribute this attitude to their general commitment to the prevailing political and economic systems. Struggles within these established frameworks did not excite their concern. It was only when the whole structure was defied that they took action, since a threat to one part of the system became a threat to every part of the system. Throughout most of the conflicts considered in this study, therefore, they were content to let the stockmen fend for themselves.

So long as the competing groups resorted to the Argentine Congress, they had to present their viewpoints to a dual audience: parliamentary delegates from nonlivestock constituencies, and—more important—the literate public at large. Under these conditions, the style of an argument assumed almost as much importance as its substance, and rhetoric became a vital instrument of combat. Within a general set of social values, doctrines shifted according to economic and political interests. The British packers pleaded for State intervention in 1913, then joined the Americans in promoting laissez-faire arguments in all the succeeding struggles. Ranchers varied their ideological offerings with more frequency. In 1913 many upheld the tenets of laissez-faire. In 1923 some breeders and small stockmen proposed a kind of traditional anti-imperialism, while fatteners and large ranchers insisted on nineteenth-century liberalism. In 1933 the fatteners helped the breeders advance a moderate anti-imperialism. But later on, a challenge from the urban lower class involved some fundamental values. The ranchers and packers then dropped their rhetorical dispute in order to meet the Peronist doctrine of modern anti-imperialism.

Whatever their intention, these ideological acrobatics all performed specific political functions.[6] In general, laissez-faire tended to keep conflicts out of the political arena and to minimize the number of participants. Anti-imperialism, on the other hand, served typically to transfer conflicts from the economic to the political sphere. On occasion, it provided rhetorical glue for urban-rural alliances. Having transformed private problems into public issues, though, traditional nationalism usually discouraged outsiders from taking part in the debates and the making of decisions; in a way it sought merely to justify the ranchers' extraordinary political power. Modern nationalism, by contrast, encouraged the expansion of conflict, and for this reason was utilized by the urban working class under the leadership of Perón.

According to this analysis, economic nationalism definitely had internal political uses. Foreign interests were not always the primary object of the attack, as seen in the Great Debate, but were sometimes employed as a means of identifying the opposition with something alien and hateful. In short, the presentation of an argument in anti-imperialist terms does not always mean that the argument is directed solely against the imperialists.

In general the cattlemen had a broad range of political weapons at their disposal, and frequently used them to offset the

---

[6] For obvious epistemological reasons, I have deemphasized the question of "conscious intention" and concentrated mainly on the functions of the various ideologies, not the motivations of their individual proponents.

economic power of the packinghouses. But these tools could also be employed by rival ranching factions. As we have seen, the functional separation of breeders from fatteners gave rise to a series of mounting conflicts culminating in the struggle over the Meat Board and the CAP. Until the latter 1930s the fatteners had the upper hand, but then the breeders turned the tables with the aid of slightly different weapons. They set up their own organizations, most notably CARBAP; and they gained influence within the Ministry of Agriculture, not the Congress, which resolved most of the conflicts in their favor. While the cattlemen had great political strength, they sometimes used it on each other. Even through the 1930s, the most important battles over beef originated within the upper-class and rural sectors.[7]

When an urban movement finally challenged the aristocracy, in the late 1930s and early 1940s, it came from lower-class groups and not the middle sectors. In launching their assault upon the upper class, the consumers and the packinghouse workers were forced to look for weapons other than parliamentary procedure, now discredited by its ineffectiveness and controlled by the cattlemen. It took the revolution of 1943—and, more specifically, the climb to power by Farrell and Perón—to give these groups some effective influence on governmental decisions. Under the military dictatorship, issues were resolved by the Executive alone. This way, consumers and laborers managed to gain redress for economic grievances through the application of political power. This process was particularly apparent in Perón's dealings with the packinghouse workers, as he repeatedly stepped in to settle labor-management disputes in favor of the union.

With this development, the pattern of alignment among the interest groups rapidly shifted. Economic considerations still formed a leading motivation for political behavior, but other factors acquired new degrees of importance. As an urban-rural

[7] As observed in Chapter II, many breeders belonged to the rural middle class, but they drew most of their leadership from the aristocracy and did not betray any significant class consciousness in their conflicts with the fatteners.

struggle, the emerging conflict had a regional dimension; as lower-class defiance of the upper class, it carried social overtones; as rising groups joined the Peronist political movement, it took on partisan implications; given Perón's magnetic appeal, it was deeply affected by charisma; and as one form of anti-imperialism confronted another, it hardened ideological lines and involved contrasting sets of social values. While Argentine politics greatly increased in complexity, the lines of division were redrawn and intensified by mutual reinforcement. As a result of this mixture in motives, one might guess, the rifts between the competing groups widened, communications broke down, and the resolution of conflict became an increasingly difficult matter.

What appears to have happened, in short, is that the transition from a society dominated by the rural aristocracy to a society with power divided between urban and rural sectors and different class groups was marked by intensified conflict along a broadening range of issues. Generally speaking, while the rural upper-class groups controlled the country, they could afford to fight among themselves over economic issues. Their concern was not the structure of the society, but the distribution of its spoils. But when the urban lower class challenged this arrangement, the attack involved the whole society: its political system, its economic system, its ideology, its values, its leadership. Then the rural groups stopped fighting with each other, and joined in a common effort to salvage their society. As Argentina moved toward modernization, a lengthy period of intraclass economic disputes within the rural sector eventually shifted to a broad urban-rural class conflict that was waged on multiple fronts.

THE DISTRIBUTION OF POWER

For the sake of generalization, the resolution of conflicts over the beef industry can be viewed in sequential terms. In schematic form, the distribution and usage of power fell into three distinct phases.

Phase One: From the turn of the century until the early 1930s, political power coincided with economic power. Effective strength was located in the rural sectors, and superiority in the economic arena brought superiority in the political arena. This was most strikingly demonstrated during the battle over the minimum price in 1923, won by the packers and the fatteners. During this period the fatteners were stronger than the breeders, and the stockmen (together) were much stronger than the consumers and the packinghouse workers.

Phase Two: In the middle and late 1930s the distribution of power within the rural upper class was altered by the organization and activities of the breeders. Through CARBAP and the Ministry of Agriculture, the breeders won some significant victories over the Rural Society. This reallocation of power permitted the breeders to use political strength to offset their comparative economic weakness, but affected the rural aristocracy only. The stockmen, as a group, were still much more influential than the workers or the consumers.

Phase Three: The rural locus of power was totally upset after the revolution of 1943, especially when Perón began his rise. After the overthrow of the longstanding political system, the consumers and (to a greater degree) the packinghouse workers managed to alter their socio-economic circumstances and bring the packers and ranchers down to political defeat. Effective power moved away from the rural areas, and political strength no longer corresponded to economic strength.

In summary, this analysis of struggles concerning the Argentine beef industry reveals a long stage of transition away from "traditional" society, during which conflict took place—and power was contained—within a dynamic rural aristocracy. Under these conditions the urban middle classes identified their interests and aspirations with the ruling groups. At the same time, the political system attained a considerable degree of modernization as it concerned the intraclass fights of these groups. Eventually, intensive urbanization and some industrial growth exerted lower-class pressures for change; but the political system, under the Concordancia, did not provide any meaningful

access to power for the new groups. Socio-economic modernization was outstripping political modernization. Eventually, the
urban lower class (not the middle sectors) issued a challenge to
the entire political and economic structure. When the State
was taken over by Perón, the lower-class groups were able to
offset economic weakness with political strength. At this point
the process of conflict underwent realignment, and a critical era
in the politics of Argentine beef came to an end.

Bibliography and Sources

THE following bibliography includes almost all the useful sources examined during the course of my research in Argentina, England, and the United States. Though most of the material is available in published form, my investigation met with several problems. I could not get into the diplomatic archives of the Argentine Government. I was unable to look at company records of the packinghouses (some of the London files were destroyed by bombs in World War II; in Buenos Aires, my requests were politely ignored). One of the hardest tasks was getting biographical information on participants in disputes over the beef industry—in all, some 700 of them; after strenuous effort, the data are usable but still far from complete.

As listed below, the sources have been placed in five different categories: books, pamphlets, and articles; official and semiofficial publications; manuscripts; periodicals and newspapers; and biographical data on political participants. I have not included interviews, most of which were quite informal.

I. BOOKS, PAMPHLETS, AND ARTICLES

Abelardo Ramos, Jorge. *Revolución y contrarrevolución en Argentina: las masas en nuestra historia*. Buenos Aires, 1957.

Alberdi, Juan Bautista. *Obras escogidas*. Ed. Hilmar D. DiGiorgio. Vols. I (*Bases y puntos de partida para la organización política de la República Argentina*) and II (*Estudios económicos*). Buenos Aires, 1952, 1956.

Alexander, Robert J. *The Perón Era*. New York, 1951.

Almond, Gabriel, and James S. Coleman, eds. *The Politics of the Developing Areas*. Princeton, N. J., 1960.

Alsina, Juan A. *La inmigración en el primer siglo de la independencia*. Buenos Aires, 1910.

Álvarez, Agustín. *South America*. Trans. Gustavo E. Archilla. New York, 1938.

Álvarez, Juan. *Estudio sobre las guerras civiles argentinas*. Buenos Aires, 1914.

Armour, J. Ogden. *Investigación sobre la industria frigorífica*. Buenos Aires, 1923.

Ashworth, William. *An Economic History of England 1870–1939*. New York and London, 1960.

Astor, Viscount, and B. Seebohm Rowntree. *British Agriculture: The Principles of Future Policy*. London, New York, and Toronto, 1938.

Baily, Samuel. *Labor, Nationalism, and Politics in Argentina*. New Brunswick, N. J., 1967.

Baquerizas, José. *Por que se creyó en Perón: políticos, militares, y peronistas*. Buenos Aires, 1957.

Barager, Joseph R., ed. *Why Perón Came to Power: The Background to Peronism in Argentina*. New York, 1968.

Barrios, Abelardo M. et al. *Las empresas de frigoríficos en juicio contencioso con el gobierno de la nación sobre la interpretación y constitucionalidad de la ley 11.226: demandas, alegatos, memoriales y antecedentes*. Buenos Aires, 1934.

Beaverbrook, Lord (William M. Aitken). *Empire Free Trade: The New Policy for Prosperity*. London, 1929.

————. *My Case for Empire Free Trade*. London, 1930.

Beltrán, Juan G. *La argentinidad*. Buenos Aires, 1919.

Benham, Frederic. *Great Britain under Protection*. New York, 1941.

Black, C. E. *The Dynamics of Modernization: A Study in Comparative History*. New York, Evanston, and London, 1966.

Blanksten, George I. *Perón's Argentina*. Chicago, 1953.

Bunge, Alejandro E. *Una nueva Argentina*. Buenos Aires, 1940.

Bunge, Carlos Octavio. *Nuestra América*. Barcelona, 1903.

Bunge, Mauricio. *Creación de un órgano intermediario oficial para la venta de hacienda gorda*. Buenos Aires, 1923.

————. "La ley de precios mínimos y máximos de la carne." *Revista de economía argentina*, Año 6, no. 63, tomo XI (septiembre de 1923), [207]–19.

Burgin, Miron. *The Economic Aspects of Argentine Federalism, 1820–1852*. Cambridge, Mass., 1946.

Capper, Arthur. "The Middle West Looks Abroad." *Foreign Affairs*, V, no. 4 (July, 1927), 529–37.

Cárcano, Miguel Ángel. *Realidad de una política*. Buenos Aires, 1938.

Carulla, Juan E. *Al filo del medio siglo*. 2nd ed. Buenos Aires, 1964.

Carver, Arthur H. *Personnel and Labor Problems in the Packing Industry*. Chicago, 1928.

Carranza, Mario A. *La ley del precio mínimo: estudio jurídico*. Buenos Aires, 1923.

Chadwick, A. et al. *The Meat Trade.* 3 vols. London, 1934.

Ciria, Alberto. *Partidos y poder en la Argentina moderna (1930–1946).* Buenos Aires, 1964.

Clemen, Rudolf A. *The American Livestock and Meat Industry.* New York, 1923.

Comisión del Comité Central del Partido Comunista. *Esbozo de historia del Partido Communista de la Argentina.* Buenos Aires, 1947.

Comité Nacional de Defensa de la Producción. *Despacho de la Comisión Especial de Asuntos Ganaderos de la H. Cámara de Diputados de la Nación.* Buenos Aires, 1923.

Compañía Swift de la Plata, S.A. *Ganadería argentina: su desarrollo e industrialización.* Text by Manuel A. Romero Aguirre. Buenos Aires, 1957.

——. *La industria frigorífica y el comercio de carnes: información ilustrativa.* Buenos Aires, 1923.

Confederación de Asociaciones Rurales de Buenos Aires y La Pampa (CARBAP). *Recopilación de las deliberaciones y resoluciones de los congresos rurales, 1932 a 1942.* Buenos Aires, 1946.

Coni, Emilio A. *Anteproyecto de abastecimiento de carne a la Capital Federal por medio de mataderos y vagones frigoríficos, efectuado por una cooperativa de estancieros.* Buenos Aires, 1922.

Consoli, Max. *Por qué soy peronista.* Santa Fe, 1946.

Cortese, Antonio. *Historia económica argentina y americana.* Buenos Aires, 1959.

Crawford, William Rex. *A Century of Latin-American Thought.* Rev. ed. Cambridge, Mass., 1961.

Critchell, James T., and Joseph Raymond. *A History of the Frozen Meat Trade.* London, 1912.

Cronshaw, H. B., and D. J. Anthony. *The Meat Industry.* London, 1927.

Dahl, Robert A. *Who Governs? Democracy and Power in an American City.* New Haven and London, 1961.

Del Mazo, Gabriel. *El radicalismo: ensayo sobre su historia y doctrina.* 3 vols. Buenos Aires, 1957.

Deutsch, Karl W. "Social Mobilization and Political Development." *American Political Science Review,* LV, no. 3 (September, 1961), 493–514.

Di Tella, Torcuato S. *El sistema político argentino y la clase obrera.* Buenos Aires, 1964.

Di Tella, Torcuato, Gino Germani, Jorge Graciarena, et al. *Argentina, sociedad de masas.* Buenos Aires, 1965.

Dorfman, Adolfo. *Evolución industrial argentina.* Buenos Aires, 1942.

——. *Historia de la industria argentina.* Buenos Aires, 1942.

Duhau, Luis. *Política económica internacional: "Comprar a quien nos compra."* Buenos Aires, 1927.

Economic Commission for Latin America (United Nations). *El desarrollo económico de la Argentina.* 3 vols. Mexico, 1959.

Edminster, Lynn R. *The Cattle Industry and the Tariff.* New York, 1926.

Eisenstadt, S. N. *Modernization: Protest and Change.* Englewood Cliffs, N. J., 1966.

[Empresas Frigoríficas]. *Memorial de las empresas frigoríficas presentado a la Cámara de Senadores, haciendo reparos al proyecto de ley de control del comercio de carnes.* Buenos Aires, 1923.

———. *Memorial de las empresas frigoríficas al Ministerio de Agricultura sobre la situación ganadera.* Buenos Aires, 1923.

———. *Presentación de las empresas frigoríficas ante el Congreso de la Nación.* Buenos Aires, 1933.

———. *La verdad sobre la industria frigorífica: memorial presentado a la Comisión Especial de Asuntos Ganaderos de la Cámara de Diputados por las Compañías Frigoríficas, estudiando la faz económica del costo de producción y de la venta de la carne.* Buenos Aires, 1923.

Enfield, R. R. *The Agricultural Crisis, 1920–1923.* London, 1924.

Farré, Luis. *Cincuenta años de filosofía en Argentina.* Buenos Aires, 1958.

Ferns, H. S. *Britain and Argentina in the Nineteenth Century.* London, 1960.

———. "Britain's Informal Empire in Argentina, 1806–1914." *Past & Present,* no. 4 (November, 1953), 60–75.

Ferrer, Aldo. *La economía argentina: las etapas de su desarrollo y problemas actuales.* 2nd ed. Mexico-Buenos Aires, 1964.

Fite, Gilbert C., and Jim E. Reese. *An Economic History of the United States.* 2nd ed. Boston-New York, 1965.

Fletcher, T. W. "The Great Depression of English Agriculture 1873–1896." *The Economic History Review,* 2nd ser., XLIII, no. 3 (1961), 417–32.

Foerster, Robert F. *The Italian Emigration of Our Times.* Cambridge, Mass., 1919.

Frondizi, Arturo. *Petróleo y política: contribución al estudio de la historia económica argentina y de las relaciones entre el imperialismo y la vida política nacional.* Buenos Aires, 1954.

Fuchs, Jaime. *La penetración de los trusts yanquis en la Argentina.* Buenos Aires, 1957.

Galletti, Alfredo. *La política y los partidos.* Mexico-Buenos Aires, 1961.

Gálvez, Manuel. *El diario de Gabriel Quiroga.* Buenos Aires, 1910.

García, Juan Agustín. *Sobre nuestra incultura.* Buenos Aires, n.d.

García Ledesma, H. *Lisandro de la Torre y la pampa gringa.* Buenos Aires, 1954.

García Mata, Carlos. *The Problem of Beef in United States-Argentine Relations.* Cambridge, Mass., 1941.

Germani, Gino. *Estructura social de la Argentina: análisis estadístico.* Buenos Aires, 1955.

————. *Política y sociedad en una época de transición: de la sociedad tradicional a la sociedad de masas.* Buenos Aires, 1963.

Gerrard, Frank, ed. *The Book of the Meat Trade.* 2 vols. London, 1949.

Giberti, Horacio C. E. *Historia económica de la ganadería argentina.* Buenos Aires, 1961.

Glauert, Earl T. "Ricardo Rojas and the Emergence of Argentine Cultural Nationalism." *Hispanic American Historical Review,* XLIII, no. 1 (February, 1963), 1–13.

González Arrili, B. *Vida de Lisandro de la Torre.* Buenos Aires, 1940.

Grant, Ross et al. *The Frozen and Chilled Meat Trade.* 2 vols. London, 1929.

Grela, Plácido. *El Grito de Alcorta: historia de la rebelión campesina de 1912.* Rosario, 1958.

Haldane, Sir William S. *Our Beef Supply: The Outlook.* London, 1929.

Hanson, Simon G. *Argentine Meat and the British Market: Chapters in the History of the Argentine Meat Industry.* Stanford, Calif., 1938.

Hayes, Carlton J. H. *The Historical Evolution of Modern Nationalism.* New York, 1931.

Hernández Arregui, Juan José. *La formación de la conciencia nacional (1930–1960).* Buenos Aires, 1960.

Hirschman, Albert O. *Journeys toward Progress: Studies of Economic Policy-Making in Latin America.* New York, 1963.

————, ed. *Latin American Issues: Essays and Comments.* New York, 1961.

Huntington, Samuel P. "Political Development and Political Decay." *World Politics,* XVII, no. 3 (April, 1965), [386]–430.

Iannini, Hugo R. *Comercio de carnes importadas en Inglaterra: mercado de Smithfield.* Buenos Aires, 1936.

Ibarguren, Carlos. *La historia que he vivido.* Buenos Aires, 1955.

Imaz, José Luis de. *Los que mandan.* Buenos Aires, 1964.

Irazusta, Julio and Rodolfo. *La Argentina y el imperialismo británico.* Buenos Aires, 1934.

Isacovich, Marcelo. *Argentina económica y social.* 2nd ed. Buenos Aires, 1963.

Íscaro, Rubens. *Origen y desarrollo del movimiento sindical argentino.* Buenos Aires, 1958.

Jefferson, Mark. *Peopling the Argentine Pampa.* New York, 1926.

Johnson, John J. *Political Change in Latin America: The Emergence of the Middle Sectors.* Stanford, Calif., 1958.

Kautsky, John H., ed. *Political Change in Underdeveloped Countries: Nationalism and Communism.* New York and London, 1962.

Korn, Alejandro. *Obras completas.* Ed. Francisco Romero. Buenos Aires, 1949.

Larra, Raúl. *Lisandro de la Torre: el solitario de Pinas.* 6th ed. Buenos Aires, 1956.

Lasswell, Harold D., and Abraham Kaplan. *Power and Society: A Framework for Political Inquiry.* New Haven, 1950.

Lazarte, Juan. *Lisandro de la Torre: reformador social americano.* 2nd ed. Buenos Aires, 1955.

Lerner, Daniel. *The Passing of Traditional Society: Modernizing the Middle East.* Glencoe, Ill., 1958.

Liceaga, José V. *Las carnes en la economía argentina.* Buenos Aires, 1952.

López, Alfredo. *La clase obrera y la revolución del 4 de junio.* Buenos Aires, 1945.

Mántaras, Eduardo C. "La ley de carnes y el problema ganadero." *Revista de Ciencias Jurídicas y Sociales* (Universidad Nacional del Litoral, Santa Fe), IV (3a. época), no. 28 (1939), 37–53.

Mariño, Octavio Augusto. *El consumo de carnes en la Capital Federal.* Buenos Aires, 1932.

———. *La ley de carnes.* Buenos Aires, 1933.

———. *Observaciones al proyecto de ley de "defensa ganadera" del Poder Ejecutivo de la Nación.* Buenos Aires, 1932.

———. *Observaciones al 2º proyecto de ley de "defensa ganadera" del Poder Ejecutivo de la Nación; el Congreso de Nueve de Julio; las sociedades rurales del interior.* Buenos Aires, 1932.

———. *Proyecto de Asociación Cooperativa Nacional.* Buenos Aires (?), 1932.

Mármol, José R., Horacio C. E. Giberti, Ricardo E. Olivari. *Por qué está cara la carne.* Buenos Aires, 1942.

Marotta, F. Pedro. *El verdadero nacionalismo económico argentino.* Buenos Aires, 1922.

Marotta, Sebastián. *El movimiento sindical argentino: su génesis y desarrollo.* Vol. II. Buenos Aires, 1961.

McGann, Thomas F. *Argentina, the United States, and the Inter-American System, 1880–1914.* Cambridge, Mass., 1957.

Merchensky, Marcos. *Las corrientes ideológicas en la historia argentina.* Buenos Aires, 1961.

Miró, Carlos A. *La intervención de los ganaderos en el comercio de carnes: reseña de las experiencias realizadas desde agosto del 1932 a mayo de 1938.* Buenos Aires, 1942.

Moore, Barrington, Jr. *Social Origins of Dictatorship and Democracy: Lord and Peasant in the Making of the Modern World.* Boston, 1966.

Nemirovsky, Lázaro. *Estructura económica y orientación política de la agricultura en la República Argentina.* Buenos Aires, 1933.

Newton, Jorge. *Historia de la Sociedad Rural Argentina.* Buenos Aires, 1966.

Nichols, Madaline Wallis. *The Gaucho: Cattle Hunter, Cavalryman, Ideal of Romance.* Durham, N. C., 1942.

Noboa, Horacio J. *Política nacional de carnes.* Buenos Aires, 1956.

Olariaga, Nemesio de. *El ruralismo argentino: economía ganadera.* Buenos Aires, 1943.

Olivera, Carlos M. *Lo que ha sido, lo que es, y lo que debe ser la Sociedad Rural Argentina.* Buenos Aires, 1946.

Ortiz, Ricardo M. *Historia económica de la Argentina, 1850–1930.* 2 vols. Buenos Aires, 1955.

――――. *El pensamiento económico de Echeverría (trayectoria y actualidad).* Buenos Aires, 1953.

Otero, José Pacífico. *Nuestro nacionalismo.* Buenos Aires, 1920.

Pagés, Pedro T. *Crisis ganadera argentina.* Buenos Aires, 1922.

――――. *Crisis ganadera argentina.* Buenos Aires, 1923.

Palma, José María. *El trust de la carne.* Buenos Aires, 1913.

Peffer, E. Louise. "State Intervention in the Argentine Meat Packing Industry, 1946–1958." *Food Research Institute Studies,* II, no. 1 (February, 1961), [33]–73.

――――. "Foot-and-Mouth Disease in United States Policy." *Food Research Institute Studies,* III, no. 2 (May, 1962), [141]–180.

[Pellegrini, Carlos]. *Pellegrini, 1846–1906: Obras.* Ed. with a biographical essay by Agustín Rivero Astengo. 5 vols. Buenos Aires, 1951.

Pendle, George. *Argentina.* 3rd ed. New York, London and Toronto, 1963.

Pereda, Horacio V. *La ganadería argentina es una sola.* Buenos Aires, 1939.

Perón, Eva. *La razón de mi vida.* 12th ed. Buenos Aires, 1952.

Perón, Juan. *Los vendepatria: las pruebas de una traición.* Buenos Aires, 1958.

Peterson, Harold F. *Argentina and the United States 1810–1960.* New York, 1964.

Pinedo, Federico. *En tiempos de la república.* 5 vols. Buenos Aires, 1946.

Prebisch, Raúl. *Anotaciones sobre la crisis ganadera.* Buenos Aires, 1923.

――――. *Información estadística sobre el comercio de carnes (primera parte: el mercado británico).* Buenos Aires, 1922.

Puiggros, Rodolfo. *Historia crítica de los partidos políticos argentinos.* 2 vols., rev. ed. Buenos Aires, 1965.

――――. *Libre empresa o nacionalización en la industria de la carne.* Buenos Aires, 1957.

Putnam, George E. *Supplying Britain's Meat,* London, 1923.

Rennie, Ysabel F. *The Argentine Republic.* New York, 1945.

Repetto, Nicolás. *Mi paso por la política.* 2 vols. Buenos Aires, 1956–57.

Reyes, Cipriano. *Qué es el laborismo.* Buenos Aires, 1946.

Richardson, J. Henry. *British Economic Foreign Policy.* London, 1936.

Richelet, Juan E. *La Argentina en el exterior.* Paris, 1930.

――――. *The Argentine Meat Trade: Meat Inspection Regulations in the Argentine Republic.* London, 1929.

――――. *A Defence of Argentine Meat.* London, 1929.

――――. *Los frigoríficos y la conferencia de los fletes marítimos.* Paris, 1929.

Richelet, Juan E. *La ganadería argentina y su comercio de carnes*. Buenos Aires, 1928.

Richelet, Juan E. *Producción, industria y comercio de la carne (proyecto para la creación de una Oficina Internacional de la Carne)*. Madrid, 1929.

Rojas, Ricardo. *Obras*. Vol. II (*La restauración nacionalista*). Buenos Aires, 1922.

Romariz, José R. *La semana trágica*. Buenos Aires, 1952.

Romero, José Luis. *A History of Argentine Political Thought*. Trans. Thomas F. McGann. Stanford, Calif., 1963.

Ruano Fournier, Agustín. *Estudio económico de la producción de las carnes del Río de la Plata*. Montevideo, 1936.

Saldías, Adolfo. *La evolución republicana durante la revolución argentina*. Buenos Aires, 1906.

Salera, Virgil. *Exchange Control and the Argentine Market*. New York and London, 1941.

Samuel, Sir Herbert. *Empire Free Trade? An Examination of Lord Beaverbrook's Proposal*. London, 1930.

Sánchez Sorondo, Matías G. *El problema ganadero ante el Congreso, 1922–23*. Buenos Aires, 1933.

Scalabrini, Pedro. *Materialismo, darwinismo, positivismo: diferencias y semejanzas*. Paraná, 1889.

Scalabrini Ortiz, Raúl. *Política británica en el Río de la Plata*. Buenos Aires, 1957. Originally published in 1939.

Schattsneider, E. E. *The Semisovereign People: A Realist's View of Democracy in America*. New York, 1960.

Scobie, James R. *Argentina: A City and a Nation*. New York, 1964.

———. *Revolution on the Pampas: A Social History of Argentine Wheat, 1860–1910*. Austin, Tex., 1964.

Silvert, K. H., ed. *Expectant Peoples: Nationalism and Development*. New York, 1963.

———. "Leadership Formation and Modernization in Latin America." *Journal of International Affairs*, XX, no. 2 (1966), 318–331.

Sinclair, Upton. *The Jungle*. New York, 1906.

Smith, Peter H. "Los radicales argentinos y la defensa de los intereses ganaderos, 1916–1930." *Desarrollo económico*, VII, no. 25 (abril–junio de 1967), [795]–829.

———. "Social Mobilization, Political Participation, and the Rise of Juan Perón." Forthcoming in the *Political Science Quarterly*.

Snow, Peter G. *Argentine Radicalism: The History and Doctrine of the Radical Civic Union*. Iowa City, 1965.

Sociedad Rural Argentina. *A propósito de una errónea información contenida en la presentación de varias Empresas Frigoríficas ante la Honorable Cámara de Diputados de la Nación*. Boletín de Divulgación No. 7. Buenos Aires, 1933.

———. *Anuario de la Sociedad Rural Argentina*. Buenos Aires, 1928.

———. *Ejecución del plan orgánico de defensa ganadera*. Boletín de Divulgación No. 6. Buenos Aires, 1933.

———. *Estatutos de la Sociedad Rural Argentina*. Buenos Aires, 1927.

———. *Plan orgánico de defensa ganadera*. Boletín de Divulgación No. 5. Buenos Aires, 1932.

———. *El pool de frigoríficos: necesidad de intervención del Estado*. Buenos Aires, 1927.

Stepan, Alfred. "Political Development Theory: The Latin American Experience." *Journal of International Affairs*, XX, no. 2 (1966), 223–34.

Subcomisión del Comercio Exterior de Carnes de la Sociedad Rural Argentina. *Comercio exterior de carnes*. Buenos Aires, 1927.

Taylor, Carl C. *Rural Life in Argentina*. Baton Rouge, La., 1948.

[Torre, Lisandro de la]. *Obras de Lisandro de la Torre*. Ed. Raúl Larra. 6 vols. 3rd ed. Buenos Aires, 1957.

Torres, Gustavo C. *Función social de la ley de carnes*. Buenos Aires, 1940.

Truman, David B. *The Governmental Process: Political Interests and Public Opinion*. New York, 1953.

Ugarte, Manuel. *The Destiny of a Continent*. Ed. J. Fred Rippy, trans. Catherine A. Phillips. New York, 1925.

Vestey, Sir Edmund. *Ottawa y la "preferencia imperial."* Buenos Aires, n.d.

Villafañe, Benjamín. *La miseria de un país rico*. Jujuy, 1926.

Wagley, Charles, ed. *Social Science Research on Latin America: Report and Papers of a Seminar on Latin American Studies in the United States Held at Stanford, California, July 8–August 23, 1963*. New York and London, 1964.

Watson, David J. R. *Los criollos y los gringos: escombros acumulados al levantar la estructura ganadera-frigorífica, 1882–1940*. Buenos Aires, 1941.

Whitaker, Arthur P. *Argentina*. Englewood Cliffs, N. J., 1964.

———. *Nationalism in Latin America*. Gainesville, Fla., 1962.

Williams, John H. *Argentine International Trade under Inconvertible Paper Money, 1880–1900*. Cambridge, Mass., 1920.

Wilson, Thomas E. et al. *The Packing Industry*. Chicago, 1924.

Zalduendo, Eduardo. *Geografía electoral de la Argentina*. Buenos Aires, 1958.

Zea, Leopoldo. *The Latin-American Mind*. Trans. James H. Abbott and Lowell Dunham. Norman, Okla., 1963.

II. OFFICIAL AND SEMIOFFICIAL PUBLICATIONS

A. ARGENTINE REPUBLIC

Boletín Oficial. April, 1940.

Cámara de Diputados de la Nación. *Diario de Sesiones*, 1900–1942.

———. *Informe de la Comisión Investigadora de los Trusts*. Buenos Aires, 1919. Also contained in the *Diario de Sesiones*, 1920, V, 999–1127.

Cámara de Diputados de la Provincia de Buenos Aires. *Diario de Sesiones,* 1910–1939.

Cámara de Senadores de la Nación. *Diario de Sesiones,* 1900–1942.

Cámara de Senadores de la Provincia de Buenos Aires. *Diario de Sesiones,* 1910–1939.

Comisión del Censo Nacional. *Censo nacional agropecuario, año 1937.* Vol. entitled *Ganadería.* Buenos Aires, 1939.

———. *Tercer censo nacional, levantado el 1º de junio de 1914.* 10 vols. Buenos Aires, 1917–1919.

———. *IVº censo general de la Nación, 1947.* 3 vols. Buenos Aires, 1948–1952.

Concejo Deliberante de la Municipalidad de Buenos Aires. *Diario de Sesiones,* 1920–1942.

Corporación Argentina de Productores de Carnes. *La Corporación en el Mercado de Liniers: hacienda para consumo.* Buenos Aires, 1937.

———. *Memorias y balances, 1935–1942.* 7 vols. Buenos Aires, 1936–42.

Departamento Nacional de Trabajo. *Boletín del Departamento Nacional de Trabajo.* 1907–1908, 1916–1922, 1933–1939. Called the *Crónica mensual* in 1922 and the *Boletín informativo* during the 1930s.

———. *Estadística de las huelgas.* Buenos Aires, 1940.

Dirección General de Estadística. *Anuario de la Dirección General de Estadística correspondiente al año 1908.* Vol. II. Buenos Aires, 1900.

———. *Anuario de la Dirección General de Estadística correspondiente al año 1912.* Vol. II. Buenos Aires, 1914.

———. *Anuario estadístico de la República Argentina.* Vol. I (*Compendio*). Buenos Aires, 1948.

Gil Navarro, Orlando, ed. *Novísima recopilación de leyes usuales de la República Argentina.* Vol. II. Buenos Aires, 1943.

Junta Nacional de Carnes. *Constitucionalidad de la ley 11.747.* Buenos Aires, 1944.

———. *Defensa de la ley de carnes (no. 11.747).* Buenos Aires, n.d.

———. *Discursos pronunciados por el Excmo. Señor Presidente de la Nación, General Agustín P. Justo, Ministro de Agricultura de la Nación, Doctor Miguel Á. Cárcano y palabras del Señor Presidente de la Junta Nacional de Carnes, Doctor Horacio N. Bruzone, con motivo de la visita al local de la entidad, el día 30 de diciembre de 1936.* Buenos Aires, 1937.

———. *Estadísticas básicas.* Buenos Aires, 1964.

———. *Informe de la Junta Nacional de Carnes a pedido del Ministerio de Agricultura con motivo de la presentación de los ganaderos del Litoral.* Buenos Aires, 1938.

———. *Informe de la labor realizada desde el 1º de enero de 1934 hasta el 30 de septiembre de 1935.* Buenos Aires, 1935.

————. *Informe de la labor realizada desde el 1º de octubre de 1935 hasta el 30 de septiembre de 1937.* Buenos Aires, 1937.

————. *La Junta Nacional de Carnes en el contralor de la industria frigorífica.* Buenos Aires, 1944.

————. *Leyes, decretos y resoluciones relacionados al régimen de comercialización de los novillos sobre la base de la clasificación y tipificación oficial de las carnes y de las normas adoptadas para la clasificación y tipificación de las carnes destinadas al consumo interno de la Capital Federal.* Buenos Aires, 1944.

————. *Reseña año 1958.* Buenos Aires, 1958.

————. *Respuestas del Poder Ejecutivo Nacional a los pedidos de informes a las HH. CC. de Senadores y Diputados de la Nación, sobre cumplimiento de la ley 11.747.* Buenos Aires, n.d.

————. *Síntesis de la labor desarrollada, 1933–1945.* Buenos Aires, 1945.

————. *Subsidio a la ganadería argentina: decretos del Poder Ejecutivo Nacional y resoluciones de la Junta Nacional de Carnes.* Buenos Aires, n.d.

Jurado, Mario, ed. *Antecedentes parlamentarios de la legislación argentina.* Vol. I (*Comercio de carnes* [*1862–1941*]). Buenos Aires, 1941.

Legón, Faustino, and Samuel W. Medrano. *Las constituciones de la República Argentina.* Madrid, 1953.

Mabragaña, H., ed. *Los mensajes: historia del desenvolvimiento de la nación argentina redactada cronológicamente por sus gobernantes, 1810–1910.* Vols. III, IV (1852–1910). Buenos Aires, 1910.

Ministerio de Agricultura. *Carnes—granos—elevadores de granos—colonización—petróleo: año 1932.* Buenos Aires, 1933.

————. *Comercio de carnes.* 3 vols. Libro Rojo, Libro Verde, Libro Azul. Buenos Aires, 1922–23.

————. *Comercio de carnes: el precio mínimo para la compra de carne bovina para exportación.* Buenos Aires, 1923.

————. *Los frigoríficos y el Ministerio de Agricultura: informes a la Comisión Investigadora del Honorable Senado de la Nación.* Buenos Aires, 1934.

————. *Informe de la Comisión Asesora Honoraria de Ganaderos, presentado al Ministerio de Agricultura de la Nación.* Buenos Aires, 1931.

————. *Informe del Comité Mixto Investigador del Comercio de Carnes Anglo-Argentino.* London, 1938.

Ministerio del Interior. *Las fuerzas armadas restituyen el imperio de la soberanía popular.* 2 vols. Buenos Aires, 1946.

Ministerio de Relaciones Exteriores y Culto. *Memoria presentada al Honorable Congreso Nacional, correspondiente al período 1933–34.* Buenos Aires, 1934.

Ministerios de Hacienda y Agricultura. *El plan de acción económica nacional.* Buenos Aires, 1934.

[Perón, Juan]. *Los mensajes de Perón.* Buenos Aires, 1952.

———. *Perón expone su doctrina: teoría y doctrina del peronismo.* Buenos Aires, 1947.

Presidencia de la Nación. *Plan de gobierno 1947–1951.* Vol. I. Buenos Aires, 1948.

Restoy, Eugenio, and Arturo Doeste, eds. *Compilación de leyes, decretos y resoluciones.* Vol. I. Buenos Aires, 1942.

Remorino, Jerónimo, Roberto Fraga Patrao et al. *Anales de legislación argentina, 1852–1954.* 5 vols. Buenos Aires, 1953–57.

Secretaría de Trabajo y Previsión. *Revista de Trabajo y Previsión,* 1944–1946 (Nos. 1–12).

B. UNITED KINGDOM

Board of Trade. *Report of the Joint Committee of Enquiry into the Anglo-Argentine Meat Trade.* London, 1938.

Department of Overseas Trade. *Report on the Financial and Economic Conditions of the Argentine Republic.* London, 1921–1945. (Title varies.)

[Foreign Office]. *British and Foreign State Papers, 1900–1945.* Vols. 94–145. London, 1904–1953.

House of Commons. *Parliamentary Debates,* 1910–1935.

Imperial Economic Committee. *Cattle and Beef Survey: A Survey of Production and Trade in British Empire and Foreign Countries.* London, 1934.

Parliamentary Papers:

Board of Trade, Inter-Departmental Committee on Meat Supplies. "Report of Committee Appointed by the Board of Trade to Consider the Means of Securing Sufficient Meat Supplies for the United Kingdom." 1919 (Cd. 456), XXV, 435–64. (Page numbers for these citations are taken from the collection in the British Museum, London.)

Committee Appointed by the Board of Trade to Investigate the Principal Causes Which Have Led to the Increase of Prices of Commodities since the Beginning of the War. "Interim Report on Meat, Milk, and Bacon." 1916 (Cd. 8358), XIV, 731–50.

Committee on Combinations in the Meat Trade. "Report of the Departmental Committee Appointed to Inquire into Combinations in the Meat Trade." 1909 (Cd. 4643), XV, 1–31.

———. "Minutes of Evidence Taken before the Departmental Committee on Combinations in the Meat Trade." 1909 (Cd. 4661), XV, 33–383.

Commonwealth of Australia. "Report (with Appendices) of the Royal

Commission on the Meat Export Trade of Australia." 1914–16 (Cd. 7896), XLVI, 1–50.

Imperial Economic Committee. "Report of the Imperial Economic Committee on Marketing and Preparing for Market of Foodstuffs Produced in the Overseas Parts of the Empire. First Report—General." 1924–25 (Cd. 2493), XIII, 799–836.

———. "Report of the Imperial Economic Committee on Marketing and Preparing for Market of Foodstuffs Produced in the Overseas Parts of the Empire. Second Report—Meat." 1924–25 (Cd. 2499), XIII, 837–71.

"Import of Meat into the United Kingdom: Statement of the Views of His Majesty's Government in the United Kingdom." 1934–35 (Cd. 4828), XVII, 755–60.

"The Livestock Situation." 1933–34 (Cd. 4651), XXI, 561–64.

Ministry of Agriculture and Fisheries. "Report of the Departmental Committee Appointed by the Minister of Agriculture and Fisheries to Consider the Outbreak of Foot and Mouth Disease Which Occurred in 1923–24." 1924–25 (Cd. 2350), XIII, 225–310.

Ministry of Agriculture and Fisheries. Departmental Committee on Distribution and Prices of Agricultural Produce. "Interim Report on Meat, Poultry and Eggs." 1923 (Cd. 1927), IX, 297–481.

Ministry of Agriculture and Fisheries and Scottish Office. "Report of the Second Inter-Departmental Committee on the Grading and Marking of Beef." 1931–32 (Cd. 4047), VI, 141–208.

Profiteering Acts, 1919 and 1920. "Interim Report on Meat, Prepared by a Sub-Committee Appointed by the Standing Committee on Trusts." 1920 (Cd. 1057), XXIII, 545–57.

———. "Final Report on Meat, Prepared by a Sub-Committee Appointed by the Standing Committee on Trusts." 1921 (Cd. 1356), XVI, 783–91.

Royal Commission on Food Prices. "First Report of the Royal Commission on Food Prices, with Minutes of Evidence and Appendices." 1924–25 (Cd. 2390), XIII, 1–223.

Royal Commission on the Importation of Store Cattle. "Report of His Majesty's Commissioners Appointed to Inquire into the Admission into the United Kingdom of Livestock for Purposes Other than Immediate Slaughter at the Ports." 1921 (Cd. 1139), XVIII, 1–15.

Royal Commission on Supply of Food and Raw Material in Time of War. "Report of the Royal Commission on Supply of Food and Raw Material in Time of War, with Minutes of Evidence and Appendices." 1905 (Cd. 2643), XXXIX, 1–216; 1905 (Cd. 2644), XXXIX, 217–704; 1905 (Cd. 2645), XL, 1–384.

Secretary of State for Dominion Affairs. "Imperial Economic Conference at Ottawa, 1932: Summary of Proceedings and Copies of Trade Agreements." 1931–32 (Cd. 4174), X, 701–95.

Secretary of State for Foreign Affairs. "Convention between the Government of the United Kingdom and the Government of the Argentine Republic Relating to Trade and Commerce, with Protocol, London, May 1, 1933." 1932–33 (Cd. 4310), XXVII, 1–15.

———. "Exchanges of Notes between His Majesty's Government in the United Kingdom and the Governments of the Argentine Republic, Brazil and Uruguay Regarding the Regulation of Beef Imports into the United Kingdom." 1938–39 (Cd. 5941), XXVII, 37–45.

C. UNITED STATES
Department of Agriculture:
Agricultural Marketing Service. *Meat Consumption Trends and Patterns* [by Gertrude Gronbech]. Agriculture Handbook No. 187. Washington, 1960.
Bicknell, Frank W. *Alfalfa and Beef Production in Argentina.* United States Department of Agriculture Report No. 77. Washington, 1904.
———. *The Animal Industry of Argentina.* Bureau of Animal Industry Bulletin No. 48. Washington, 1903.
Bureau of Animal Industry. *Foot-and-Mouth Disease.* Farmers' Bulletin No. 666. Washington, 1952.
Holmes, George K. "Argentine Beef," *The Agricultural Outlook,* Farmers' Bulletin No. 581, 30–40. Washington, 1915.
Melvin, A. D. "The South American Meat Industry." *Yearbook of the United States Department of Agriculture, 1913* (Washington, 1914), 347–64.
Melvin, A. D., and George M. Rommel. "Meat Production in the Argentine and Its Effect upon the Industry in the United States." *Yearbook of the United States Department of Agriculture, 1914* (Washington, 1915), 381–90.
Olitsky, Peter K., Jacob Traum, and Harry W. Schoening. *Report of the Foot-and-Mouth Disease Commission of the United States Department of Agriculture.* U.S.D.A. Technical Bulletin No. 76. Washington, 1928.

[Department of State]. *Papers Relating to the Foreign Relations of the United States, 1900–1943.* Washington, 1902–1965. In 1947, for the edition corresponding to the diplomatic year 1932, the title was changed to *Foreign Relations of the United States, Diplomatic Papers.*
Federal Trade Commission. *Maximum Profit Limitation in the Meat-Packing Industry.* Washington, 1919.
———. *Report of the Federal Trade Commission on the Meat-Packing Industry.* 6 vols. Washington, 1919.
United States Congress. *Congressional Record.* 66th Cong.—81st Cong., 1919–1930.

III. MANUSCRIPTS

A. DIVISIÓN DE ARCHIVO, MUSEO, Y PUBLICACIONES DEL CONGRESO NACIONAL,
BUENOS AIRES
These archives were used to consult the original texts of petitions to
the Argentine Congress.

B. PUBLIC RECORD OFFICE, LONDON
At the time research was conducted (June–September 1967), Foreign
Office documents were open through the year 1923.

Board of Trade. Correspondence and Papers. (Series B.T. 11, B.T. 55.)
Department of Overseas Trade. Correspondence and Papers, 1918–1922.
(Series B.T. 60.)
Foreign Office. Commercial, 1906–1919. (Series F.O. 368.)
———. Consular, 1906–1922. (Series F.O. 369, 566.)
———. Embassy and Consular Archives, 1900–1922. (Series F.O. 118, 347.)
———. General Correspondence, 1900–1905. (Series F.O. 6.)
———. General Correspondence: Political, 1906–1923. (Series F.O. 371.)

C. NATIONAL ARCHIVES, WASHINGTON
Bureau of Foreign and Domestic Commerce. Reports of Commercial At-
tachés: Buenos Aires, 1932–1934. (Record Group 151.)
Department of Agriculture. Foreign Agricultural Relations: Reports, 1918–
1938. (Record Group 166.)
Department of State. Foreign Service Posts of the Department of State:
Correspondence of the American Legation/Embassy in Buenos Aires,
1910–1936. (Record Group 84.)
———. General Records of the Department of State: Decimal File, 1910–
1936. (Record Group 59.)

D. UNPUBLISHED PAPERS
Arner, George B. L. "The Cattle Situation in Argentina." Mimeographed.
Washington, 1923; rev. 1924.
British Empire Producers' Organization. "Comments on the Meat Trade's
Manifesto." Manuscript dated October 7, 1930 in the Biblioteca del
Banco Tornquist.
Economic Commission for Latin America (United Nations). "El desarrollo
económico de la Argentina." Mimeographed. Santiago de Chile, 1958.
Instituto de Investigaciones Económicas y Financieras de la Confederación
General Económica. "Elementos para la historia de una moderna acción
empresaria." Mimeographed. Buenos Aires, 1965.
Mariño, Octavio Augusto. "Discurso pronunciado en el acto inaugural
de la 43a. exposición y 5o. concurso de novillos gordos, realizada en

Gualeguaychú el día 11 de octubre de 1936." Manuscript in the Biblioteca del Banco Tornquist.

Ras, Norberto. "El problema argentino de las carnes." Manuscript in the library of the Argentine Rural Society. N.p., n.d.

Ryan, Tomás Patricio. "El festín de los buitres." Manuscript given to me by the author. Buenos Aires, n.d.

Wright, Winthrop R. "Argentine Railways and the Growth of Nationalism." Ph.D. Dissertation, University of Pennsylvania, 1964.

IV. PERIODICALS AND NEWSPAPERS

A. PERIODICALS

Anales de la Sociedad Rural Argentina, 1900–1947.

Annual Review of the Chilled and Frozen Meat Trade (W. Weddel & Company, Ltd., London).

The Argentine Review (London), 1932–34.

Boletín de la Unión Industrial Argentina, 1900–1945. The title varies: from November 1925 to the end of 1936 it was called the *Anales;* from January 1937 to January 1944 it was known as *Argentina Fabril;* after that it became the *Revista.*

Buenos Aires y La Pampa, 1935–1948.

Cold Storage and Produce Review, 1913–1933.

La Res, 1933–1945.

Review of the River Plate, 1912–1946.

B. NEWSPAPERS

Most newspapers were consulted only for times of particular crisis or tension in the Argentine beef industry.

Buenos Aires Herald.

C.G.T. (Buenos Aires).

The Daily Express (London).

Edición Rural (Buenos Aires).

La Nación (Buenos Aires).

La Prensa (Buenos Aires).

La Tierra (Rosario).

The Times (London).

The Times Imperial and Foreign Trade Supplement (London). (Title changed in August 1922 to *The Times Trade and Engineering Supplement.*)

V. BIOGRAPHICAL DATA ON POLITICAL PARTICIPANTS

For Argentine participants in the politics of beef, I have tried to gather biographical information on their date of birth, regional identification, occupation, class origin and status, and political parties. While gleaning some data from above-cited sources (especially the *Anales de la Sociedad Rural Argentina* and Ministerio del Interior, *Las fuerzas armadas*) as well as from personal informants, I have mainly relied on the works listed here. Incidentally, the material employed in this study is on file and open to researchers in a "data bank" on Argentine leadership at the Centro de Sociología Comparada of the Instituto Torcuato di Tella in Buenos Aires.

Echevarrieta, Marcelo. *Argentina, sus hombres.* Buenos Aires, 1934.

Guillermo Kraft Ltda. *Quien es quien en la Argentina.* 1939, 1941, 1943. Buenos Aires, 1939, 1941, 1943.

Piccirilli, R., F. Romoy, and L. Gianello. *Diccionario histórico argentino.* 6 vols. Buenos Aires, 1953–54.

Santillán, Diego Abad de. *Gran encyclopedia argentina.* 8 vols. Buenos Aires, 1956–1963.

Sociedad Inteligencia Sudamericana. *Hombres del dia 1917, el diccionario biográfico argentino.* Buenos Aires, 1917.

Sociedad Rural Argentina. *Nómina de socios.* 1932, 1939, 1946, 1956. Buenos Aires, 1932, 1939, 1946, 1956. Previous membership lists were occasionally published in the Society's *Anales.*

Udaondo, Enrique. *Diccionario biográfico argentino.* Buenos Aires, 1938.

For American and British politicians, the following sources were helpful:

United States Congress. *Biographical Dictionary of the American Congress, 1774–1961.* Washington, 1961.

Whitaker, Joseph. *Almanack,* 1910–1933. London, 1910–1933.

Index